Risk in Child Protection

Assessment in Childcare Series
An accessible series that explores the key challenges facing frontline professionals in child protection. Each book offers a concise overview of a specific subject area, such as risk or domestic abuse, and suggests practical frameworks for undertaking effective assessments. The series conveys the reality of contemporary casework and provides the missing link between conceptual statutory guidance and practical instruction for facing the day-to-day issues that arise. Martin C. Calder is Director of Calder Training and Consultancy Limited.

of related interest

Practical Guide to Child Protection
The Challenges, Pitfalls and Practical Solutions
Joanna Nicolas
ISBN 978 1 84905 586 4
eISBN 978 1 78450 032 0

The Common-Sense Guide to Improving the Safeguarding of Children
Three Steps to Make A Real Difference
Terry McCarthy
ISBN 978 1 84905 621 2
eISBN 978 1 78450 092 4

Eradicating Child Maltreatment
Evidence-Based Approaches to Prevention and Intervention Across Services
Edited by Arnon Bentovim and Jenny Gray
Foreword by Harriet Ward
ISBN 978 1 84905 449 2
eISBN 978 0 85700 823 7

Good Practice in Assessing Risk
Current Knowledge, Issues and Approaches
Edited by Hazel Kemshall and Bernadette Wilkinson
ISBN 978 1 84905 059 3
eISBN 978 0 85700 252 5

Putting Analysis Into Child and Family Assessment
Undertaking Assessments of Need
Third Edition
Ruth Dalzell and Emma Sawyer
ISBN 978 1 90939 123 9
eISBN 978 1 90939 127 7

The Child's World
The Comprehensive Guide to Assessing Children in Need
Second Edition
ISBN: 978 1 84310 568 8
eISBN: 978 0 85700 183 2

Improving Child and Family Assessments
Turning Research into Practice
Danielle Turney, Dendy Platt, Julie Selwyn and Elaine Farmer
ISBN 978 1 84905 256 6
eISBN 978 0 85700 553 3

Social Work with Troubled Families
A Critical Introduction
Edited by Keith Davies
ISBN 978 1 84905 549 9
eISBN 978 0 85700 974 6

Risk in CHILD PROTECTION

ASSESSMENT CHALLENGES AND FRAMEWORKS FOR PRACTICE

Martin C. Calder
with Julie Archer

Jessica Kingsley *Publishers*
London and Philadelphia

First published in 2016
by Jessica Kingsley Publishers
73 Collier Street
London N1 9BE, UK
and
400 Market Street, Suite 400
Philadelphia, PA 19106, USA

www.jkp.com

Library of Congress Cataloging in Publication Data
Calder, Martin C.
  Risk in child protection work : frameworks for practice / Martin C. Calder.
    pages cm. -- (Assessment in child care)
  Includes bibliographical references and index.
  ISBN 978-1-84905-479-9 (alk. paper)
  1. Child welfare--Great Britain. 2. Child abuse--Prevention.
3. Child sexual abuse--Prevention. 4. Risk
management. I. Title.
  HV751.A6C24 2015
  362.7--dc23
                          2015024546

British Library Cataloguing in Publication Data
A CIP catalogue record for this book is available from the British Library

ISBN 978 1 84905 479 9
eISBN 978 0 85700 858 9

Printed and bound in the United States

Contentment cultivates creativity
A reflection of Janet, Stacey and Emma and our family life.

Martin C. Calder May 2015

Contents

Standardised chapter guidance

Each chapter will have an introduction and a key messages section at the end along with some key issues for first-line managers and also senior managers and trainers. It will also feature reflective questions for the practitioner.

CHAPTER 1

Introduction

Policy Background

My entire career in child protection work has been spent making millions of risk judgments that affect the lives of children, families, social workers and many other professionals. My experience mirrors thousands of other professionals operating in the child protection sphere.

It is with considerable alarm, therefore, that such an everyday and critically important task lacks any formally issued guidance from central government to the hugely accountable local safeguarding children's boards and local authorities. Risk is so important that it has always been a key performance indicator for the government and a focus for the increasingly punitive Ofsted regime of inspection. It is a central consideration in thresholds at all stages of the intervention continuum – from initial concern through to decisions to make Care Orders – and examination of options to import from elsewhere to guide our risk assessment and management practice are few and far between.

This book reflects my journey from ignorance through to innovation in the risk assessment world and includes how my frameworks for risk assessments have evolved – both due to an emerging evidence base coupled with changes in practice and professional context. The goal is to encourage people to critically reflect on the materials to see if they can be utilised in their own work or to apply them in practice if they think they are useful.

It is with pride that I have been asked to author this book as the inaugural text in a new series of books commissioned by Jessica Kingsley Publishers spanning 'Assessments in Child Care'. The need for a series also clearly highlights that, whilst risk can be isolated as a generic concept, the reality for front-line practice is that we also have to be clear about the specific (and frequently multiple) risks that emerge in the caseloads we manage.

I coined the term 'toxic context' (2012) to frame the environment in which many committed workers are attempting to undertake ever-increasingly complex risk assessments and where the civil courts are imposing an ever-higher threshold for 'beyond reasonable doubt' in the adjudication of court cases (see Figure 1.1). In reality, the civil court threshold approaches that of the criminal court. It is debatable whether this is due to a desire to head off appeals, in recognition of the human rights legislation (with an emphasis on preserving the right to family life), or due to the growing problems for social care departments to present plans that offer something better for the children than remaining at home. The previous regime of bureaucracy has most definitely been joined (but not replaced unfortunately) by a butchery from Cameron's Conservative government that has culled the social care and allied professionals resource landscape, and with it acutely limited the options available.

Figure 1.1 Toxic context

Some of the ingredients of each level of toxicity are identified in Table 1.1.

TABLE 1.1 THE TOXIC CONTENT

Political	Organisational	Professional
Outputs outweigh outcomes	Staff shortages due to recruitment failure	Collusion with families
No acknowledgement of ever-increasing complexity of task and caseloads	High levels of staff turnover and sickness	Emotional impact of work:
	Lack of cover for leave and sickness	▸ High levels of stress
		▸ Inadequate reflection
Deletion of child protection vocabulary	Inadequate levels of skill and specialist knowledge	▸ Reduced sensitivity
Ofsted operating outside knowledge base	Inadequate resources, such as administrative and clerical assistance	▸ Defensiveness
		▸ Detachment
	Inadequate premises for workers and public	▸ Dangerous decision-making

(Calder 2012)

At a political level, the agenda dictates the approach rather than the problem inviting a tailored solution. In this sense, the initiatives from the Labour government from 1997 throughout their term focused upon:

▸ Market forces

▸ Business focus

▸ Economy: Value for money

▸ Efficiency

▸ Transparency

▸ Performance management

▸ Embrace technology

▸ Change, change and more change…

▸ Change without evaluation or consultation.

One of the most significant problems emerged from a performance management approach to a complicated, ever changing world.

The real concept of performance management is associated with an approach to creating a shared vision of the purpose and aims of the organisation, helping each employee understand and recognise their part in contributing to them, and in so doing, manage and enhance the performance of the individual and the organisation. (Fletcher 1993)

At one level there are many positive aspects to this approach:

- ▶ Modern performance management is an inclusive process; it's not just about checking up on people

- ▶ It is a multi-dimensional activity and the measurement varies depending on a variety of factors

- ▶ It is complex and brings in its train a whole range of specific techniques and methodologies.

Consultation with front-line staff across Scotland as part of the Supporting Front Line Staff Initiative revealed that staff wanted more performance management; they wanted to know how well they were doing, how they could improve and to be assured that what they were doing was making a difference. In their words they wanted clear standards and expectations, supervision and appraisal, their personal development addressed, to know the reasons behind changes to working practices or services and to know if they could influence changes.

At the other end of the continuum is the impact on the practice of this approach and this includes:

- ▶ Being Blinkered: when it becomes the sole criterion for evaluating individual performance

- ▶ Terror at the numerical fixation focus

- ▶ Naming and shaming an individual if they fall short, with punitiveness prevailing

- ▶ Waning Motivation and willingness to commit or go the extra mile, and goodwill evaporates

- ▶ Constricted managerial focus

- ▶ Reduced risk taking and creative practice

- ▶ Outputs outweighing outcomes – tick-box mentality returns

- ▶ Leadership challenges reduced to manage the achievement of centrally-set goals

- Practitioners, 'hitting the target and missing the point' as well as 'playing the numbers game'
- Decreased effectiveness of service delivery
- Contradicting ethical values – the system rather than the person matters and users feel short-changed or pawn-like
- Randomly identified targets – measureable
- Few 'baskets' of indicators to promote interagency collaboration exist.

Overall, this creates a culture where resources are diverted from areas where they are needed, leading to a drop in service integrity and resulting in perverse behaviours to achieve targets. This may encourage a management culture that pursues results and targets at the expense of both quality and integrity, a drop in commitment to tackling poor or unethical practices, as well as seeing 'fast but sloppy work' and a concern with quantity over quality. It therefore becomes clear that *context* changes the goals towards which workers, managers and organisations work. Context shapes the nature of leadership.

Workers and agencies stand or fall by their child protection practice and risk management is at the heart of good child protection work. The concept of risk was purposefully and very deliberately jettisoned from official guidance spanning all children and their families (DH 1999, 2000). The Munro review (2011b) challenged the deletion of risk when it was a core activity, the timescales dictating practice and the unhelpful conflation of Section 47 inquiries and core assessments. It also suggested that the continuing expansion of safeguarding procedures was unhelpful and invited abbreviation.

Ayre and Calder (2010) argued that the overwhelming response by welfare states to child deaths and other system failures has been to seek bureaucratic solutions by introducing more and more laws, procedures and guidelines. The more risk and uncertainty has been exposed, the greater the attempts to close up the gaps through administrative changes. While these are valid concerns, the problem surrounds the one-dimensionality of the approach and the relentless focus on new forms of organising child welfare work as the key to solving problems. Here, practice is regarded as little more than rule following.

Ayre and Calder (2010) also pointed out that because of the many attempts to reform and recast provision which have taken place, public confidence in the ability of the English child protection system to keep children safe has remained stubbornly and alarmingly low. More alarming still, this lack of confidence has, over recent years, come to be shared by the ministers, managers and practitioners responsible for devising and delivering these services (Clark 2009; Parton 2004). They concluded that unless we initiate substantial and fundamental change in both policy and practice, child protection services are in danger of entering a vicious spiral of decline from which it will be very difficult to recover. Work in the field of abuse and neglect in England has been greatly affected during the first decade of the twenty-first century by a government-mandated change of focus from child protection as narrowly defined to a more broadly defined concept of child safeguarding (Munro and Calder 2005). This concept sees child protection not as a distinct activity but as located firmly within a wider range of issues affecting children's wellbeing. However, this chapter focuses not on this, but on the de-professionalisation of the workforce charged with meeting this challenge.

The result of so many inquiries into fatal child abuse has been to foster a blame culture in child protection work. This is often the approach of politicians and the media. It is difficult to see how the benefits from inquiries positively inform policy, practice, and learning. What is clear is that policy changes, as a result of recommendations made by child death inquiries alone, do not ensure improved practice and better outcomes for children. Although the findings from inquiries provide insight and can be a tool for developing evidence-based practice, in a blame driven environment they divert attention from the day-to-day dilemmas with which child protection practitioners work. In environments where blame is individualised and society seeks scapegoats when errors and wrong decisions are made, practitioners are likely to develop defensive attitudes, which do not lead to ongoing improvement in the service provided.

At an organisational level, Laming (2003) was clear that there is a level of accountability required as they create the local working environment within which workers practice. He was also clear that anxiety undermines practice.

The inability of social services and other agencies to protect children known to them who were suffering abuse, sometimes for prolonged periods, is frequently underpinned by significant systemic as well as practice failures. Indeed, in some instances, where additional harm was caused to children by institutional action during child protection investigations, systemic failures appear to be the most significant factors. What we see arise from this is a reactive dangerousness:

- ▶ Blame and fear of getting it wrong initiating lower thresholds for child protection and LAC (looked after children)
- ▶ No consideration about:
  - » The impact of resource allocation/rationing
  - » Whether we can offer anything better than supporting safety for children in birth family
  - » Divisiveness between professional groups
  - » Premature self-protective practice.

Laming noted that the factors that predispose the likelihood of tragedies occurring include the repeated failure of individual workers to perform their roles adequately, allied to an organisational framework that lacks the managerial rigour and the will or robustness to ensure that responsibilities are discharged and that effective multi-agency working happens. When these factors occur in tandem, conditions are created that increase the probability of system failure.

Organisational issues raised by inquiries include:

- ▶ Staff shortages due to recruitment failure
- ▶ High levels of staff turnover and sickness
- ▶ Lack of cover for leave and sickness
- ▶ Inadequate levels of skill and specialist knowledge
- ▶ Inadequate resources, such as administrative and clerical assistance
- ▶ Inadequate premises for workers and public.

Laming noted that senior managers and others spent far too much time not taking responsibility and not appreciating the nature of the work that was going on in 'the front office'. A major focus of the report is to try to ensure that, in the future, issues concerning responsibility and accountability are addressed, and thus what are the most appropriate forms of governance. Incompetent practices identified by Laming included:

- ▸ Evidence of profound organisational malaise and an absence of leadership as exemplified by senior managers' apparent indifference to children's services, which were under-funded and neglected.

- ▸ Local child protection procedures were way out of date and this was compounded by major staffing problems and low morale among staff who were invariably over worked and 'burning out'.

- ▸ Front-line workers got little support or quality supervision and were uncertain about their role in child protection.

- ▸ Extremely poor administrative systems existed for tracking referrals and case information.

Perhaps the most significant overall contribution of this report, especially when seen in the context of all the previous inquiries, is how it connects up the experiences of front-line workers with poor management and a lack of accountability right up to the highest levels. We are left in no doubt that the workers involved in Victoria Climbié's case were over-worked and under-supported.

Laming also identified concerning aspects of organisational culture. The social workers did not just have to deal with menacing and manipulative clients, but similar kinds of colleagues, including managers, who acted out distorted and abusive patterns with one another. The report's descriptions of the internal politics of the social work teams demonstrate that there was little comfort or release for the workers. One social worker recalled that the 'team was much divided, and there were a lot of deep conflicts. At times the working environment felt hostile, and it was not a comfortable place to work comfortably in'. Professional relationships come to mirror the distorted and abusive relationships within families. Lisa Arthurworrey, the social worker who had most contact with Victoria Climbié, actually referred to her team manager as 'the headmistress. I was a child who was seen but not heard, and had seen what had happened to those who challenged (manager)'.

There is a critical issue that requires exploration in the area between organisational and professional dangerousness; the issue of the role of the first-line manager in the child protection arena. It is clear when there are consequences of not acting as a shock absorber for front-line staff from the political and organisational requirements. These include:

- One-dimensional performance management culture. One social worker referred to the culture of 'conveyer belt social work' and how the 'ethos seemed to be particularly about getting the cases through the system and meeting the targets, meeting the statistics, getting them through the system', rather than doing the work that needed to be done.

- Others spoke of the 'bombardment factor' of the relentless work that came into the office. Cases were just 'plonked on social workers' desks', with no attention to the workers' needs, feelings, worries, or the degree to which the level of difficulty in the case reflected their experience or competence. There was a complete lack of attention to process and feelings, no space for reflection, for slowing things down, as the social work office itself was not a safe or nurturing space.

- Pressure to get cases 'through the system' creates a situation where attention, time and resources are diverted from doing in-depth, needs-driven work with children and families in ways which can promote child safety, welfare and healing.

- The soul is being squeezed out of the work, pulling workers' and entire systems' attention away from understanding and developing the kinds of deep relationships with the self, children and carers, which are required in order to do meaningful child protection and welfare work.

- Organisational situations and cultures have developed where some systems operate to impede effective intervention. Some of these actually create greater conditions of risk for children, families, workers and agencies. Lack of clarity from government regarding children in need, wellbeing, child protection and safeguarding.

Calder (2008) pointed out that:

> Too often the apex of the organisation doesn't have a clue of what child protection work is like and are much more preoccupied with value for money and performance indicators than they are with their most valuable asset – the workers. Also, I often see performance indicators being collected just for the sake of it. Findings are seldom fed back in an analysed format that might inform practice. It leaves workers persecuted for statistical information but none the wiser when it comes to its interpretation. (p.117)

> 'Front-line managers are the keystones of the organisation.'
> Chief Inspector of Social Services (DH 2000, p.10)

> They have a key role in determining whether standards of practice are consistently maintained, in supporting staff engaged in complex, personally demanding practice, and ensuring staff are continually developed in knowledge-based practice. Without this, they can add to the separation that can occur within an organisation and the poor or non-existent collaboration with others. (DH/SSI, 2006, pp.10–11)

There is a clear and positive relationship between the quality of services and an effective management structure. Calder (2010) articulated the core conditions for effective service delivery, barriers to good practice and here in Tables 1.2, 1.3 and 1.4 I add what we have been given to work with.

TABLE 1.2 CORE CONDITIONS FOR EFFECTIVE SERVICE DELIVERY

Organisational	Core condition	Client/Worker
The agency has effectively researched and understood client need. It is clear about its goals and working methods	Clarity	Good assessment Clear agreement as to goals of intervention, time scale, and working methods

Other people, especially consumers, understand what the agency is offering	Congruence	The intervention being used is appropriate
Recruitment, training, and staffing levels are correct	Competence	The worker is skilled, knowledgeable, and experienced
The worker is well supervised and supported with adequate working conditions	Confidence	The consumer is willing to be helped, believes he/she will be helped, and trusts the worker concerned. The worker is confident about his/her role/task
Local services are co-ordinated and planned effectively. Some elements or agreement exists *vis-à-vis* working methods and core philosophy, agencies trust and respect each other's work	Continuity	Long-term support is available to those who need it. The consumer can move/be referred between agencies without disrupting his/her confidence or progress

(Gawlinski and Otto 1985)

TABLE 1.3 BARRIERS TO GOOD PRACTICE

Politics	Central government is confused or ambivalent about services. Speaks with forked tongue: i.e. expects much, gives too little, changes mind often
Policy	There is an absence of agreed policy about services at a national, regional and local level
Planning	No clear plan exists for services nationally, regionally or locally. Investment in buildings, people and services is haphazard
Professional	Different professional groups are competing for power, mystique, status and collectively devaluing clients' views, needs and opinions
People	Managers, planners, researchers and fieldworkers are personally uncommitted, disenchanted, tired and cynical
Practice	Working methods are ill defined. Research findings are ignored and no good theoretical basis for work exists. Training is poor or non-existent. Intervention is likely to be misplaced, confused, inappropriate or non-existent

TABLE 1.4 WHAT WE ARE WORKING WITH?

Organisational	Current conditions	Client/Worker
The organisation is constrained in creative approaches due to the 'what works' culture. It does what it must to attain targets set by government	Cloudy cultural conditions	Culture of assessment is mandated and governed by inflexible timeframes that force staff to strip essential processes of planning and client engagement
The agency is more interested in whether clients meet pre-set criteria rather than having the capacity to respond to the real need	Containment criteria	Interventions come from a localised menu that is often driven by access to ring-fenced pots of money
The workforce is insufficient in number and experience	Culled	The worker access to post qualifying courses is constrained and contingent on them sacrificing their own time to do the necessary work and allow for reflection
The manager's role continues to change and grow and they are now meeting themselves coming back	Complicated contortionism and chameleon-like appearance	The current climate is a breeding ground for more difficulties in engaging resistant clients who are lacking trust and respect for social care staff
Organisations are confused about whether to prioritise staff and client needs to enhance outcomes, or meet, targets that are output-based	Confused	The dichotomy between the plethora of early intervention programmes and the professional panic about getting things wrong have led to more child protection activity and an explosion of care proceedings
Organisations are compliant with governance dictated by performance management	Compliant and controlled	Client need and a staff desire to provide for this is often contained by inflexible performance indicators

Organisations are restructuring in response to government dictates and the separation of adult and children's services has dislocated effective planning	Compartmentalised	The workers are struggling to come to terms with what is going on within their own directorate so they often have no time or inclination to look beyond their own remit to embrace skills and resources in other directorates – compromising care packages
'Damned if you do, damned if you don't' – the media and political interest in children's services is more intense and critical than before and this adds an added dimension to organisational governance	Crucifixion	Clients are not immune from public and media coverage and views, and there is a greater scepticism about the value of social work intervention
Few performance targets are cross-agency or directorate and this acts against meaningful and high-priority collaborative practice	Collaborative dislocation	Workers and other professionals are working at two different parts of the system, child in need and child protection (CIN and CP), and the fluidity of transition is loaded with worker protection worries
Organisations are so busy digesting things that defy easy resolution, coupled with initiative explosion that they end up becoming constipated – with few solid outputs!	Constipation	Staff often struggle to have an understanding of the details of the initiatives and how they impact on their day-to-day work so that duplicated or contradictory messages from professionals act as a barrier to good practice

cont.

Organisational	Current conditions	Client/Worker
Whilst there is a common outcome via *Every Child Matters* there is a range of individual departmental (government and local) and agency response systems and frameworks that defy easy consolidation	Contradictory commonalities	The advent of the Common Assessment Framework (CAF), far from providing a common framework for assessment, has added confusion and fuelled discontent across professional groups, which is tangible and can be played out in the families they are working with
There is a constant need to build capacity strategically (especially in smaller authorities) and this has provided for the growth of independent consultants	Consultancy enhancement	Consultants are used to try and equip front-line staff with the tools to do the job; consult on individual cases to try and facilitate the engagement of professionals and the family in the required work

It is important to acknowledge the changing role and competing demands for front-line managers. Some of the key changes and demands include:

- ▶ Increased central government control
- ▶ Performance targets
- ▶ Performance management
- ▶ External audit, inspection and league tables
- ▶ Multiple initiatives from government
- ▶ Widening spans of control for managers
- ▶ Uncertainty about funding
- ▶ Rising public expectations especially about the management of risk
- ▶ Quality of social workers
- ▶ Increased use of litigation by service users

- Continual restructuring of services

- Turnover of staff and recruitment problems

- Rising service thresholds resulting in more chronic presenting problems

- Reduced demarcation between public and private sectors

- Movement towards integrated services.

See Table 1.5 for an overview of how the current systems, structures and priorities impact on first-line managers and the staff they manage.

TABLE 1.5 IMPACT OF THE CURRENT SYSTEMS,
STRUCTURES AND PRIORITIES UPON...

The first-line manager's role	The staff they supervise and manage
Steer staff through changes in structure and philosophy	The erosion of the value of individual skills and 'professional judgment' within the workforce
Motivate them to work with change	It stifles creativity and discourages risk-taking
More time spent working with other agencies concerned about the elevated threshold for the provision of a social work service	Skews assessment task (e.g. Integrated Childrens Systems (ICS) as a business process)
Being distracted from their ever-expanding front-line roles	Evaporation of good will
An expanding public relations role	Confusion re focus of interventions

Statham (2004) pointed out that the role of team manager had grown incrementally and its complexity was often not recognised by the organisation. As a consequence, many first-line managers are under severe pressure, and the support systems they need are not in place. Equally significant is that there is no qualification for them, although first-line managers are aware that moving from front-line worker to first-line manager is a very significant professional and personal step. For many, the entry qualification is that of practice teaching. This at least enables the first-line manager to think through supporting adults learning to practice and to be accountable for performance to standards of practice and service. However, it does not assist directly in being accountable to the organisation for the quality of practice of workers with a range of qualifications and experience, or managing staff who may have more experience than they do.

Learner and Statham's (2004) review of research on the context of managing front-line practice, found an increasing necessity to focus on the external as well as the internal and the policy environment. In part this is due to the imperative to provide integrated assessments and services. A second complication is the proposed development of 'integrated' service delivery. To achieve this, the management of practice requires an awareness and understanding of:

- ▶ The overall structure and interconnection between the social care services
- ▶ The implications of multi-agency approaches
- ▶ The composition and nature of teams in today's environment
- ▶ The nature of evidence-based decision-making
- ▶ Diversity and equality.

This sets the very broad context for the new first-line management role.

The role of supervision is critical in maximising the chances of achieving safe outcomes for all. Supervision is a process by which one worker is given responsibility by the organisation to work with another worker(s) in order to meet certain organisational, professional and personal objectives. These objectives and functions are:

- ▶ Competent accountable performance (managerial function)
- ▶ Continuing professional development (developmental/formative function)
- ▶ Personal support (supportive/restorative function)
- ▶ Engaging the individual with the organisation (mediation function).

The Children's Workforce Development Council (CWDC) (2007) points out that professional supervision can make a major contribution to the way organisations ensure the achievement of high quality provision and consistent outcomes for people who use services (adults, children, young people, families, carers). High quality supervision is also vital in the support and motivation of workers undertaking demanding jobs and should therefore be a key component of retention strategies. Supervision should contribute to meeting the performance standards and expectations of people who use services, and of carers and families, in a changing environment.

The quality of the relationship between workers and the people who use services is the essential ingredient of effective services. People who use social care and children's services say that services are only as good as the person delivering them. They value workers who have a combination of the right human qualities as well as the necessary knowledge and skills. Supervision must enable and support workers to build effective professional relationships, develop good practice, and exercise both professional judgment and discretion in decision-making. For supervision to be effective it needs to combine a performance management approach with a dynamic, empowering and enabling supervisory relationship.

Supervision should improve the quality of practice, support the development of integrated working and ensure continuing professional development. Supervision should contribute to the development of a learning culture by promoting an approach that develops the confidence and competence of managers in their supervisory skills. It is therefore at the core of individual and group continuing professional development. Table 1.6 shows the effects on workers and clients of poor supervision.

TABLE 1.6 THE EFFECTS OF POOR OR NO SUPERVISION

Services to patients/clients and carers	You, the worker and supervisee
Loss of professional direction Reduced sensitivity/empathy Inappropriate use of authority Poor planning	Reduction in confidence Build-up of feelings of anxiety Training needs not identified Practice not reviewed
Staff/management relations and the organisation as a whole	**Multidisciplinary working and interagency relations**
Increased sickness, disaffection, distrust Poor internal communication Organisational goals, values and policies unclear	Role confusion Poor communication Inappropriate services

(Wonnacott 2012)

In a climate of rapid and imposed change, organisations and individuals may be forced to relinquish previous certainties, assumptions and practices, in accepting the inevitability of continuous change. For some this may provide exciting new and creative opportunities. Organisational change and fragmentation also mean that many organisational structures are embryonic and immature, and therefore potentially more available to influence, and in need of development.

One of the main challenges arising from this poisonous environment is a fear of being left alone and making mistakes which result in being pilloried. This has also fuelled the hot potato of practice where professionals feel anxious or under-skilled and pass on referrals for fear of being held culpable if something goes wrong and they are left holding the case. This is a recipe for confusing and alienating families and there is little point in a good risk assessment that doesn't engage the family and encourage them to join you in redressing the causes for concern. This also fuels professionally defensive practice that adds to the problems as opposed to resolving them. For example, we have seen a massive increase in the number of referrals from agencies into social care, which has produced a domino effect: an increasing number of children subject to interagency child protection plans and an increase in the number of children subjected to care proceedings. This creates very real personal and practical demands on front-line staff and resources. This then limits preventive work. This fuels a system that awaits crisis. The prognosis is poorer when we have this as our starting point. It demoralises staff, bewilders judges and sets families up to fail.

In recent times we have seen an explosion of media and professional interest in the catalogue of sexual abuse crimes perpetrated by many men who had access to, and an opportunity to exploit, vulnerable children. The need for a historical abuse inquiry has in and of itself raised very real concerns that politicians had had either an awareness of the concerns or an active involvement. There have been claims for many years about sex offenders in powerful places and establishment attempts to cover up their actions.

The government's principal probe – a sweeping, independent inquiry looking at how public bodies dealt with these types of allegations – ran into problems before it had even started work. Baroness Butler-Sloss stood down from chairing the inquiry saying she did not believe any victims of abuse could have full confidence in her given that her late brother, Lord Havers, was Attorney General for much of the 1980s and was the government's senior legal officer at the time the Dickens dossier (upon which many of the allegations were founded) was considered. Home Secretary Theresa May then chose Dame Fiona Woolf to replace her, but she also stood down after questions were raised over her experience and personal connections with the ex-Home Secretary Leon Brittan.

The late Conservative MP Geoffrey Dickens had compiled files relating to concerns about sexual abuse by some powerful and famous figures, including politicians, and passed them to the Conservative Home Secretary Leon Brittan in the 1980s. There is a reported concern that at least 20 prominent figures – including former MPs and government ministers – abused children for 'decades'. Those files were lost.

There are currently a number of other high-profile inquiries in existence, which include Operation Fairbank: London Metropolitan Police's umbrella inquiry into historical child sex abuse claims involving politicians and other public figures. It began in 2012 as a 'scoping exercise' to establish evidence for formal investigation and went on to establish a number of criminal investigations: Operations Fernbridge, Midland, Cayacos and then later Athabasca.

Hopkins and Morris (2015) reported that an undercover police operation that gathered evidence of child abuse by Cyril Smith and other public figures was scrapped shortly after the MP was arrested, BBC Newsnight was told. The Liberal MP, who died in 2010, was held during a 1980s probe into alleged sex parties with teenage boys in south London, a source told the programme. The source said Smith was released from a police station within hours. The order to scrap the inquiry, made after Smith and others had been arrested, came from a senior officer whom the undercover team had never met before, the source said. Officers were then ordered to hand over all their evidence – including notebooks and video footage – and were warned to keep quiet about the investigation or face prosecution under the Official Secrets Act, the source claims. He said the intelligence-led operation started in 1981 involving a team of undercover regional crime squad officers, including some from Yorkshire who were based in London for the secret inquiry (Hopkins and Morris 2015).

This landscape of inquiries into high profile politicians and others does provide a relevant backdrop to the current state of child protection as they are the people who direct the policies and procedures as well as hold the purse strings for organisations. Monies are released when targets have been met. Many targets are not child focused. Inspection regimes are politically driven.

The call by Eileen Munro for a lighter-touch approach has backfired. Ofsted's *Social Care Annual Report* (2015) highlights that many local authorities and their partners are struggling to provide a good enough standard of help, care and protection for some of England's most vulnerable children. Their findings draw upon more than 5,000 inspections of a range of social care services, including local authority children's services, children's homes, fostering services, adoption support agencies, secure training centres, and residential family centres. Of the 43 inspections of children's social care provision carried out in 2013/14, seven local authorities were found to be inadequate, with a further 26 requiring improvement (Ofsted 2015).

Ray Jones (2015) highlighted that Ofsted have been castigated by the Commons Education Select Committee for its apparent inability to identify problems in Birmingham's Operation Trojan Horse schools, and for downgrading its ratings from outstanding to inadequate once the schools were at the centre of a media and political furore. The chair of the Select Committee is also quoted as saying, 'Questions have been raised about the appropriateness of Ofsted's framework and the reliability and robustness of its judgments' (Jones 2015).

Ofsted has also recently been criticised by the communities and local government select committee for its failure to identify issues in Rotherham in regard to the sexual exploitation of children and young people. It had given an adequate rating to the local council before revising and reversing its judgment at the time of media and political outrage over children being left unprotected. The committee chair stated that Ofsted's, 'credibility is now on the line' (Betts 2015).

Professionally dangerous practice

Traditionally, front-line workers have been the fall guys when something goes wrong, allowing the organisation, interagency network and politicians to remain immune from criticism or consequence. When we talk about toxic families we cannot divorce them from their context. This does not excuse culpability for harm but neither can it be side-lined or ignored. The same is true for front-line professionals. Their operating environment is resource bare, volume and complexity accumulative, and multiple impacts are unquestionable.

Grasping the reality of 'professional dangerousness' helps workers from all disciplines to be more aware that our protective intentions and actions can inadvertently contribute to extending dangerous behaviour in some families. It has been variously defined as: 'The risk of being caught in a system where the professional is psychologically and emotionally battered by clients, by colleagues, by the system and defensively may make inappropriate and sometimes destructive responses' (Fletcher 1978) and 'The process by which individual workers or multidisciplinary networks can, most unwittingly, act in such a way as to collude with, maintain or increase the dangerous dynamics of the family in which the abuse takes place' (Reder, Duncan and Gray 1993).

There are a number issues that arise in practice as a result:

► Collusion with the family to avoid the real issues, and to avoid having to raise concerns with the parents

► Over-identification with the needs and difficulties of the adults in a family whilst giving scant regard to the needs of the children

► Over-involvement and over-identification with a family so that professional boundaries become unclear and practical needs are addressed whilst potentially dangerous and risky patterns of behaviour may be missed or ignored

► Avoiding contact with the family because of unacknowledged fears about violence and personal safety

► Avoidance of discussion of workers' feelings and values, especially in relation to race, culture, class, religion and gender

► Working with a family in an unsystematic, incoherent way without clear objectives so that real concerns are not addressed

► Unresolved and undisclosed interagency differences of approach or assessment

► Over-reassuring a child or parent about the unlikelihood of removal from home may subsequently lead to overlooking or ignoring evidence of abuse and neglect.

Workers operating in the child protection arena continually experience exposure to emotionally challenging experiences; attention has to be paid to this as it can become dangerous if left unattended. Some of the real emotional issues include:

► High levels of stress

► Reduced sensitivity

► Detachment and denial

► Inadequate reflection

► Blunted emotional responsiveness

► Dangerous decision-making

► Defensiveness, de-personalisation.

Professional Accommodation Syndrome

Professional Accommodation Syndrome (Morrison 1997) offers a theoretical framework to understand the damaging effects of this process on staff (see Figure 1.2). It is an adaptation of Summit's Child Sexual Abuse Accommodation Syndrome. It is transferable to staff because it helps to explain the experience of staff in terms of what is known about the processes of victimisation and discrimination.

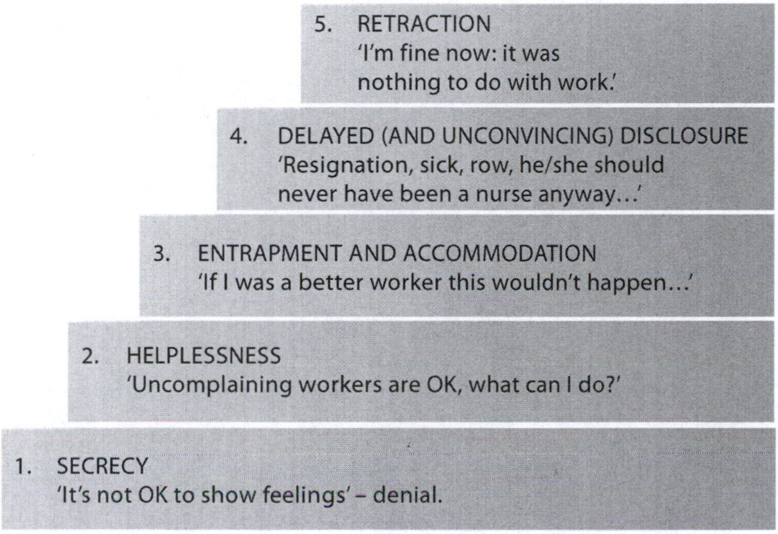

5. RETRACTION
'I'm fine now: it was nothing to do with work.'

4. DELAYED (AND UNCONVINCING) DISCLOSURE
'Resignation, sick, row, he/she should never have been a nurse anyway...'

3. ENTRAPMENT AND ACCOMMODATION
'If I was a better worker this wouldn't happen...'

2. HELPLESSNESS
'Uncomplaining workers are OK, what can I do?'

1. SECRECY
'It's not OK to show feelings' – denial.

Figure 1.2 Professional Accommodation Syndrome
(Morrison 1997)

Heasman (2008) offered a useful framework for considering professionally dangerous practice in context by adding a professional domain to the principal operating assessment framework in England. He started from a premise that if we can better recognise and understand the professional domains and dimensions of both 'risk' and 'safety' then perhaps strategies may be developed to identify and 'accentuate the positive', the frequently unsung safeguarding work that occurs day in day out, by and between professionals, and 'eliminate the negative' of, at best, ineffective and, at worst, dangerous individual, agency and interagency practice.

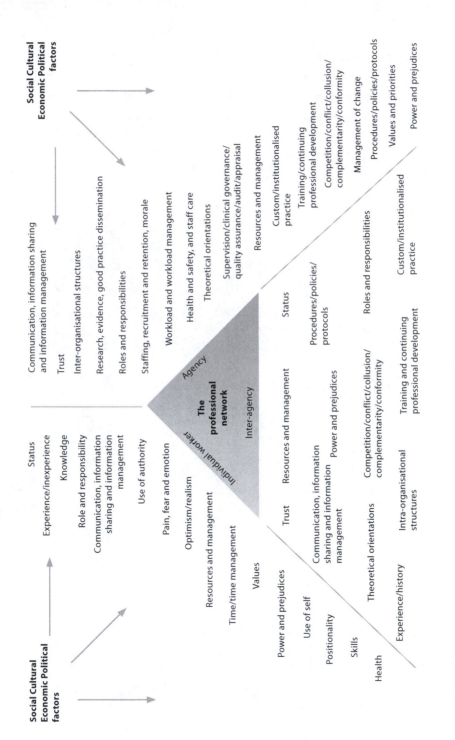

Figure 1.3 The professional network
(Heasman 2008)

Figure 1.3 offers us Heasman's revised triangle and this is followed with a fuller exploration of the key issues in Table 1.7.

TABLE 1.7 ESSENTIAL CONSIDERATIONS

Worker domain	
Dimension	**Characteristics/considerations**
Experience	For potential consideration: ▸ Personal and professional experience ▸ An accumulation (and testing/validation) of 'practice wisdom' ▸ Levels of confidence in relation to what works ▸ Levels of competence – knowledge, skills and values ▸ A range of working knowledge that informs individual practice in the context of multi-agency work from within a specific agency and in a particular community, in partnership with parents and carers and with children and young people
Knowledge	For potential consideration: ▸ A typology of seven areas of knowledge: 　» know what 　» know when 　» know why 　» know how 　» know who 　» know self 　» know others ▸ Knowledge that is conscious and articulable; sub-conscious, accessible with prompting; unconscious or latent knowledge ▸ Residual messages informing how a worker: analyses, assesses, 'makes sense', theorises in relation to the situations he/she is involved in; and how he/she 'forms a response' that leads to a plan and actual implementation/intervention to promote change, maintain or manage decline ▸ Levels of commitment to evidence-based approaches – knowledge of 'what works' ▸ Consideration of relevance of general evidence-based findings applied to particular circumstances

cont.

Worker domain	
Dimension	**Characteristics/considerations**
Role and responsibility	For potential consideration: ▸ Actual role expectations and responsibility linked to post and position, self and others (both specific to a worker's agency, legislation, statutory requirements and profession e.g. compliance with professional codes of conduct) ▸ Worker's perception of their role and responsibility
Communication, information sharing and information management	For potential consideration: ▸ Ability to communicate effectively through various appropriate media ▸ Understanding of the boundaries of confidentiality ▸ Understanding information sharing protocols: what, when, to whom, why ▸ Understanding data protection issues ▸ Processes of analysis and decision-making
Use of authority	For potential consideration: ▸ Understanding of the authority that they have by virtue of their position (personal and professional), status, legislation ▸ Appropriate exercise of that authority: to maintain a child focus, to communicate and engage appropriately, to ask difficult questions, to respond to threats, to challenge others (including other professionals, colleagues, line managers if required), to 'make a case', to influence, to direct others
Status	For potential consideration: ▸ Formal status accorded a particular worker linked to job title and role ▸ Informal status rooted in either workers' perceptions and/or others' perceptions ▸ Perceived status resulting from social position
Time and workload/time and workload management	For potential consideration: ▸ Appropriate balance between workload and time to manage it effectively ▸ Realistic identification and recognition of all aspects of work: direct practice, administration, continuing professional and personal development/training, supervision, networking ▸ Skills, strategies and guidance to manage finite (including personal) resources effectively

Resources/ resource management	For potential consideration: <ul><li>Availability of appropriate, quality assured, effective resources (preventative, responsive)</li><li>Skills, strategies and guidance to manage finite resources effectively</li></ul>
Optimism/ realism	For potential consideration: <ul><li>Workers' knowledge/understanding of explanations and factors contributing to an 'at risk' aetiology</li><li>Workers' knowledge/understanding in relation to protective or safeguarding factors</li><li>Workers' knowledge/understanding in relation to the capacity for potential for change and improvement</li><li>Consideration of the dynamic of hope and the reality of experience</li></ul>
Health	For potential consideration: <ul><li>Workers' own health (physical and emotional – see below) and implications for optimal effectiveness</li><li>Levels of stress and the effects</li></ul>
Pain, fear and emotion (vulnerability and resilience)	For potential consideration: <ul><li>The impact of challenging, complex and potentially distressing aspects of work with children and young people and the circumstances that they face</li><li>Varying responses from different workers according to the emotional vulnerability or resilience of the worker</li><li>Fear of violent or threatening parents/carers</li></ul>
Emotional intelligence, reflexivity, use of self-confidence, sensitivity/de-sensitivity	For potential consideration: <ul><li>Empathy, compassion, self awareness</li><li>Relational, reflective and reflexive practice</li><li>Communicate, engage, work in partnership, promote participative approaches, recognise expertise rooted in experience</li><li>Ability to respond and adapt in the here and now, in dialogue, in congruence</li><li>Ability to make a case and persuade</li><li>Workers' relative perceptions, feelings ('gut instinct') of risk and safety/safeguarding'factors</li><li>Keeping a focus on 'this' child/young person when characteristics of a situation are shared amongst a number of 'similar' children/young people</li><li>The importance of a maintaining a 'fresh pair of eyes'</li><li>An ability to recognise changing circumstances</li></ul>

cont.

Worker domain	
Dimension	**Characteristics/considerations**
Skills and agency	For potential consideration: ▸ Appropriate and corroborated/endorsed sense of competence, confidence and agency – further key element required for effective practice ▸ Workers' actual capacity to act, influence, respond (proactively, preventatively, reactively) using a range/repertoire of evidence/practice wisdom informed tools and strategies; recognising and making the most of opportunities ▸ Workers' perceptions of their capacity to act, influence and respond (proactively, preventatively, reactively)
Values	For potential consideration: ▸ Recognition of the social, cultural, political, professional and personal construction of values ▸ Adherence to professional codes and statements of values ▸ Anti-discriminatory, anti-oppressive practice, promoting equality of opportunity and access, valuing diversity ▸ A key element of competence
Positionality	For potential consideration: ▸ Workers' awareness of their own position (gender, class, orientation, ethnicity, culture, disability status, etc.) and the potential impact on their understanding and responses ▸ Workers' ability/willingness to consider others' positions and the potential impact on their understanding and responses
Power and prejudice	For potential consideration: ▸ Recognition, understanding and response to power differentials, prejudice and discrimination: personal, organisational, institutionalised, structural, social, political

Agency/organisation domain	
Dimension	**Characteristics/considerations**
Communication, information sharing and information management	For potential consideration: ▸ Ability to communicate effectively through various appropriate media ▸ Understanding of the boundaries of confidentiality ▸ Understanding of information sharing protocols: what, when, to whom, why… ▸ Understanding of data protection issues ▸ Processes of analysis and decision-making
Trust	For potential consideration: ▸ Respect and confidence between staff in relation to competence, respective roles and responsibilities, processes and procedures, etc.
Intra-organisational structure	For potential consideration: ▸ Comprehensive, complementary, coherent, transparent and accountable (checks and balances) levels and layers of service provision and management within the agency
Research, evidence, good practice dissemination for effective policy and practice	For potential consideration: ▸ Effective strategies for dissemination of research findings/good practice initiatives to critique and challenge current policy and practice and to inform, develop and promote effective future policy and practice
Roles and responsibilities	For potential consideration: ▸ Clear, transparent, agreed, negotiated and accepted shared understanding of respective complementary roles and responsibilities between agencies
Staffing, recruitment, retention and morale	For potential consideration: ▸ Realistic appraisal of required capacity ▸ Retention strategy including opportunities for continuing professional development, progression, flexible working arrangements and appropriate benefits ▸ Commitment to agreed staffing levels at appropriate differentiated levels ▸ Effective recruitment strategy to minimise vacancies ▸ Recognition that public and voluntary services are probably effectively maintained by goodwill and unpaid overtime

cont.

Agency/organisation domain	
Dimension	**Characteristics/considerations**
Workload and workload management	For potential consideration: ▸ Appropriate workloads – volume, range of work, using complementary strengths ▸ Sophisticated and responsive workload weighting systems to recognise all aspects of workers' (changing) roles and responsibilities ▸ Effective management, advice and guidance
Health and safety and staff care	For potential consideration: ▸ Recognition that the workforce is perhaps the most valuable asset that an agency has ▸ Strategies to protect staff, to fulfil 'duty of care', to promote and protect health and welfare (physical and psychological), to prevent health and safety being compromised, to protect and provide support as appropriate
Theoretical orientations	For potential consideration: ▸ Adoption and promotion of appropriate theoretical approaches underpinning practice and policy – complementary and shared – following critical appraisal of effectiveness/what works ▸ Promoting key priorities such as participation, partnership working, anti-discriminatory/anti-oppressive strategies, equal opportunities, etc.
Supervision, clinical governance, quality assurance, audit, appraisal	For potential consideration: ▸ Comprehensive (multi-function), regular, child-centred/focused supervision including appropriate practice critical analysis, reflection, guidance and direction, decision-making and SMART goals linked to anticipated outcomes and signs of success defined in relation to child/young person's health and development (optimal outcomes), rooted in awareness of 'what works' ▸ Critical, independent (where appropriate) structures and processes for clinical governance, quality assurance, audit and appraisal ▸ Meeting internal and external/local and national standards, benchmarks, priorities and performance indicators

Resources and management	For potential consideration:
	▶ Realistic, planned and monitored allocation of resources to achieve goals linked to anticipated outcomes and sign of success defined in relation to child/young person's health and development (optimal outcomes), rooted in awareness of 'what works'
	▶ Effective management of resources – with both fixed and responsive capacity
Custom and institutionalised practices	For potential consideration:
	▶ Critical recognition of the strengths and especially the limitations of practice (personal and organisational) and policies that may be pursued and perpetuated as a matter of custom or may be institutionalised (including hidden, structurally embedded discriminatory practice)
	▶ The danger of organisational malaise (Laming 2003)
Training and continuing professional development	For potential consideration:
	▶ Opportunities for training and continuing professional development:
	» A range of courses, activities and events (individual, team, agency, multi-agency)
	» Differentiated and targeted (linked to roles and responsibilities)
	» Clear aims, objectives and well-defined learning outcomes
	» Referenced to contemporary key benchmarks and documents (e.g.: *Every Child Matters: Change for Children Outcomes Framework* (DfES 2006); *National Occupational Standards for Social Work* and related Statement of Expectations of Service Users and Carers (Topss 2004); Codes of Professional Conduct; learning outcomes; *UN Convention on the Rights of the Child* (1989); Post-qualifying/Post-registration frameworks; legislation; policies and procedures, etc.)
	» Promoting diversity, equal opportunities
	» Promoting children and young people's/parents' and carers' participation
	» Promoting multi-agency practice and integrated working
	» Research-informed (including findings from serious case reviews) and promoting research-informed practice
	» Resulting in realistic (SMART/goal-based) action plans linked to learning outcomes
	» Evaluated (baseline, added value, impact on participants, impact on service users)
	» Accredited where possible and appropriate

Agency/organisation domain	
Dimension	**Characteristics/considerations**
Competition, conflict, collusion complementarity, conformity	For potential consideration: ▸ Recognition that intra- and inter-personal and group dynamics may operate within an agency overtly and/or covertly to impede effectiveness
Management of change	For potential consideration: ▸ Recognition and management of continuing processes of change and development: participatory, transparent, clearly communicated, emotionally intelligent
Procedures, policies and protocols	For potential consideration: ▸ Up to date, clear, accessible, agreed, complied with, embedded and supported by people, structures and processes across an agency ▸ Reviewed and developed
Values and priorities	For potential consideration: ▸ Recognition of the social, cultural, political, professional and personal construction of values ▸ Adherence to professional codes and statements of values ▸ Anti-discriminatory, anti-oppressive practice, promoting equality of opportunity and access, valuing diversity
Power and prejudice	For potential consideration: ▸ Recognition, understanding and response to power differentials, prejudice and discrimination within an agency or organisation: personal, organisational, institutionalised, structural, social, political, cultural, etc.

cont.

Interagency domain	
Dimension	**Characteristics/considerations**
Trust	For potential consideration: ▸ Respect and confidence between staff and in relation to competence, respective roles and responsibilities, processes and procedures, etc.
Resources and management	For potential consideration: ▸ Realistic, planned, monitored, allocation of complementary resources to achieve shared goals linked to anticipated outcomes and sign of success defined in relation to child/young person's health and development (optimal outcomes), rooted in awareness of 'what works' ▸ Effective management of resources – with both fixed and responsive capacity between and across agencies
Status	For potential consideration: ▸ Formal status accorded workers linked to job titles and roles ▸ Informal status rooted in either workers' perceptions and/or others' perceptions ▸ Perceived status resulting from social positions
Communication, information sharing and information management	For potential consideration: ▸ Ability to communicate effectively through various appropriate media ▸ Understanding the limits of confidentiality ▸ Understanding information sharing protocols: what, when, to whom, why ▸ Understanding data protection issues ▸ Processes of analysis and decision-making
Power and prejudice	For potential consideration: ▸ Recognition, understanding and response to power differentials, prejudice and discrimination between agencies and organisations: personal, organisational, institutionalised, structural, social, political

cont.

Interagency domain	
Dimension	**Characteristics/considerations**
Procedures/policies/ protocols	For potential consideration: ▸ Up-to-date, clear, accessible, agreed, complied with, embedded and supported by people, structures and processes across agencies ▸ Individual agency procedures and policies to be complementary and compatible ▸ Reviewed and developed
Theoretical orientations	For potential consideration: ▸ Adoption and promotion of appropriate theoretical approaches underpinning practice and policy – complementary and shared following critical appraisal of effectiveness 'what works' ▸ Promoting key shared priorities such as participation, partnership working, anti-discriminatory/anti-oppressive strategies, equal opportunities, etc.
Competition, conflict, collusion complementarity and conformity	For potential consideration: ▸ Recognition that intra- and inter-personal, group, agency and organisational dynamics may operate between agencies overtly and/or covertly to impede effectiveness
Roles and responsibilities	For potential consideration: ▸ Clear, transparent, agreed, negotiated and accepted shared understanding of respective complementary roles and responsibilities between agencies
Experience/history	For potential consideration: ▸ The sum of individual experience that may be pooled, shared and accumulated such that the whole is greater than the parts, or may be fragmented and unshared, such that the whole is less than the individual parts ▸ The accumulated experience of working together
Interagency/ organisational structure	For potential consideration: ▸ Comprehensive, complementary, coherent, transparent and accountable (checks and balances) levels and layers of service provision and management between agencies

Training and continuing professional development	For potential consideration: ▸ Opportunities for training and continuing professional development: » A range of courses, activities and events (individual, team, agency, multi-agency) » Differentiated and targeted (linked to roles and responsibilities) » Clear aims, objectives and well-defined learning outcomes » Referenced to contemporary key benchmarks and documents (e.g: *Every Child Matter: Change for Children Outcomes Framework* (DfES 2006); *National Occupational Standards for Social Work* and related Statement of Expectations of Service Users and Carers (Topss 2004); Codes of Professional Conduct; 'W.T.' learning outcomes; *UN Convention on the Rights of the Child* (Unicef 1989); Post-qualifying/Post-registration frameworks; legislation; policies and procedures, etc.) » Promoting ADP, diversity, equal opportunities » Promoting children and young people's/parents' and carers' participation » Promoting multi-agency practice and integrated working » Research-informed (including findings from serious case reviews) and promoting research-informed practice » Resulting in realistic (SMART/goal-based) action plans linked to learning outcomes » Evaluated (baseline, added value, impact on participants, impact on service users) » Accredited where possible and appropriate
Custom and institutionalised practice	For potential consideration: ▸ Critical recognition of the strengths and especially the limitations of practice (personal and inter-organisational) and policies that may be perpetuated as a matter of custom or may be institutionalised (including 'hidden' discriminatory practice) ▸ The danger of inter-organisational malaise (Laming 2003)

Positive pathways to protection

The ultimate aim for all organisations is to achieve a desired outcome with minimal adverse consequences. The severity of potential adverse outcomes and the likelihood of this occurring influence the degree of risk-taking that is felt to be appropriate in any given situation. However playing safe by making no decision does not eliminate risk and in some circumstances can increase the probability of adverse outcomes.

Organisational safety includes:

▶ Psychological factors that include employees' shared attitudes, perceptions, beliefs, norms, values and behaviours

▶ Organisational factors such as rules, regulations, equipment, structures and policies in relation to risk and safety.

A weak safety culture can increase the risk of an incident, and the identification of an organisation's safety culture can serve to identify risk areas and enable the organisation to take steps to avoid an adverse incident.

Commercial organisations typically view risk as an inherent part of their business and indeed most businesses probably could not exist without some form of risk-taking. Commercial organisations typically place more emphasis on organisational issues surrounding risk and risk events than is evident in recent literature examining health and welfare organisations.

Latent and active failures

Reason introduced the related concepts of 'active failures' and 'latent failures' to express the multi-level nature of accident causation. Active failures or errors are felt almost immediately. They are associated with the actions of front-line workers – i.e. errors of judgment and lapses in performance. Latent failures are found deeper in the system. They only become visible when they combine with other factors to create error. They are more often due to the actions of people not in front-line work: policy-makers, senior managers and designers. Active failures are neither necessary nor sufficient in and of themselves to cause an accident. Latent failures include:

- ▸ Cultures that foster blame and create defensiveness
- ▸ An unwillingness to admit to mistakes or to ever deviate from procedures even when the individual case circumstances justify it
- ▸ Supervision that is blame-apportioning rather than reflective.

There are serious consequences that include:

- ▸ Defensive attitudes from staff
- ▸ Climate of fear
- ▸ Isolated practice to avoid exposure to others
- ▸ Back covering practice predominating
  - » At an organisational level
  - » Within the management structure
  - » Across agencies
  - » Across workers.

Positive learning organisations ideally have an organisational culture that:

- ▸ Promotes openness, creativity and experimentation among members
- ▸ Encourages members to acquire, share and process information
- ▸ Provides the freedom to try new things, risk failure and learn from mistakes
- ▸ Creates opportunities for members to think and reflect and to learn from new evidence and research
- ▸ Celebrates and shares good practice
- ▸ Systematically gathers views from service users and carers and uses them to influence service planning.

Building an Emotionally Competent Organisation

Morrison (1997) states that in order to become more emotionally competent, an organisation must:

▶ Integrate the feeling and thinking aspects of agency life with the doing/task focus

▶ Move from secrecy to openness

▶ Move from helplessness to empowerment

▶ Move from accommodation to clarity

▶ Undertake an organisational cultural audit.

Morrison (2005) also pointed out that:

▶ Organisational cultures powerfully influence and determine the dominant styles of problem-solving, reward systems, role models and how change is managed

▶ Social care organisations are highly sensitive to the wider political context in terms of change, accountability and control.

Table 1.8 outlines six important factors for effective safeguarding.

TABLE 1.8 SIX FACTORS FOR EFFECTIVE SAFEGUARDING

Acting on concerns	Staff Support	Knowledge
The capacity and ability of managers and staff to recognise and respond effectively to anything that may give rise to concern about the wellbeing of service users	How staff are supported to deliver and sustain effective safeguarding	Staff's knowledge of safeguarding practice
Accountability and roles Management roles and responsibilities for effective safeguarding	**Participation** Capacity and opportunity to pick up children's and other service users' safeguarding concerns	**Partnership** Working with partner agencies to achieve effective safeguarding

In Figure 1.4 Morrison also offers us a preventative framework in relation to the Professional Accommodation Syndrome.

5. Prevention
    Prevent secrecy
    Maintain openness
    Identify patterns

4. Prevention
    Understand the problem
    Identify process
    Act to restore the worker

3. Clarify
    Define roles and responsibilities
    Identify distortions around responsibility

2. Empowerment
    Ensure role clarity, competence, training, feedback

1. Openness
    Permission – it's OK to show feelings and talk about stress.

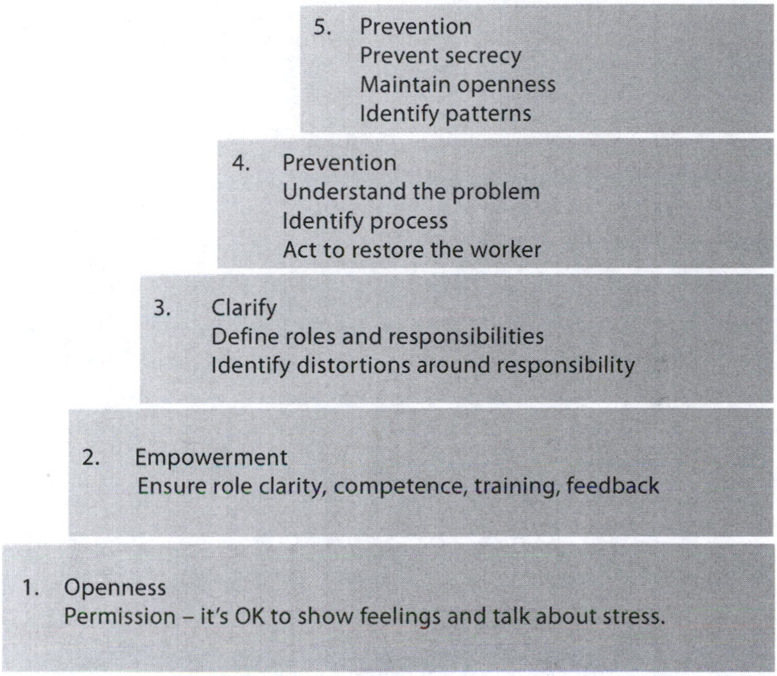

Figure 1.4 Professional Accommodation Syndrome: Prevention building blocks
(Morrison 2005)

Laming (2009), in his progress report reminded us that it is important to recognise the stressful and emotional content of social work and to create an environment that enables social workers to share their feelings and anxieties without being labeled as inadequate. Laming states, 'Such a support system needs to be reinforced by a system of good line management that is creative, empowering and sensitive to the individual needs of front-line staff, yet confident enough to set and secure high standards of delivery' (p.20).

There are many risks for staff that require recognition and then management, they include:

- The demands of the job
- The amount of control workers have over their work
- The support they receive from managers and colleagues
- Relationships at work (this includes bullying)
- Roles in organisations
- Change and how it is managed.

The role of emotional intelligence is critical here – defined as, 'The innate potential to feel, use, communicate, recognise, remember, describe, identify, learn from, manage, understand and explain emotions' (Hein 2007). Goleman (1996) argued that it included:

- Being able to motivate oneself and persist in the face of frustration
- To control impulse and delay gratification
- To regulate one's moods and keep distress from swamping the ability to think
- To empathise and to hope.

Emotional intelligence is the process of thinking individually and collectively about how emotions shape our actions and of using emotional understanding to enrich our thinking. Emotional intelligence involves using whatever relationships are available to help transform feelings that incapacitate to feelings that empower.

Elements of emotional intelligence include: self-awareness, emotional resilience, motivation/drivers, empathy sensitivity, influence/rapport, intuitiveness re: decisions, and conscientiousness.

TABLE 1.9 ELEMENTS OF EMOTIONAL INTELLIGENCE

Self-awareness	Self-management
The characteristics of good self-awareness:	The characteristics of good self-management:
▸ Being tuned to inner feelings	▸ Being able to control own emotions
▸ Recognising how feelings affect behaviour	▸ Staying calm in a crisis
▸ Being attuned to values which guide behaviour	▸ Being transparent – living their values – having integrity
▸ Being open and authentic	▸ Being flexible
▸ Being able to speak openly about emotions	▸ Learning continually
▸ Having good intuition about best course of action	
▸ Knowing strengths and limitations	
▸ Being able to laugh at oneself	
▸ Welcoming constructive criticism and feedback	
▸ Welcoming challenges	
▸ Being self-confident	
▸ Having a sense of presence	
Social awareness	**Relationship management**
The characteristics of good social awareness:	The characteristics of good relationship management:
▸ Being empathic: sensitive to what others are feeling	▸ Inspirig others to work together with a shared vision and sense of common purpose
▸ Listening to others' perspectives	▸ Being able to engage attention of and influence group
▸ Being aware of political forces at work in the organisation	▸ Cultivating people's abilities
▸ Being aware of guiding values and unspoken rules that operate amongst people	▸ Being able to deal with conflict, understanding people's perspectives and agreeing a way forward
	▸ Encouraging collaboration and teamwork

Social Work Task Force (Gibb 2009)

The Social Work Task Force was set up by the DH and the Department for Children, Schools and Families to undertake a comprehensive review of front-line social work practice and to make recommendations for improvement and reform of the whole profession, across adult and children's services.

When social workers have confidence in their own skills, purpose and identity, and in the system in place to back them up, they have a huge amount to offer. They collaborate effectively with other professionals and adapt to new roles and expectations. Most importantly, they forge constructive partnerships with people who find themselves vulnerable or at risk and make a sustained difference in their lives. At present, however, social work in England too often falls short of these basic conditions for success. Weaknesses in recruitment, retention, front-line resources, training, leadership, public understanding and other factors are all compounding one another. They are holding back the profession and making service improvement difficult to achieve.

The task force acknowledged that social workers play an essential role in protecting children and young people from harm and in supporting people of every age. The work they do can be difficult and very demanding, requiring careful professional judgments that can make all the difference to those they serve. However, putting a multitude of problems right was never going to be easy.

Feedback from employers, practitioners, practice assessors and from independent research strongly suggests that there are certain areas of knowledge and skills which are not being covered to the right depth in social work initial training. These include: assessment frameworks, risk analysis, communication skills, managing conflict and hostility and working with other professionals.

We are in no doubt that too many social workers are carrying caseloads which can be too high and make it hard for them to do their job well. There is very strong evidence that the absence of effective workload management makes practitioners feel de-skilled, lowers their morale and can lead to poor health. In these circumstances, service users can end up with a patchy, unreliable service. In cases of serious risk, the judgment and decision-making of social workers can be impaired.

They also identified the centrality of managers for staff. Unfortunately, however, we are also concerned about the overall quality and consistency of front-line management, and the pressures under which managers and supervisors are working, on a number of counts.

- ▶ Professional supervision is often inadequate because line managers do not have access to training and development to help them to carry it out well. Even where training is available, managers are often too busy once in post to take it up.

- ▶ It is rare for the training offered to front-line managers to focus on how they support practitioners in becoming resilient in dealing with the emotional impact of the work, or on how they manage the performance of staff. In both areas, managers report feeling inadequately prepared.

- ▶ Time pressures on managers, and high numbers of staff reporting to them without any method for mitigating this, result in a need to focus narrowly on tasks and processes and on meeting indicators, at the expense of concentrating on outcomes for service users and the quality of service.

The task force reported on the impact for workers of public perceptions and expectations of their roles. They have expressed their anger at how social workers often appear singled out for blame in the aftermath of the tragedy of a child's death. They have also expressed their frustration at the reluctance – and in some cases blanket resistance – among some employers to allow them to engage with the media about the positive difference they are making or to talk (within agreed boundaries) about the pressures, dilemmas and difficulties of the job.

The public image of the profession seems therefore to be unremittingly negative, with damaging consequences for recruitment, morale and public perceptions. It is compounded by low levels of understanding of the exact role and purpose of social workers and of the real demands of front-line social work. The media focus on harrowing cases of child abuse has also led to worries that social work has been reduced to high-end child protection in popular understanding, thus disregarding other important aspects of social work. This lack of understanding affects not just the wider general public. Colleagues from other professions and service users can also be unclear or confused about what they should expect of social workers, leading to misunderstanding and frustration on all sides.

The preface to Munro and the battle to reclaim child protection

In June 2009, Professor Eileen Munro, from the London School of Economics, was invited by the Secretary of State to conduct an independent review of child protection in the UK. She did so against a backdrop of further high-profile child deaths and media reporting, a crisis in social work and working together across professional groups, the gap between aspiration and reality growing by the day, and a disabling toxic environment. It followed the progress since the Laming review, a social work task force and an ongoing crippling climate of austerity, coupled with a growing practice of no one wanting to be named as having failed to protect children. The hot potato of managing concerns was growing and no one wanted to accept responsibility for taking a decision not to act.

I had some years earlier co-authored a paper entitled 'Where Has Child Protection Gone?' (Munro and Calder 2005) with Eileen Munro, to try and generate a political debate about what was needed. Safeguarding had replaced child protection and as such had diluted a critical task. We made several observations of note:

> ▶ It is very puzzling to read the flood of official publications lacking words of 'child protection', 'child abuse', and 'risk' and being replaced by 'safeguarding', 'needs', and 'strengths'. This change is part of an attempt to transform the culture of children's services. The government wants to see a fundamental shift in focus from what have become predominantly reactive, crisis services for a small group of children to a preventive range of services for all children with needs.

> ▶ These new policies have admirable goals of maximising the life chances of all children and 'ensuring each child fulfils their potential'. However, within this agenda, the victims of abuse are in danger of being lost. They are being merged with all other groups of children in need; 'a child at risk of significant harm' has been

re-named 'a child in need of protection'. This is stylistically elegant but carries a very real danger of losing sight of the distinctive nature of child abuse work and the specific difficulties of working with suspected abusive parents.

▶ The safeguarding agenda is intended to solve both sets of problems but it fails to do this, focusing too strongly on preventive services and giving insufficient attention to the deficiencies in child protection and how they might be resolved. Moreover, by widening the remit of children's services, it threatens to distract time, resources and attention from the specific difficulties of identifying and helping the children who are being abused. Although introduced as the government's response to the Climbié report, it may, paradoxically, reduce the chances that a future Victoria will receive the protection she needs.

▶ The 'safeguarding agenda' has impressive goals of increasing services for both lower level problems and a wider range of problems than the current focus on serious abuse and neglect. The new term 'safeguarding' is not a synonym for 'protection' but applies to all the problems that may disrupt a child's health and development – from whatever cause. The new Local Safeguarding Boards that replace Area Child Protection Committees have a range of responsibilities that reflect this broader meaning. The range of challenges it faces includes:

» Broader definition of safeguarding – maximising outcomes for all children

» Building collaborative structures and services that are best placed to deliver on the agenda

» Establishing clear relationships including scrutiny and commissioning arrangements across the various strategic planning forums

» Developing work across agencies including: planning, screening, and auditing arrangements

» Involvement of communities and users

> » Equipping the workforce – managing structural and cultural change, accountabilities, training requirements, thresholds, and implementing the Common Assessment Framework (CAF).

▶ The safeguarding agenda requires a fundamental transformation of the culture of children's services to shift the emphasis from child protection to a wider concern for all children.

▶ It is not that social workers or health visitors are averse to supporting families. Indeed, most of them would welcome the opportunity to work in a more constructive and less confrontational manner. Managing risk not only for the child but also for oneself, and the agency, has become a major preoccupation in front-line work.

▶ The main strategy in the safeguarding agenda is preventive: to intervene at an earlier stage and so prevent the build-up of family stresses that are the precursor, in some cases, to abuse. Realistically, however good the preventive services become, some cases of abuse will still occur so there will always be some need for a child protection service.

▶ It is hard to see which of the many proposed changes could be expected to improve the identification and protection of victims of abuse. The government has rightly seen that an assessment that focuses mainly on risk of abuse is partial and that good work should include a wider assessment of the child's wellbeing and needs. However, it is in danger of creating the opposite problem. It is introducing the CAF, to be used by all professionals, to improve needs assessment and inter-professional collaboration. However, the government seems to recognise that the assessment of need and risk of abuse are different tasks and the CAF is explicitly not for use in child abuse cases and does not help professionals decide when cases of need should become cases 'in need of protection'. The predecessor of the CAF, the Assessment of Need Framework, which is used by social workers, also focuses exclusively on need, failing to capture the reality that most cases active in social services are of a child protection nature. The Integrated Children's

Services programme does not explicitly address the integration of risk assessment with needs assessment. There are two new forms that are relevant to child abuse: the Section 47 inquiry form and the Child Protection Conference form. These, however, are intended to record the work that has been done but do not in themselves address the deficiencies in practice that lead to poor decision-making.

▶ At a high level of abstraction, it is possible to group the victims of abuse with other children but, for those directly involved, they are a significantly different group. For the children themselves, there is clearly a big difference between living in a home where you are frightened and hurt and in a home which is a safe haven. For the parents, there is a vast difference in dealing with professionals who regard you with suspicion, thinking you may be the cause of your child's problems and professionals who trust you and think you have your child's best interests at heart. For the professional, there are many differences in working in partnership with a family to solve a problem and regarding them with caution, needing to check the information they give you.

▶ In our conclusions we argued that there is a huge gap between aspiration and delivery at all levels of the system, from central government to front-line practitioner, and this is disabling for the workforce and potentially dangerous for the vulnerable children it seeks to safeguard. Professional judgment can only be exercised when there is clarity of context and clarity of task. Both are glaringly lacking at the present time. There are major problems in attracting and keeping staff in children's services. The safeguarding agenda, with its conflicting messages, is likely to drive even more away.

Multiple Munro manuscripts and missed opportunities

On 10 June 2010, Michael Gove MP, Secretary of State for Education, commissioned Eileen Munro, Professor of Social Policy at the London School of Economics and Political Science, to lead a review aimed at improving child protection in England and Wales. By the time the

Review concluded its work in April 2011, it had published three reports: two interim reports with a narrow focus, and a final report published on 10 May 2011.[1]

The Munro review of child protection was published in three parts between autumn and spring 2010–11. *Part One: A Systems Analysis* (Munro 2010) was published on 10 October 2010, receiving considerable media attention. In this report, Munro engaged in a consultative process of speaking to service users, children, young people, families and social workers in an attempt to understand 'why previous well-intentioned reforms, have not resulted in the expected level of improvements' (Munro 2010, p.3). Thus, this could be viewed as a baseline report, engaging in policy analysis of recent reforms to child protection, with some discussion of implications for social work practitioners. The report is structured in three parts: section one detailing a systems approach to child protection, section two focuses on early prevention and intervention and section three sets out the next steps for the second report.

The second report, *Part Two: A Child's Journey* (Munro 2011a) was published on 10 February 2011. This report, structured in four chapters, is a descriptive account of child protection systems as experienced by a young person, from seeking help to receiving it, from initial needs assessment to final evaluation of interventions. While Munro insists that the report, 'will not seek a series of superficial quick fixes' (Munro 2011a, p.8), the interim report in many ways does suffer from a superficial treatment of a complex issue. In the second report, Munro expands on her systems approach and details the need for good practice including early intervention and prevention, the role of multi-agency working and effective management of front-line social workers in safeguarding children.

The final report, *A Child Centred System* (Munro 2011b) was published on 10 May 2011 and is organised into eight chapters. With much signposting to the previous two reports, the final review presents a guide for an effective child protection system, embedded within professional values and shared accountability and transparency

---

1   See more at: http://www.systemicleadershipinstitute.org/the-munro-review-of-child-protection/the-munro-review-of-child-protection/#sthash.QvSvbqWR.dpuf

in practice. By attacking the compliance culture, and promoting learning cultures within organisations, the report presents as a departure from previous policy reforms which laid the blame of child death as a failure of professional judgment, rather than looking deeply into its causes.

The recommendations put forth mirror much of Lord Laming's (2009) report, including the removal of over-bureaucratised lengthy assessment procedures. In addition, suggestions are made to overhaul the assessment process by removing distinctions between initial and core assessments, creating greater leeway for professional judgment, removing constraints to local innovation and creating new and more effective inspection procedures for good practice to support children on their journey through the child protection system. Thus, by sharing accountability for child protection across agencies, the child-centred system proposed by Munro, attempts to create a more efficient, less bureaucratised system of procedures (Rajan-Rankin and Beresford 2011).

Munro (2008) defined risk assessment as the ability to predict future behaviours of parents, weigh up protective and risk factors, and assess the potential for change in a family, or with parents. This is an essential element of the continuing assessment of the family. These are difficult judgments made in complex situations and demand a combination of reasoning skills and practice wisdom. This is a core skill of children's social workers.

Interestingly, Munro also considered the adoption of police risk assessment methods for all child protection workers. The Child Risk Assessment Matrix (CRAM) model, developed by the Metropolitan Police after the Baby P case, was seen to be a good example: breaking down children's situations into the categories of 'victim', 'suspect' and 'household'. Within each, officers must answer a series of risk factor questions to record how much they know about the child. The aim is to quantify concerns and ensure areas of risk do not go unnoticed (Cooper 2010).

The reports do talk about uncertainty, problems in accurate prediction, source and nature of errors, and issues in the exercise of professional judgment but alarmingly it does not address risk or risk assessment directly.

Whilst all these recommendations are helpful and partially address the contextual concerns set out in this chapter, there are critical and noticeable omissions and, in the time since its publication, consequences that include:

- ▶ The growing number of Ofsted inspections culminating in an inadequate grading.

- ▶ Real difficulties in assembling a multi-agency inspectorate team capable of working together.

- ▶ Uncertainty and risk need to be accepted as intrinsic to the work alongside a recognition that abuse and neglect do not present in unambiguous ways. Risk needs recapturing and reframing away from a belief held by many that uncertainty in child protection work can be eradicated.

- ▶ A lack of guidance from central government and most Safeguarding Children's Boards about how to conduct a risk assessment and what they should include.

- ▶ A lack of any clear and work-orientated teaching on risk or risk assessment for social workers.

- ▶ A lack of follow-up from the recapturing of the word risk in *Working Together* (DfE 2013).

- ▶ Some of the frameworks highlighted in the reports are being used as simple solutions to complex problems, and in isolation[2] coupled with inflexibility. Also, some systems are being introduced not to enhance practice but to achieve reduced costs in a climate of austerity.

- ▶ The continued duality of systems: early help (funded by the parallel initiative 'troubled families') reworking Common Assessment Framework (CAF) to deal with cases below the social work threshold whilst social work develop a single assessment framework (joining initial and core assessments) but with a lack of focus upon risk in each.

---

2   http://news.bbc.co.uk/1/hi/uk/8029832.stm

> ▶ The requirement for all child protection cases to be managed by qualified social workers is unhelpful since many are accumulative and it is right and proper that other agencies deal with some risk whilst trying to prevent a deterioration, and also acknowledging that for families, risk assessment and management should be incremental and proportionate.

Working Together 2013: too little, too late

Working Together to Safeguard Children (DfE 2013) has been described as '...a radical shift in the way that the child protection system will operate in England. This includes a new approach to the oversight of serious case reviews, new guidelines for assessing the needs of vulnerable children, and a huge reduction in the level of national child protection guidance' (Dean 2013). It represents a fundamental shift in national child protection policy, placing greater emphasis on local areas to develop their own processes and encouraging stronger reliance on the professional judgment of individual practitioners.

Within this significantly shortened version of the statutory guidance (97 pages down from 700+) we see a loss of all indicators of abuse for professionals to recognise and act upon, but we do see for the first time in nearly 15 years, the resurrection of the word *risk*. We can now name the work that we do.

> ▶ All professionals who come into contact with children and families are alert to their needs and any risks of harm that individual abusers, or potential abusers, may pose to children.

> ▶ Assessment should be a dynamic process, which analyses and responds to the changing nature and level of need and/or risk faced by the child.

> ▶ Practitioners should be rigorous in assessing and monitoring children at risk of neglect to ensure they are adequately safeguarded over time.

> ▶ Social workers, their managers and other professionals should be mindful of the requirement to understand the level of need and risk in a family from the child's perspective and ensure action or

commission services which will have maximum impact on the child's life.

▶ No system can fully eliminate risk. Understanding risk involves judgment and balance. To manage risks, social workers and other professionals should make decisions with the best interests of the child in mind, informed by the evidence available and underpinned by knowledge of child development.

▶ Social workers and managers should always reflect the latest research on the impact of neglect and abuse when analysing the level of need and risk faced by the child.

===== **Key messages from the chapter** =====

Risk is an integral part of all professionals' work

It is increasingly seen as a social work exclusive activity

There has been a long history of removing the vocabulary necessary to help workers protect children

There have been multiple contributors to a toxic context from which workers operate

There has been some attention to try and name and offer options to address the contextual concerns

There are no risk frameworks available from central government to guide social workers

Risk pervades the workforce – personally, inter-professionally and with families

There are and remain real voids for workers, managers and organisations in trying to capture risk

The blame culture fuels defensive decision-making

Munro advocates being risk-sensible

We must include national guidance on risk assessment similar to what has emerged in neighbouring countries.

CHAPTER 2

Ten Key Challenges for Practice

This chapter will build on the issues raised in Chapter 1 and examine certain challenges in further detail, they will include the following areas:

- ▶ The challenges of professionals working together
- ▶ Authority, and the challenges of partnerships with parents, carers and children
- ▶ Capturing and retaining the child as central to the decision-making processes
- ▶ Worker challenges from the work
- ▶ Leadership challenges
- ▶ Thresholds, eligibility criteria and assessment practice
- ▶ Barriers and blocks to identifying and managing risk
- ▶ The challenges of evidence-based practice
- ▶ Errors and their impact on workers and outcomes
- ▶ The exercise of professional judgments.

Chapter 1 has reinforced the systems theory importance of cross-over influences across political, organisational and professional domains. In reality, the hierarchy is a top-down one and it is only from front-line articulation of the problems that this has created a ripple-effect upwards to review the procedures and performance culture that has contributed to worker incapacity to act creatively and protectively for the children it serves. Ruch (2013) describes the current context as being akin to rabbits in headlights. Several obstacles remain to be changed and include impoverished and malnourished practitioners, box ticking, and professional vulnerability, sensitivity and omnipotence. Social work has been caught between a rock and a hard place: on the one hand it is encouraged to move into a more proactive, strengths-based mode; on the other, a political, public and media expectation remains that it should have a 100 per cent safety record when it comes to the protection of children. Social work serves as the sponge that mops up society's anxiety, and consequently, according to Munro (2005), it bears its guilt for disaster and becomes the target for its frustration. There is no room for error as the level of tolerance is low – the general expectation is that social workers must protect all children 'track jumping' between strength and risk approaches to case management (Calder 2007).

The challenges of professionals working together

The call for multidisciplinary working and interagency working has had a long and distinguished history, despite the serious limitations uncovered in practice by a succession of child abuse inquiries into child deaths.

The ongoing focus on working together is based on a belief that it has the potential for achieving more than the sum of the collaborating parts operating individually. The central goal of working together is the achievement of some degree of consensus by a group of individuals about a plan of action and its execution. It usually includes an interpersonal process in which members of a group contribute, each from their knowledge and skill, to the accomplishment of a task, yet are responsible as a group for the outcome. A process of cross-fertilisation of ideas is presumed to occur, which encourages new perspectives and reformulations of difficult problems and solutions that exceed the boundaries of separate disciplines. The more generalised the task and the more the individual professional is dependent on the co-operation of others in its accomplishment, the greater their motivation will be for collaborative activity (Mailick and Ashley 1989).

In light of this belief, central guidance has been repeatedly issued, becoming more prescriptive in nature, in order to achieve this desired outcome. Child protection is not the exclusive province of any one agency.

Unfortunately, different constituent agencies of the child protection system are guided by different legislation and government guidance, and these, at times, seem to pull in different directions (Margetts 1998). Working together among different professionals and between different agencies is also not a uniform activity. It can range from the face-to-face contact between a doctor and a health visitor concerned about a shared patient, to a network of professionals employed by different agencies to meet the needs of a particular client group (Loxley 1997).

Calder (1999) identified a range of contributory problems to working together that included:

- ▶ Differences in background and training: Professionals bring a range of personal and professional experiences combined with extensive differences in temperament and views of life and society. They will differ greatly in their educational experiences, particularly their professional training, which has a profound socialising effect upon them.

- ▶ Varied attitudes to family life: Individual attitudes to family life are shaped by personal experiences, ethnic origin, culture and social class combining with the effects of professional socialisation. It follows, therefore, that attitudes will vary over issues such as what constitutes good/bad family life, normal behaviour, etc.

- ▶ Stereotypes and prejudices: Are a pervasive feature held by us in relation to disciplines we rarely encounter, and have the potential to damage trust and create stress and confusion about what skills and responsibilities they actually have to offer. The different approaches necessarily adopted by professional groups may give rise to stereotypical 'cardboard' images of each other. Such stereotyping can be dangerous when it allows us to distance ourselves from others, and to fail to see the individual through the distorting lens of our own prejudices. It can be used defensively to convince ourselves that we do not need to take their ideas, understandings and values seriously, and to reinforce our own superior knowledge.

- ▶ Role identification and socialisation: Each professional will have been socialised into their particular role, and will have a value system and language unique to their particular profession. These value systems are constant sources of potential conflict, which affect how professionals view each other's work and the level of risk acceptable to their respective professions. This has a profound effect on how they see each other, on the nature of their interaction and on their perceptions of specific family situations and the action taken.

▶ Differences within and between professionals: No individual is the same, whether they are from the same agency or from a different one. Subsystems exist – each with different aims and values relating to personal and social characteristics (such as class and gender). Not all individuals hold the same interests, beliefs or expertise.

▶ Status and power: Differences in contracts of employment, the different types and standards of professional training, occupational status and prestige, gender, race, class, language, and public image all contribute to the real and felt power differentials within the interagency network. Working together means contact between different emotional realities, different systems of meaning and different types of bias. At its most acute, the statutory responsibility of social services for the protection of abused children is at odds with its low status, salary and less certain identity. Professionals working together require significant personal investments, inducing a sense of vulnerability, such as exposing practice to peer scrutiny and with it the prospect of being assessed as being incompetent. Such anxieties can become infectious and compound the presenting problems. One profession may regard another as hostile or inferior to their own and shape their attitudes accordingly. Status affects performance: those who perceive themselves of low status may offer no contribution or feel unable to question information or comments made by those of seeming high status or power.

▶ Professional and organisational priorities: The nature of the work undertaken by the various agencies varies greatly. Those with statutory and lead procedural responsibilities will spend much of their time doing child protection work, compared to other agencies where it plays one part of a much more generic caseload. For example, Hallett (1995) found that teachers only spent half a day a month on child protection and thus remain detached from the system. The importance of staff training will be given different emphasis by the various agencies (varying from essential to being seen as a luxury).

▶ Structures, systems and administration: The variety of structures, and the systems within them, of the different agencies create difficulties and make co-ordination difficult. Agencies hold different powers and duties, and some do not have coterminous geographical boundaries. Accountability and authority is fragmented, with individuals have differing degrees of authority with which to speak for their agencies. All these differences affect co-operation and inhibit the transfer of information between agencies.

▶ Different roles and responsibilities: The issue of role clarity is important, particularly when their blurring can relieve staff of knowing who is doing what and why, and who should be held accountable in the event of failure. Social services have a broad role in the management of child abuse, ranging from partnership and rehabilitation to investigation and removal. The police have a duty to prosecute (punitive), whilst probation has a crime prevention role, plus working with those convicted of sexual offences.

▶ Lines of authority and decision-making: Social services are the lead agency in child protection, joined by the police and others. Only recently has the law required key agencies to co-operate with social services in the investigation of child abuse. The problem with such mandated working together is that people and agencies will not necessarily collaborate just because someone tells them to do so. Different agencies and individuals may have varying degrees of acceptance of, or commitment to, co-operate and differing capacities to resist.

► Different perspectives: Professionals define and explain child abuse in different and sometimes conflicting ways and adopt quite different stances about the way work should be undertaken. Different theories often emerge from particular disciplines and are maintained without reference to, or acknowledgement of, parallel theories. This blinkered approach to problem definition affects our ability to provide a problem resolution.

► Complexity and co-ordination: Rai (1994) defined complexity as the degree of structural differentiation or internal segmentation, as reflected by the number of divisions, number of hierarchical levels, and the number of geographical locations of the organisation. He found a very clear negative relationship between complexity and co-ordination in child welfare agencies, particularly relating to communication.

► Communication: Information is power and sharing it symbolises some ceding of autonomy. Disagreements exist both as to the content of what is to be shared and about the actual value of talking together at all. What seems essential to communicate for one, may seem a breach of confidentiality or peripheral to another. Professionals from different fields are used to working within their own particular culture and organisational structure with their established rules on issues such as confidentiality. The very differences in language and traditions can lead to a breakdown in communication, especially when dominated by technical terms and/or jargon. The differences in status, position and hierarchy inhibit communications among members of an organisation, particularly inter-level. These concerns have been aggravated further by the recent introduction of the Data Protection Act (1998) and the impact on information exchange outside of the child protection banner. There is a belief that accompanying legislation to the Children Act (2004) will resolve this issue, although the degree of anxiety about being held personally accountable for sharing information inappropriately will remain for some time.

▶ Underlapping service provision: is a tactic employed by agencies where they choose the narrowest possible view of their duties and then they discharge them in as perfunctory a way as possible. Once one agency has taken this view, others may do so to avoid 'dumping', thus depriving the client of any service, rather than a complementary interagency response (Margetts 1998).

▶ Changes in philosophy: is a pervasive feature of current child protection work. Following the Children Act (1989) and the introduction of parental responsibility and partnership (see Calder 1995); and the report *Child Protection: Messages from Research* (DH 1995b), which recommended that we review the balance between family support and child protection approaches, there has been conflict between agencies on how to respond to these concepts.

▶ Organisational restructuring: Reforming legislation has occurred in social services, health, education, and criminal justice sectors, in pursuit of greater efficiency and effectiveness with the introduction of market principles against a backcloth of fiscal retrenchment. This has led to agencies redefining their core business and basing collaboration on fiscal as opposed to interprofessional arrangements. The result is that:

> Collaboration is currently dangerously overdependent on the commitment and skills of individuals, rather than organisations, and thus too easily disrupted by their departure. Unfortunately, this means that whilst the quality of response may be very good if it involves individuals committed to collaboration, it cannot guarantee it maintains that response across populations or over time. (Morrison 1997)

Morrison (1997) also notes that the organisational context has therefore become less predictable, less stable and more conflicting in the short-term, as the competition for resources becomes even more acute. Whilst the emphasis on contractual, accountable and targeted services may in the longer term result in strategic interagency partnerships for the planning, commissioning and evaluating of child protection services, in the short term at least, partnerships across agencies are under severe strain. Morrison (1997) concluded that these cumulative forces have, 'placed an almost intolerable strain on interagency work and the ethos of collaboration which has been the heart of modern child protection work. Given that, even under reasonable conditions, multi-agency work is not easy, current conditions mean that this is its sternest test since its importance was first recognised in the early 1970s.'

▶ Anxiety and child protection: Morrison (1995) has argued that anxiety runs like a vein throughout the child protection process. This can relate both to the work as well as the struggle to survive in the current external climate of change. If it is not contained, learning cannot take place. Failures at an organisational level to appropriately contain anxiety can permeate all aspects of the agency's work, as well as affecting its relations with the outside world and other agencies.

Morrison (2004) has also identified the need to look at the organisational and system influence on creating the necessary atmosphere for working together to be attained. He identified the following factors associated with risky systems:

▶ Over-ambitious goals

▶ Philosophical/legal conflicts

▶ Lack of clear policy

▶ Pace/newness of change

▶ Role confusion or ambiguity

▶ Inexperienced or wrong staff

▶ Inadequate focus on quality

▶ Poor training and supervision.

Morrison (1998) explored the implications of the partnership ethos for interagency collaboration using an organisational partnership model (see Table 2.1).

TABLE 2.1 ORGANISATIONAL PARTNERSHIP MODEL

	Involuntary	Voluntary
No participation	Strategic Us vs. the world Adversarial approach	Paternalism You need us Medical model approach
Participation	Play fair Involving others Social justice approach	Developmental Working and learning together Psychological approach

(Morrison 1998, p.129)

This model allows us to look at the differing perceptions of collaboration between organisations. In the paternalism position, collaboration is viewed as an activity which is engaged in, as and when the agency deems fit, and only on its own terms. It involves others when it chooses. It sees collaboration as a benefit it confers on other agencies rather than being an obligation.

In the strategic/adversarial position, collaboration is approached with considerable wariness and caution, fuelled by the belief that it will involve more losses than gains, that other agencies will exploit the process in order to gain territory or acquire resources at the expense of one's own agency. Territorial behaviours dominate interaction. The result is that collaboration is often conflictual, and endless time is spent on negotiating the terms of engagement. Interaction between agencies is through bureaucratic modes rather than informal or personal communication.

In the play fair position, there is a basic belief that clients both need and have an entitlement to an effective multidisciplinary service. Agencies are therefore concerned to ensure that all are clear about their roles and responsibilities. There is a focus on clarity of mutual expectations, processes of working together and about how clients will be involved in this. An appreciation and respect exists for the different roles played by different agencies/disciplines.

In the developmental position, it has a broader vision than that held by the 'fair play' camp. It sees collaboration as providing a dynamic model of positive and developmental processes which are intended to motivate both staff and clients to work for change. There is a place for active informal multidisciplinary networks designed to enhance how we work and learn together, and there is a greater focus on outcomes as well as process.

The advent of performance targets for individual agencies and the costs associated with failure to attain highly with them has meant that agencies have frequently become very insular and only work outwards once their own house is seen to be in order. In parallel with this has been the shift from child protection to safeguarding, in which the remit has seen the integration of prevention and protection. Whilst this is helpful in that some agencies can no longer distance themselves from a child protection role, as everyone has a part to play in safeguarding children, it has meant that they have been stretched and so thresholds are often set at a higher child protection threshold. Perversely, the drive to recapture child protection might actually allow some of the agencies to step back from their responsibilities once again. The correlated concern of sharing information is explored later in this chapter, but again the persistent confusion appears to be around what constitutes child protection – at the point of actual, or the earlier likely, significant harm.

Understanding communication

Good communication is an essential prerequisite for building and maintaining purposeful supportive relationships. Issues relating to poor communication within and between agencies can be particularly problematic in a child protection context. Reder and Duncan (2003), proposed a very useful model for understanding communication in child protection. While communication is normally understood as a process by which information is transferred from the sender to the receiver, for it to be effective communication the information must also be understood as it was intended. These authors maintain that events seen in serious case reviews and child death inquires illustrate how catastrophic it can be when practitioners located in different agencies and from different professional backgrounds fail to pay sufficient attention to the meaning behind what is actually said and agreed to verbally, either face-to-face or over the telephone, or what is meant in written correspondence, or sent in email communications. The interpretation of the intended meaning is critical, but there are many interpersonal factors in the sender and receiver that can obscure or distort the meaning of information. These of course include non-verbal communication, such as the tone of voice, facial expression and body language, but also more subtle factors that may not be as readily observed.

Child protection practice frequently involves communicating data or information; however, this is not a neutral action. The cognitive and affective dimensions of practice are so important that practitioners must also be consciously aware, as senders and recipients of communication, that it is the means by which people convey their feelings about themselves and their experiences. 'Information' in this sense encompasses feelings, attitudes, beliefs, intentions and desires, and, if these are not correctly interpreted in the communication process, it can be highly problematic.

The advantages of effective inter-agency communication include:

- ▸ Focusing energies and resources of different agencies on a common problem
- ▸ Enabling a coherent and holistic approach to complex, cross-agency problems
- ▸ Credibility and authority through the involvement of different agencies and the community
- ▸ Access to finance
- ▸ Help in improving the co-ordination of policy and developing a better understanding of the work of other agencies
- ▸ Help in spreading the responsibilities for taking risks.

And, on the other side of the coin, the disadvantages include:

- ▸ A perception of collaboration when the reality can continue to be one of competitiveness and defensiveness
- ▸ Requiring high levels of time, energy and resources to maintain, which small organisations do not possess and which could be used more effectively if directed at the problem itself

- ▶ The promotion of consensus which can lead to the avoidance of difficult decisions

- ▶ The promotion of conflict and the danger that no one will move beyond this

- ▶ Adopting the culture of the largest agency, or the lead agency, and thereby often not developing cultures that promote the involvement of non-traditional agencies, including agencies operated by minority ethnic groups

- ▶ Too narrow a focus on effectiveness as measured by the achievement of outputs at the expense of a focus on the problem itself

- ▶ The need for people to 'get on' at a personal level – personal relationships are as important as structures

- ▶ The potential for conflicts of interest where some agencies are members of a partnership and also rely on the partnership itself for funding (Harrison *et al.* 2004).

Authority, and the challenges of partnerships with parents, carers and children

Authority derives from power, but the two are not synonymous. Power is the capacity to control the behaviour of others, either directly by fair means, or indirectly by manipulative means. Whereas authority – the established right to make decisions on pertinent issues – is a transactional concept and includes the committed consent of another person who is responsive to that authority. Authority is not only present but is the foundation of the relationship because potential clients do not become fully engaged until they grant authority to the worker. Authority has negative connotations for many social workers because they associate it with power, which they perceive as an impediment to the helping relationship. However, authority recognises rights, responsibilities and obligations and is a positive force in relationships with clients. It should be applied humanistically rather than omnipotently. Where it is applied with understanding, warmth and helpfulness, it should be experienced as being supportive in nature.

Jane Gilgun (1999) has argued that authoritative practice means that professionals are aware of their professional power, use it judiciously and that they also interact with clients and other professionals with sensitivity, empathy, willingness to listen and negotiate, and to engage in partnerships. They respect client autonomy and dignity while recognising that their primary responsibility is the protection of children from harm and the promotion of their wellbeing.

The autonomous and authoritative practitioner exercises professional judgment, is confident in the face of facts and challenges, shares information appropriately, contributes effectively to assessments, conferences, core groups (does not avoid responsibility), and analyses facts, asks questions, explores hunches and considers outcomes and impact.

Five levels of authority can be identified according to the power vested in the worker:

▶ Legally constituted authority, as in child protection and custodial settings

▶ Institutionally constituted authority, as in adoption and public assistance

▶ Authority inherent in a position as in hospital social work and family services

▶ Authority of expertise, which pertains to all types of social work

▶ Authority inherent in the person, which is dependent on the personality of the individual social worker.

Calder (1995) examined the concept of partnership in some detail since he could find no agreed working definition in the literature. The essence of partnership is sharing. It is marked by respect for one another, role divisions, and the right to information, accountability, competence and value accorded to individual input. In short, each partner is seen as having something to contribute, power is shared, decisions are made jointly and roles are not only respected but are also backed by legal and moral rights. The objective of any partnership between families and professionals must be the protection and welfare of the child. Partnership should not be an end in itself. Partnership consideration should be grounded on openness, mutual trust, joint decision-making and a willingness to listen to families and capitalise on their strengths. It is likely that workers will have different approaches to different family members and that these will change over time.

White and Grove (2000) suggest that four vital elements must exist within a true partnership. These elements are: respect, reciprocity, realism and risk taking. They argue that, without respect between partners there can be no hope of achieving partnership: 'The essence of respect is the ability to see a person or a party as they really are, not as I or my organisation would like them to be'. Reciprocity requires that partners contribute what they can to the partnership: 'If one party has all the power, the finance and the ability to define and label, partnership is absent'. Realism 'requires a realistic appraisal of the challenges, tasks and resources'. Risk-taking requires that we 'court failure', even though, they argue, this goes against the grain.

Calder (1995) argued that it is useful to see partnership as a continuum, with a basic requirement at the beginning of a working relationship, the provision of adequate information and a willingness on the part of professionals to listen without pre-judging the situation. However, relationships thereafter may fluctuate and move backwards and forwards along the continuum. Inevitably there will be conflicts between the views and needs of children and those of adults, and often also between adults who are important in a child's life. It may be possible to work in partnership with part of the family whilst only providing information to others. He also went on to identify a number of partnership models in evidence in child care and protection work, none of which constitute an equal relationship between families and workers. At different stages of the intervention process, workers may move between the following models.

The expert model: where the professional takes control and makes all the decisions, giving a low priority to parents' views, wishes or feelings, the sharing of information, or the need for negotiation.

The transplant (of expertise) model: where the professional sees the parent as a resource and hands over some skills, but retains control of the decision-making.

The consumer model: where it is assumed that parents have the right to decide and select what they believe to be appropriate, and the decision-making is ultimately in their control.

The social network/systems model: where parents, children and professionals are part of a network of formal and informal development, and social support for the family and the child. They are capable of supplementing existing resources via the facilitation of the social worker who should draw more on the extended family while complying with statutory requirements.

Words such as equality, choice and power have limited meaning at certain points in the child protection process, such as when professionals are conducting a Section 47 investigation. In such circumstances it is rare that the family views the process as a partnership and they may feel angry and refuse to co-operate. Partnerships can vary from family to family. Some adults are relieved to know that the ultimate power to protect the child rests with the professionals, and others chafe against the use of authority. It may be easier to establish partnerships with those family members who are less implicated in the abuse or those who are more consistently stable.

Research identifies clearly some successful features of partnership (Calder 1995): a shared commitment to negotiation and actions about how best to safeguard and promote the child's welfare; mutual respect for the other's point of view; good communication skills by professionals; the establishment of trust between all parties; integrity and accountability on the part of both parents and professionals; shared decision-making; joint recognition of constraints on services offered; recognition that partnership is a process and is not an end in itself but a means to an end.

There are also a number of blocks to effective partnership:

- ▶ The need to invest considerable time and resources
- ▶ Building capacities within service provider agencies
- ▶ Achieving changes in organisational cultures and professional attitudes to children and young people's participation

- ▶ Conventional professional styles of meetings and the use of inaccessible language

- ▶ Timing of meetings in conventional working hours

- ▶ The need to prepare children, young people and parents for participation.

Kirby *et al.* (2003) identified a number of key processes that need to be unlocked culturally if partnership is to be attained:

- ▶ Unfreeze existing attitudes, procedures and styles of working

- ▶ Catalyse change through the use of champions of participation, through developing a vision for children and young people's participation and through partnership working

- ▶ Internalise change through communicating and developing a shared vision and understanding of participation

- ▶ Institutionalise by mainstreaming practice.

Partnerships with men

In the most vulnerable families there is a pressing need to address the role of fathers, in particular how to enhance their participation in child protection. Research regarding child protection in the UK has not thoroughly covered the role of fathers in the child protection system. Ryan (2000) reviewed Department of Health research into child protection, and her findings suggested that this is partly reflective of the apparent lack of focus on fathers in child protection practice itself. Gibbons, Conroy and Bell (1995) followed referrals through the child protection system. At the referrals stage, natural fathers and stepfathers were noted as playing a part in the lives of most of the children, and by the stage of registration they were still mentioned as significant in 65 per cent and 25 per cent of registrations respectively. Two-thirds of natural fathers mentioned as significant at this stage were resident, as were nearly nine in ten of the stepfathers. Yet despite this, Ryan's research found professionals do not routinely examine how these men are significant in their children's lives, and whether their involvement in subsequent planning would be of benefit.

Several questions arise when considering what part fathers might play in child protection proceedings. Are they resident? Are they a risk or could they contribute to protection? Are they interested in the child's life or are they remote? Other research gives us a fuller picture about the fathers and father figures in families where there are child protection concerns, and the difficult relationships many fathers in this population have with their children. The majority of families that are subject to a referral have no wage earner, and even where two parents are present, a high percentage of the fathers are unemployed.

A number of reasons emerge as to why fathers are not currently engaged with child protection work. Men tend to play a smaller role in the lives of their children, leading professionals to conclude that they are less significant in the process of protecting children. Among fathers who are not particularly involved in the lives of their children, the presence of social work professionals tends to exacerbate these distant relationships rather than address them. Fathers generally, can perceive the involvement of social workers negatively. Non-offending fathers of sexual abuse victims may believe they should avoid physical and other forms of contact with their children, or don't know how they should respond (i.e. they do nothing to avoid doing any harm). Fathers, both abusive and non-abusive, may leave the home for a variety of reasons. Where parents have separated, mothers are often resistant to their former partners' involvement. Professionals can perceive men, particularly those implicated in abuse, as a threat both to their clients and to themselves. This reduces the potential for working constructively with all those significant in the lives of the children, and relevant to their abuse.

Partnerships with children

'We have everything to gain and nothing to lose
by forging partnerships with children.'

(Calder 1995)

The Children Act sets a moral, legal and practical obligation to involve children in our work by setting out a philosophy of empowerment via the extension of the duty to ascertain their wishes and feelings, and to give consideration to them (in the light of age and understanding), before making any decision. There is a wide range of additional reasons for involving children in our work and these include upholding children's rights; fulfilling legal responsibilities; improving services; improving decision-making; enhancing democratic processes; promoting children's protection; enhancing children's skills; empowering and enhancing self-esteem. Children's wishes and priorities may be different from those of adults and they need to be taken into account.

Children and young people report mixed experiences in relation to being given information, allowed space to discuss anxieties and being encouraged to participate in meetings. Whilst some children have felt let down, others have appreciated the genuineness, warmth and empathy of workers who made them feel valued and more than just 'a case'. It will be possible to work more closely with some children than others depending on the level of their development and the experiences which they have undergone. It should also include consideration as to the child's needs and abilities and each child's wish to be involved in the decision-making.

Workers need to find the most appropriate balance between enabling children to be involved whilst at the same time protecting them from exposure to stresses and conflicts inconsistent with their welfare. They will be capable of different levels of involvement and participation at different times. Age is a consideration: advice is against formal inclusion of children under ten in formal processes because of the presence of strangers, language, formality, and influence of parents on what they can and cannot say, etc.

Thomas (2002) has proposed a 'climbing wall' where the following key aspects are taken into account:

- ▶ The choice a child has over participation
- ▶ The information he/she has about their situation and rights
- ▶ The control he/she has over the decision-making process
- ▶ The voice he/she has in the decision
- ▶ The support he/she has in speaking up

- ▸ The degree of autonomy he/she has in speaking up
- ▸ The degree of autonomy he/she has to make decisions independently.

This suggests participation is highly complex in that a child feels able to speak up and is supported to do so but still has limited information and little control over decisions. There is no prescriptive way of securing children's participation although it is increasingly viewed as a requirement. We need to move toward meaningful participation and avoid tokenism and misrepresentation. Representative participation, involving diverse communities of children and young people will remain challenging. Participation can require considerable local cultural change.

There are a number of critical factors that need to be taken into account when considering involving children and young people in the decision-making process:

- ▸ The importance of information for children and young people to make an informed decision
- ▸ Time and explanation for children to properly understand the issues
- ▸ Ongoing consultation: decision-making is a process not to be confined to a one-off meeting
- ▸ The availability of support for the child or young person to talk through options in a non-judgmental environment
- ▸ Appropriate settings for decision-making are accessible, comfortable, private and appropriate to the young person's culture. Many children find the usual style of meetings uncomfortable
- ▸ Opportunities to prepare beforehand and talk about things afterwards are important
- ▸ Even-handedness is needed in the handling of different points of view
- ▸ Attention needs to be given to the child's priorities
- ▸ Access to an advocate or supporter is helpful

- ► Attention to any special needs of the child, including communication needs

- ► Feedback and discussion on outcomes is important.

It has been recognised that the children try to communicate through actions rather than words and that they cannot be relied upon to challenge explanations offered by the parents or parent figures, especially when the latter are present. However, the theme running throughout the inquiries in the late 1980s is that children do tell; children's telling begs the question of how to understand, and to interpret what they say. There are some useful suggestions for creating participatory processes for children and young people, which include consideration of:

- ► Clarifying objectives; Why participation? What goals are being set? What levels of participation are desired?

- ► Setting realistic timescales – planning and preparation

- ► Meetings or not? Are these the most appropriate forum for children and young people? How can they be child-friendly?

- ► Investing resources for participatory processes, training, support and skills development for staff and young people

- ► Supporting young people and staff – both will need information and skill development

- ► Building in involvement – participation should not be an afterthought (McNeish and Newman 2002).

Capturing and retaining the child as central to the decision-making processes

To any lay person it must be baffling how professionals so frequently seem to lose sight of the child, all too often allowing the focus to be on the parents. Why is it hard to keep the child in focus? Some of the reasons frequently cited include organisational structure, resources, capacity to implement change, work roles, the economic and political climate and prevailing community attitudes. Practitioners have expressed concern about the day-to-day demands of the job, large caseloads, competing priorities within cases and staff shortages. Increasingly complex and procedurally driven protection processes mean that there is a risk that the child's experience of these processes become lost.

The Victoria Climbié Inquiry found that procedural guidance could obscure rather than illuminate the child's perspective. Winkworth and McArthur (2006) observe that with so many agendas running concurrently it is easy to lose sight of the child in these processes and to allow other interests to dominate, and they concluded that, 'Being child-centred means being guided by contemporary knowledge about the welfare of children and young people and includes keeping the child and young person's perspective and experience uppermost in all considerations' (p.5).

Individual attributes are also contributory. A person's own values, beliefs, assumptions and experiences are likely to influence the manner in which individuals practice and the way in which they react to the nature of the work. Personal risks and safety are also contributory as workers are routinely expected to visit the homes of violent people, and potential harm to them is a real risk; threats of violence and hostility associated with home visits are stressful.

There is also the emotional labour of child protection work and workers need to manage their feelings (internal) and emotional expression (external) in interactions with multiple others (managers, colleagues, parents, and children). The emotional labour of engaging with children and developing a relationship may impact on child-focused practice. Therapeutic collusion raises a further challenge of balancing empathy for the parent/s, who may be trying to cope with their own difficulties and making some effort to change, with the needs of the child. There may be desire on behalf of the parent for change but progress to address serious adverse impact on the child has been insufficient. Workers' normal ways of coping can de-centre the child, whilst individual reactions to the nature of the work and strategies for maintaining physical and emotional safety (conscious and unconscious) may contribute to decisions not to visit the family home to see and talk with the child. Focus on, and empathy for, parents may prevent practitioners from seeing that parents have not been able to make changes or to progress fast enough to meet the needs of their children.

The Scottish Assessment Framework (2012) is the embodiment of keeping the child central. Rather than simply having the word 'child' in the triangle, it sets out three dimensions of a child's experience and articulates outcomes for them to attain (see Figure 2.1).

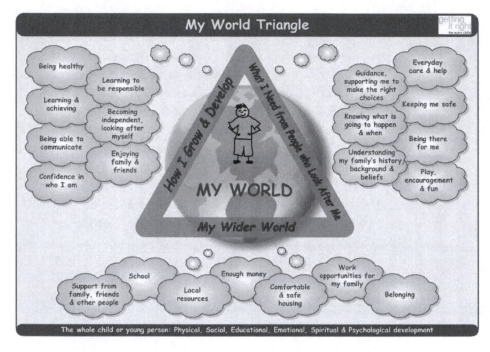

Figure 2.1 My world triangle
(Aberdeen Getting it Right 2012)

Worker challenges from the work

Andrew Cooper (2006) noted that social workers, and other professionals engaged in complex child care and child protection work, are charged by society with the job of thinking certain kinds of unthinkable thoughts, of facing emotional realities from which most of us are shielded most of the time. He argues that a central part of their role is about having the capacity for a certain kind of knowledge – knowledge rooted in a readiness to tolerate emotional experience of extreme mental pain, suffering, damage and dangerousness.

He refers to the emotional aliveness to the situation facing the worker. Something troubling, and perturbing is registered and is being thought about. This speaks to what it means to have, and make use of a professional relationship in child protection work. Through your own relationship with the family, you access something of the nature of their relationship. Through your own sense of disturbance, you register the potential risks, dangers and disturbances in the family relationships.

Emotional experience announces itself as a kind of disruption (be it ever so slight) to our emotional equilibrium. Whether the source of the emotion is primarily internal – in a thought or recollection that causes anxiety or the sudden eruption of a sense of grief, or relief, or joy – or primarily external – arising from the direct impingement of our environment upon us, if a colleague seems angry or unusually happy we register it as emotion through our bodies. Whatever thought processes arise from, or accompany such experiences, I want to suggest that if this bodily dimension is absent, then we lose contact with a vital source of information about what is taking place. As professionals, we of course must ask the question, 'Well, what exactly do such experiences tell us? How can we know whether they tell us more about ourselves than they do about the other person?'

Our ability to name emotional states – our own and others' – to have a language of emotion that is rooted in experience is fundamental to our everyday human functioning. The generalised lack of such a capacity even has a technical psychiatric name. At a simple level, what the proponents of the 'emotional intelligence' thesis are saying, is that this level of experience is necessary, ordinary, and an essential component of what we usually call 'thinking'.

> *In a sense we have two brains, two minds – and two different kinds of intelligence: rational and emotional. How we do in life is determined by both … it is emotional intelligence that matters …feelings are typically indispensable for rational decisions.* (Goleman 1996, p.28)

So also, 'There is intelligence in the emotions (and) intelligence can be brought to emotions' (Goleman 1996, p.40).

Of, course when we move to consider the emotional and intellectual complexity of doing child care work, then matters are indeed much more complex. But I want to try to illustrate that it is perfectly possible, as well as important, to approach these levels of our experience in a systematic and professionally attuned manner.

Hostage theory (Stanley and Goddard 1997)

The hostage theory describes where, under conditions of extreme threat, isolation and feelings of powerlessness, the hostage or victim of violence may unconsciously utilise ego-defences or engage in self-deception, with the result that the relationship with the perpetrator may move from one of fear or anger to ambivalence and then perhaps to understanding, friendship or attraction. Once this pathological relationship is established, it is likely to become self-reinforcing. Co-operation with the abuser may increase the person's safety, but at the cost of distorted thinking, increased feelings of helplessness, loss of control, possible feelings of guilt and anger, and where the victim is the child protection worker, an increased risk of re-abuse to the abused child. Figure 2.2 is a summary of the characteristics of a hostage relationship.

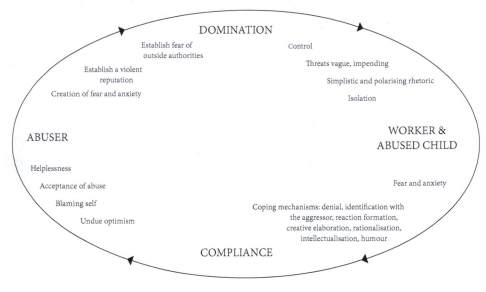

Figure 2.2 Characteristics of a hostage relationship
(Horwath 2000)

The hostage theory is increasingly being supported by a reinterpretation of the literature and empirical studies. At times the child protection worker is subject to direct violence and threats (explored later in this chapter in its own right). Workers who fear organisational blame become anxious and defensive encouraging entirely negative interpretations of risk, the pursuit of risk elimination and the growth of a 'cover your back' culture, can contribute to professional isolation and a fear of encouraging positive risk taking for fear of failure.

It has been suggested, then, that child protection work in England has in recent decades been beset by issues of competence and confidence. The competence of the child protection system and its workers has been questioned widely, and there has been an associated loss of confidence on the part of the general public, successive secretaries of state, the managers of safeguarding services and, crucially, safeguarding workers themselves. It has also been argued that many of the well-intentioned steps which have been taken to address problems of competence have, in reality, diminished rather than enhanced the capabilities and the self-belief of those involved, and that, as a consequence the child safeguarding system is in danger of entering a vicious spiral of decline.

Leadership challenges

Child protection is a highly pressured environment. To ensure that managers remain thoughtful, they need to manage their time and cope effectively with the demands, rather than become overwhelmed. The stress associated with a pressured work environment can be contagious. A manager needs to make sure that they are not a source of stress, support others under pressure, encourage a low-stress environment and attend to the sources of stress (SCIE 2009).

Gibbs, Dwyer and Vivekananda (2009) identified that the role of emotions in management and leadership has received increasing attention recently, as research has demonstrated the importance of relational models of management. Morrison (2007, p.8) argued that emotional intelligence is not an end in itself, rather a means to enrich thinking, action, service delivery and outcomes. It is apparent therefore that the emotional and cognitive resources required in child protection work, make it imperative that managers have a high capacity to understand and utilise emotions. Interestingly, emotion is frequently seen as the less reliable, undisciplined little sister of thinking. However, there is substantial evidence that emotions play an important role in decision-making and that using both emotional and cognitive sources of information and analysis are important if we are to make effective decisions. Morrison (2009b) has explored this issue in some detail. He cites research demonstrating that the presence of emotion can enhance the processing of information: subjects who were asked to view a distressing movie had greater recall when allowed to attend to their emotional responses than those asked to suppress them. Since the processing of information, much of which is emotionally laden, is vital to the task of child protection, it follows that usefully attending to feelings assists thoughtful analysis and assessment. Morrison goes on to argue that the, 'research suggests that the boundary between feeling and thinking, and the oft-heard call for the removal of emotions from so-called objective or professional decisions, needs reassessment' (p.12).

The research evidence that emotions contribute to effective practice has demonstrated expanded and creative thinking, the ability to make links between different sources of information, greater flexibility in negotiations and improved assessment and diagnostic skills (Morrison 2009).

Being aware of intense feelings, understanding these and managing them are vital to practitioners at every level of practice. Although emotions are present in decision-making (even if unacknowledged) in the face of overwhelming feelings, it is common for practitioners to attempt to suppress or avoid feelings. Managers need to be able to understand, process and use their own emotions effectively and assist others to do the same (Heifetz, Grashow and Linsky 2009).

There are many influences on how we think and feel; in working with people in distressing life circumstances, we will focus on three primary influences: what we bring with us, including our personal and professional experiences; our interaction with individuals and systems around us, and the nature of the work and its impact on our lives.

Managing one's feelings has a direct impact on developing mental agility. Being flooded with intense feelings particularly those that arouse fear, distress and anxiety, inhibits the brain's ability to process information cognitively. This processing allows for abstract consideration and a response that integrates information from all sources, including affective and cognitive. Perry (2006) noted the way that a fear-driven state prevents children from managing their own feelings and being free to engage in their environment. This in turn inhibits learning. The same is true for child protection practitioners and managers. We cannot learn and make thoughtful decisions if we are in an unprocessed emotional state.

Thresholds, eligibility criteria and assessment practice

Barry (2007) argued that the relationship between worker and client is paramount to effective working in risk assessment and management and yet it is being eroded by the language and politics of risk. There is an overall preoccupation with thresholds and short-term crisis intervention, resulting in risk-averse management, minimal scope for learning from mistakes and a lack of user involvement in decision-making. In English speaking countries, the preoccupation is with thresholds and short-term crisis intervention, resulting in risk aversion and a questioning of the professional role. In European countries, however, it is the relationship with the family that engenders trust and risk taking and validates the professional role. Technical manuals tend not to work because they become part of the system rather than external to it. Human relationships cannot be predicted like machines can and manuals are also static instruments which can never fully or effectively measure dynamically evolving human processes.

One of the key challenges for organisations is how to ration an ever-decreasing resource base yet deliver the same or even an enhanced level of service as indicated statutorily. One of the ways this is achieved is by adopting a restricted approach to assessment. For example, Smale *et al.* (1993) identified the following three models of assessment:

> ► *The questioning model*: the professional is assumed to be the expert in identifying need. The worker's behaviour is dominated by asking questions, listening to and processing the answers. There may be an assessment form to be filled in which guides the worker, although the questions reflect the worker's agenda, not other people's. This model assumes that questions can be

answered in a straightforward manner or that the professional is able to accurately interpret what is said and not said. Complexities of communication across cultural and other boundaries – race, gender, class and disability tend to be under estimated or even ignored. It may be enough to identify need but not if goals include increasing choices, maintaining independence and maximising people's potential, as other skills are required to achieve the above.

► *The exchange model*: the professional concentrates on an exchange of information between themselves and the service user and as such the question and answer pattern will be avoided as the worker seeks to engage the service user. The behaviour of the professional is crucial in establishing the respect and trust of the others and will vary over time. Definition of the problems and their resolution are arrived at through the initiative of the service user, and the professional follows or tracks the service user – to lead is to assume that the professional knows where to go. Any communication has to be checked out carefully – responding to the meaning that each person puts on the language used – and people are empowered by professionals who assume an all encompassing expert role. The model is supported by consumer studies and at its heart is the belief that people are and always will be the expert on themselves.

► *The procedural model*: the goal of the assessment is to gather information to see if the client fits or meets certain criteria that will make them eligible for services. With resources being increasingly scarce, so have tighter thresholds for the provision of a service emerged. The criteria pre-define what sort of person should get what resources and so the worker will complete a form with or without the service user. Questions are asked, and what is or is not a relevant question is determined by those setting the criteria for resource allocation. The agenda is set not by the worker or the client but by those who develop the forms, and the process is service driven.

Walker and Beckett (2010) noted that consumer studies and outcome research into helping relationships in social work, and other professional supportive relationships, support the principles underlying the exchange model of assessment. The questioning and procedural models are based on management imperatives about service allocation from finite resources.

They all raise questions about the notion of expertise and the use of power, especially in risky situations where a measure of short-term control may result in longer-term empowerment or vice versa. It may be that in practice there are elements of each appearing during different stages of a piece of work, or at different times with several contacts with a client. In adopting a questioning model, the challenge is to ensure we are taking an accurate snapshot of the problems, as we may be driven to focus on the presenting problem and quantify according to its severity rather than examining whether it is a problem that stands alone, or rather is part of a wider set of problems that may interact negatively with each other. This may be a practice of necessity but it does reinforce the snapshot approach as opposed to a more holistic approach. We know in many areas of work that problems rarely present singularly although the true risk is never quantified if we view all the problems through the primary or presenting one. This is evident in scarce specialist resources, where a young person presenting with sexually harmful behaviour may be referred to a service dealing with this problem, but they may not have a portfolio of knowledge, skills or assessment frameworks to deal with the problem holistically.

Jan Horwath (2000) has offered us an excellent road map for looking at thresholds. She developed a threshold diamond (see Figure 2.3).

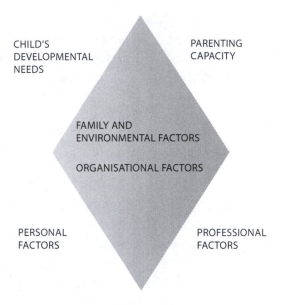

Figure 2.3 Threshold diamond
(Horwath 2000)

She argues that subjective factors influence judgments about thresholds such as organisational, professional and personal (detailed in Table 2.2).

TABLE 2.2 SUBJECTIVE FACTORS INFLUENCING JUDGMENTS ABOUT THRESHOLDS

Organisational	Professional	Personal
Staff vacancies	Understanding the assessment task	Stress
High staff turnover		Burnout
Absenteeism	Attitude towards child welfare	Low morale
Inexperienced staff	Deficit or empowerment approach	Past experiences
Organisational change		Personal demands and issues
Management style	Level of knowledge and skills	Support networks
Performance targets	Ability to keep abreast of practice developments	
Work setting	Level of experience	

Horwath, J. (2000)

Left unresolved, this renders threshold considerations a lottery for the child, with decisions often depending upon which worker on which team, with which manager makes a judgment. Thresholds, like judgments, are subjective.

We also know that there are different points in the process where a threshold is applied and this clearly impacts upon how informed a decision can be. We also know that the advent of thresholds across agencies, set to reflect their priorities and resources, often does not collectively offer a safety net for children, and it is known for some to slip through.

In the context of resource limitations and budgetary constraints, eligibility criteria provide a framework to help in determining appropriate levels of service response to identified needs. Eligibility criteria must have regard to those responsibilities laid upon social services by statute. At the same time, limited resources inevitably mean that it is not possible to fully discharge all of the duties and responsibilities laid upon local authorities. This means that individual authorities need to refine further the very widely defined concept of children in need as set out in the Children Act.

Eligibility criteria cannot be applied in too rigid and bureaucratic a fashion, and flexibility in their application is required in order to allow for the exercise of some degree of professional discretion. At the same time, it has to be recognised that such discretion must be applied in the context of political and managerial decisions about the overall allocation of resources and the application of the criteria. Inevitably, there will be variations in the perception of need and judgments about the appropriate service response.

Barriers and blocks to identifying and managing risk

Barriers to identifying and managing risk include:

- ▶ The unknown: inadequate knowledge of signs and symptoms or law policy and procedure
- ▶ The 'busy screen': the need to identify what is (e.g. air traffic controllers) important from a 'flood of data' including relevant

and irrelevant factors swirling around from one's own and other's cases

▶ Interpretation: being able to correctly interpret information in the context of assessing risk

▶ Status of information (e.g. the expert witness Professor Roy Meadow): failure to distinguish fact from opinion, being too trusting and uncritical

▶ Need to separate personal and professional values and opinions

▶ Unappreciated data: information may not be appreciated if it has come from a source which is distrusted (e.g. the agency or worker who routinely over- or under reacts

▶ The decoy of dual pathology: information may be missed if the receiver is decoyed by a different problem; it is difficult keeping an eye on several issues at the same time

▶ Focusing on just one problem and missing the oblique one that's more important (e.g. long-term neglect case; social worker had no recollection of young women's disclosure of sexual abuse)

▶ Investigators may have a false sense of security about a particular interpretation (e.g. medical assessments of sexual abuse in Cleveland)

▶ Competing tasks within the same visiting schedule, e.g. fostering and child protection

▶ The known and not assembled: individuals may hold information which they can withhold or which is not pieced together with the rest

▶ Not fitting the current mode of understanding: this has also been described as a loss of objectivity, and the importance of supervision is highlighted

▶ Long standing blocks: assumptions made at an early stage which influenced later interpretation of information (extended from Cleaver, Wattam and Cawson 1998, p.9).

Other considerations might also include the following:

- ▶ threats and intimidation
- ▶ time frames and system structuring to manage
- ▶ training disconnected from practice
- ▶ lack of reflection time
- ▶ fashionable models e.g. SOS and resolutions
- ▶ insufficient time to scrutinise previous files
- ▶ a lack of professional consensus on risk and focus differences
- ▶ a lack of an agreed understanding of key concepts – such as emotional abuse
- ▶ an expectation that workers fulfil a 'Jack of all trades' approach
- ▶ lack of access to evidence-based assessment materials
- ▶ frameworks for analysis being non-existent.

Blocks to recognising risks include:

- ▶ Information treated discretely:
  - » The unknowns
  - » The known but not fully appreciated
  - » The known and not assembled.
- ▶ Selective interpretations include:
  - » 'Rule of optimism'
  - » Desensitisation: The more familiar the situation the less risky it seems
  - » Denial as a defence
  - » Decoy of dual pathology
  - » Narrow focus on one aspect of concern
  - » Translation of low probability to impossibility
  - » Tendency to minimise delayed risks
  - » Verbalisation of risk does not reduce it.

Pervasive belief systems:

- ▸ Assumptions made at early stage influence later interpretations
- ▸ Evidence discounted to confirm validity of a previous plan.

Concrete solutions:

- ▸ Reliance on practical measures to deal with emotional problems
- ▸ Practical indicators used as sole measure of whether care taking has improved.

Dale, Green and Fellows (2002) also highlighted other important sources of information bias as including emotional factors which play a crucial role in the interpretation of information and formation of judgments. These influences stem from personal past experiences (ranging from privilege to abuse), present circumstances (satisfactions, dissatisfactions, stresses) and future expectations (aspirations and fears). These may be complicated by less conscious processes of projection, transference and countertransference which can impact strongly as sources of bias. Emotional status, countertransference and mood can have a major impact on professional perceptions, behaviour and judgments. Also, cognitions are thinking processes of the 'is the glass half full or half empty?' variety that affect how the world is interpreted. Cognitive styles, belief systems and levels of knowledge affect what a person notices and ignores, how such observations are construed, and the degree of importance that becomes attached to each interpretation and its implications. A powerful source of bias lies in the operation of selective interpretations in favour of a confirmatory hypothesis. Evidence is only observed and incorporated when it supports a pre-existing belief or inclination. Evidence that does not support the interpretation is either not noticed, ignored or discounted. Belief systems also introduce significant sources of bias. One example is divergent views regarding parental potential for change.

Taylor (2015) talked about the dangers of overestimating risk but notes it is largely driven by a fear of making mistakes, of underestimating risk or simply missing something. The impact on professional careers is very real: disciplinary action, the media, and now the threat by Mr Cameron to introduce jail sentences for those who fail to identify risk situations. Taylor also pointed to the reality that there are few negative consequences for estimating risk too highly – whilst a low estimation of risk can be disastrous on all fronts. It might mean more paperwork and sometimes more input is required, but this frustrating exercise is simply part of the risk-averse deal. The concern remains, of course, that attention will be distracted from a really dangerous situation and something of great importance is missed.

The challenges of evidence-based practice

There has been a growing political expectation that public sector programmes should be able to objectively and scientifically demonstrate programme success and client satisfaction (Rist 1997), partly as a consequence of a growing focus on demonstrating service cost-effectiveness and cost efficiency, and ongoing concerns regarding the social cost of poorly performing programmes (Tomison 1999). Curtis (1997) also argued that it was, 'the seductive appeal of absolute certainty' thought to result from the use of quantitative, economically-focused performance criteria that has led to the domination of scientific or experimental evaluation methods. Thus, in the 1990s, following a trend evident across a variety of fields, including medicine, welfare and education, there was a growing shift to adopting an evidence-based approach to child protection practice. Based on the view that, 'Formal rationality of practice based on scientific methods can produce a more effective and economically accountable means of social service' (Webb 2001, p.60), the intention is to make policy and practice decisions informed by a critical appraisal of the best evidence available rather than merely, 'accepting famous ideas just because they are famous' (Sheldon 2001, p.803). This has been keenly embraced by the judiciary: 'Expressions of opinion must be supported by detailed evidence and articulated reasoning' (Munby J 2003).

'Evidence is the apple pie of decision-making. Who could be against it?' (Peterson 2001). Evidence-based practice can be defined as, 'the conscientious, explicit, and judicious use of current best evidence in making decisions about the care of individuals' (Sackett, Richardson, Rosenberg and Haynes 1997, p.2). More specifically, it involves, 'integrating individual practice expertise with the best available external evidence from systematic research as well as considering the values and expectations of clients' (Gambrill 1999, p.346).

The evidence-based practice movement therefore urges practitioners to seek out and critically assess relevant research literature and findings. 'Evidence-based practitioners should themselves collect data systematically, specify outcomes in measurable terms and systematically monitor and evaluate their interventions' (Hill 1999, p.20). Throughout this process, judgments need to be made about the research, its methods, sampling and analysis. In this way, the research evidence should support practitioners in their professional judgments, rather than undermine them.

Evidence from research can provide information to help us to understand needs, to understand causes and to understand what works. All evidence has the potential to provide information that can help practice decisions. By making research work better for service delivery it is possible to improve outcomes for service users, improve accountability to stakeholders, increase objectivity and fairness in decision-making, increase confidence and quality of decisions, as well as gaining more skilful practitioners.

Some forms of evidence are more trustworthy than others, because steps are taken to reduce bias. Evidence-based practitioners need to be discerning about the evidence they use. Sources of research evidence include:

- ▶ Systematic reviews: reliable succinct summary of key messages
- ▶ Overviews: summary of a review of literature
- ▶ Good practice guidelines
- ▶ Peer reviewed journals
- ▶ Research presented as conferences
- ▶ Professional journals
- ▶ Performance and evaluation data for your team.

Unfortunately, many have taken evidence-based practice to mean, 'that practice should be based upon the evidence of randomised control trials alone and that all other practice is either not evidence-based or of a lower quality… This narrow approach is a common misunderstanding of the paradigm' (Ramchandani, Joughin and Zwi 2001, p.60). In actuality, 'The phrase evidence-based practice draws attention to the kind of evidence needed to rigorously test different kinds of practice-related claims. What is needed to critically appraise data regarding a question depends on what kind of question it is, (e.g. question concerning effectiveness, validity of a measure, predictive accuracy of a risk assessment measure') (Gambrill 1999, p.344).

There are also a number of very real obstacles to evidence-based practice that include inadequate access to research information, lack of knowledge about how to find or appraise research, insufficient time or resources and competing priorities, lack of support from colleagues, a culture of acting before reflecting, poor communication of research within organisations, perceived threats to professional autonomy and lack of relevant and timely evidence.

We also have to acknowledge that not all decisions are based on evidence, because good quality evidence is not available, or evidence is not available in a relevant, accessible and compelling way or decision-makers, and/or their organisations, are not committed to evidence-based practice.

What evidence can be brought before the court?

The purpose of evidence is to put information before the court to prove 'facts' that are at issue in proceedings. Evidence can be divided into three categories; while all three are admissible, each will be given different weight by the court.

- ▶ Primary: direct knowledge, i.e. the witness's own knowledge and observation

- ▶ Secondary: hearsay, i.e. information passed to the witness by someone else

- ▶ Tertiary: evidence given by an opinion witness from secondary and other sources from which the witness forms an opinion.

When a case reaches care proceedings, social workers may present recommendations that are likely to mean significant and often permanent change in the lives of children, young people and families. It is the responsibility of the local authority – and the social worker as its representative – to make recommendations only on the basis of the best available evidence of what is likely to produce the best (or least harmful) outcome. Otherwise, our actions are not alleviating significant harm. 'Meaning well' is not enough.

Over the last decade, debates about the quality of decision-making in social care have led to the development and critique of evidence-based practice, which aspires to eliminate wrong, harmful (and costly) interventions. Evidence-based practice has been criticised for being too mechanistic and not reflecting the complexity of the decision-making process (see Webb 2001).

Evidence-informed practice includes the best available evidence about what is effective (including research), practice wisdom (built up through learning from operational experience) and feedback from, and views of, service users (e.g. about expectations, preferences, the impact of their problems and our interventions). Being 'evidence-informed' in the workplace implies a number of things:

- Asking challenging questions about current practice
- Knowing how and where to find relevant research
- Understanding key messages about what works
- Reflecting on your values and experiences in order to learn
- Developing methods of measuring the impact your work is having on users
- Listening to what users have to say about services
- Being explicit about how research, experience and user views have informed your conclusions, proposals and decisions.

Social workers will often talk of 'gut feeling' when they describe their work with children and families, and it is in this that they have knowledge and expertise usually beyond the reach of other professionals

(Brophy *et al.* 2001). This gut feeling is an important consequence of observation and time spent with families and it constitutes much of what a social worker will represent as evidence. However, it is important to understand exactly what social workers mean by gut feeling, and how it does (or does not) fit with the principles of research.

There are many definitions of research. It might be defined as an extension of common sense – finding out about things, looking for information about them, trying to make sense of them. This definition makes a link between research and its role in critically appraising your gut feeling and observations. On its own, gut feeling is not robust and can be criticised as culturally determined; however, critically appraising your gut feeling is a crucial process to achieving objectivity. You may or may not confirm your feeling, but you will gain the necessary evidence to articulate to the court the evidence on which your statement and oral evidence is based. Your gut feeling must stand up to testing and it is the role of the court to ensure this happens.

Research is more than just an extension or process of common sense, however. Research evidence can also be defined as, '[referring] to the results or findings of systematic, robust and trustworthy empirical enquiry' (Becker and Bryman 2004). So a social worker also needs to judge the quality and reliability of the research, what theoretical standpoint has been taken, and how robust the methodology is in relation to judging findings. Understanding methodologies and applying critical analysis to findings is the key to understanding research. Reading skills must be supplemented with an ability to appraise critically.

Expertise is a combination of skill and knowledge that helps you provide opinion. In social work it should include:

▶ Academic or formal knowledge

▶ Practice knowledge

▶ Personal skills that relate to practice.

Figure 2.4 identifies a model of professional knowledge forms.

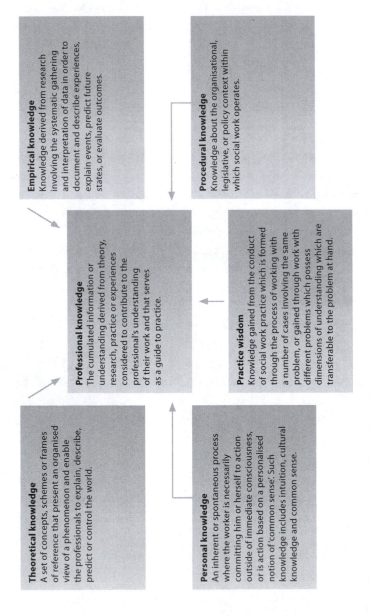

Empirical knowledge
Knowledge derived from research involving the systematic gathering and interpretation of data in order to document and describe experiences, explain events, predict future states, or evaluate outcomes.

Procedural knowledge
Knowledge about the organisational, legislative, or policy context within which social work operates.

Professional knowledge
The cumulated information or understanding derived from theory, research, practice or experiences considered to contribute to the professional's understanding of their work and that serves as a guide to practice.

Practice wisdom
Knowledge gained from the conduct of social work practice which is formed through the process of working with a number of cases involving the same problem, or gained through work with different problems which possess dimensions of understanding which are transferable to the problem at hand.

Theoretical knowledge
A set of concepts, schemes or frames of reference that present an organised view of a phenomenon and enable the professionals to explain, describe, predict or control the world.

Personal knowledge
An inherent or spontaneous process where the worker is necessarily committing him or herself to action outside of immediate consciousness, or is action based on a personalised notion of 'common sense'. Such knowledge includes intuition, cultural knowledge and common sense.

Figure 2.4 Model of professional knowledge forms

Pros and cons of using research evidence in the court arena

Arguments in favour of using research in evidence in the family court	Arguments against using research in evidence in the family court
▶ There are examples in case law where research has been used well by social workers (e.g. in relation to domestic violence) and the use of research evidence affected the outcome positively and set the precedent for future cases. ▶ Research evidence can alert social workers to new ideas and help them challenge current policies and procedures that may not be in the best interests of the child, even though they are established. ▶ Complex cases leading up to care proceedings are hugely challenging; research is essential in helping inform best outcomes. ▶ Social workers wishing to use research can learn lessons from the literature on the use of research by expert witnesses. ▶ Relying on experts is expensive, particularly if they are not from the local area; and the necessary experts are not always available. ▶ Case discussion groups can help social workers think broadly about a particular case (confidentiality is an issue, but there are solutions to this), including reflection on research in discussions can help achieve better outcomes for children.	▶ Research is too general and ambiguous; decision-making in child cases is highly complex. ▶ There is a drive towards streamlining content and procedure. One aim of the protocol is to reduce the length of statements and reports; incorporating research would lengthen statements. ▶ Social worker confidence levels and skills are low; this applies even more so in the family court, where the profile of the social worker is low. ▶ Social workers are often out of their depth when it comes to incorporating research into reports and decision-making; the key is embedding an evidence-informed approach throughout the agency. (This view was contentious; others supported a combination of evidence-informed policy and individual use of research in reports.) ▶ The work conditions and career structure of social work is not conducive to aiding best practice among social workers. Individual social workers are overburdened with cases; there is little time for the quality of approach that is necessary to be evidence-informed.

Critical thinking

> To have a better chance of understanding the risks of harm that children face, practitioners should be encouraged to be curious and to think critically and systematically. Being aware of the way in which separate factors can interact to protect from harm or cause increased risks of harm to the child is a vital step in this process. Since in many of the cases families were known to adult services and not just to children's services, the wellbeing of children and whole families must also be a priority for those working in services for adults. (Brandon *et al.* 2008, p.2)

'Critical thinking' is a notion that can assist in making sense of (research) evidence and its practice implications. Gambrill (1997) offers the following definition: 'Critical thinking involves the careful examination and evaluation of beliefs and actions in order to arrive at well-reasoned ones' (Gambrill 1997, p.125). She argues that critical thinking encourages us to examine the context in which problems occur, view questions from different points of view, identify and question our own assumptions and to consider the possible consequences of different beliefs or actions. In this way the notion of critical thinking values independent thinking and, 'encourages intellectual modesty rather than pomposity, by emphasising the importance of our being aware of what we don't know. It discourages arrogance as well as the assumption that we know better than others, or that our beliefs should not be subject to critical evaluation' (Gambrill 1997, p.128).

Critical thinking is also associated with reasoning which includes having reasons for what we believe and do, and being aware of what they are, critically evaluating our own beliefs and actions and being able to present to others the reasons for our beliefs and actions (Cottrell 2005). Critical thinking incorporates an attitude of mindfulness – that is, an awareness of one's own thoughts, feelings, motivations, actions – that links very readily to the practice of reflection. Skills and attributes required include curiosity, open-mindedness, the ability to manage uncertainty and not knowing, being able to question one's own as well as others' assumptions, the ability to hypothesise, self-awareness, observation skills, problem solving skills, the ability to synthesise and evaluate information from a range of sources, creativity, sense making and the ability to present one's thoughts clearly, both verbally and in writing. Gambrill (1997) claims that critical thinkers can identify the elements of thought involved in tackling a problem and routinely ask the following kinds of questions:

- ▶ What is the precise purpose (goal) of my thinking?
- ▶ What precise question (problems) am I trying to answer?
- ▶ Within what point of view (perspective) am I thinking?
- ▶ What am I taking for granted, what assumptions am I making?
- ▶ What information am I using (research evidence, data, facts, observation)?
- ▶ How am I interpreting that information?
- ▶ What conclusions am I coming to?
- ▶ If I accept the conclusions, what are the implications for my practice?
- ▶ What would the consequence be if I put my thoughts into action?

So, critical thinking in respect to research can help to identify the ways in which research, and a person's interpretation of it, may become distorted. It seeks to identify the weaknesses and limitations of one's own position, highlighted by the research evidence. It relies on an acceptance that there are many valid points of view, each of which may lead to insight:

- ▶ Could I be wrong?
- ▶ Have I considered alternative views?
- ▶ Do I have sound reasons to believe that this plan will help this service user?

Some examples of critical thoughts about research:

- ▶ How do I know that this claim is true?
- ▶ Who presented it as accurate? Are vested interests involved? How reliable are the sources?
- ▶ Do the facts/perspectives presented stand up to scrutiny?

▶ Is there evidence that the evidence is reliable? How many critical tests have been performed? How have they been affected by bias? Have the results been replicated? How representative were the samples used?

▶ Have any facts or perspectives been omitted?

▶ Are there any other promising points of view? Have these been tested?

Gambrill (1997) states that the critical thinker is more likely to:

▶ Clearly describe problems

▶ Discover problem related resources

▶ Think contextually and see the links between individual and wider problems

▶ Focus upon outcomes related to service users' problems

▶ Accurately assess the likelihood of attaining outcomes

▶ Select interventions that address problems, select effective plans

▶ Use resources wisely

▶ Respect and have empathy for others

▶ Continue to learn and enhance skills.

Gambrill (1990) identifies the benefits of critical thinking as increasing the accuracy of decisions, avoiding cognitive biases, recognising errors and mistakes as learning opportunities, accurately assessing the likelihood of attaining hoped-for outcomes, making valuable contributions at case conferences, selecting effective plans, respecting and having empathy for others, continuing to learn and enhancing one's skills and increasing self-awareness.

Barriers to critical thinking in practice include the already well established point of child protection work making heavy demands on reasoning skills. With an issue as important as children's welfare, it is vital to have the best standard of thinking that is humanly possible, and mistakes are costly to the child and the family (Munro 2008).

Here are some errors that can occur if we act on inaccurate accounts: overlooking client assets, describing behaviour unrelated to its context, misclassifying clients, continuing intervention too long, focusing on irrelevant factors, selecting ineffective intervention methods, increasing client dependency, withdrawing intervention too soon and not arranging for the generalisation and maintenance of positive gains.

Errors and their impact on workers and outcomes

Mistakes are inevitable, yet they can offer valuable learning opportunities if corrective feedback is received. We should recognise that mistakes will be made – it is impossible to avoid making mistakes; recognise that it is our duty to minimise avoidable mistakes; be on the lookout for mistakes; embrace a self-critical attitude; welcome others pointing out our mistakes, and accept objective criticism when it is specific and provides clear reasons why specific statements or specific hypotheses appear to be false or specific arguments invalid.

In acknowledging mistakes we should accept that openness is a precondition for learning; complaints, oversights and errors are logged and replayed, mistakes are acknowledged, even celebrated as a source of information, everyone wants to do better in future and a 'learning organization' develops.

Decision errors are deviations from some standard decision process that increase the likelihood of bad outcomes. Human error involves investigating how knowledge was or could have been brought to bear in the evolving infinite. Experts do not make errors because they are doing the best that could be done under the circumstances. Reason (2000) distinguishes among mistakes, violations, lapses and slips that may occur during planning, carrying out a task or monitoring. A violation entails knowingly omitting an important step; a lapse involves not recalling an intention to carry out an important task at the time needed and a slip entails unwittingly omitting an important task in a sequence and not detecting it.

Reason (1997) offered a number of helpful examples of possible contributing factors to errors: unfamiliarity with a potentially important situation which is novel or occurs infrequently, shortage of time for error detection and correction, a mismatch between real and perceived risk, operator inexperience (for example, a new employee), an impoverished quality of information conveyed by procedures and person-to-person interaction, little or no independent checking or testing of output and a conflict between immediate and long-term objectives.

If we focus specifically on errors in child protection practice we can include an over-reliance on self-report, an over-reliance on strengths-loaded frameworks and processes. Incident-led (reactive) practice identifies uncollated process of concern historically, over-optimism to dynamic processes without anchoring in static records, a focus on the adult losing sight of the child, individual agency blinkered practice, records don't match casework, snapshots, misinterpreting cues and information, or collecting too much (irrelevant) information.

Common errors of reasoning in child protection reported by Munro (1999) include a failure to revise risk assessments – difficulty in changing minds, considering alternative perspectives, a failure to look at own files, past information overlooked, a failure to take a long-term perspective, to note emerging patterns, written evidence being overlooked in preference to direct reports, scepticism about new evidence that challenges existing views, being uncritical about evidence that supports existing view, taking the parents reactions during the assessment as representative, a failure to check facts and information and a tendency to groupthink and conformity.

In errors of commission, we do something that decreases the likelihood of discovering valuable options. We may look only for data that confirm our beliefs, jump to conclusions, stereotype people or theories, misinterpret cues, assume that correlation reflects causation or prematurely discard a valuable option. Conversely, with errors of omission, we fail to do something, which decreases the likelihood of discovering valuable options. We may not question initial assumptions; fail to pose well-structured questions related to information needed to make decisions; fail to seek out critically appraised problem-related research findings; ignore the role of environmental causes; overlook cultural differences or overlook client assets. Howitt (1992) identified further errors in relation to the process and processing of information. Templating involves checking the individual against a 'social template' to see whether he or she fits a particular pattern. An instigating event, such as a bruise on a child, leads to the suspect person being compared with the template. Justification refers to using theory to justify decisions rather than critically examining the beliefs and evidence that have influenced the decisions. For example, some child protection errors result from views that justify contradictory courses of action. Consider the assumption that a family or family member is only 'treatable' if they understand the implications of and admit responsibility for what has happened. If they say they did abuse the child, the child is removed; if they say they did not, they are assumed to be lying and the child is removed. Thus the outcomes from truthful or false denial are the same, the family is damned if it does and damned if it doesn't. The view justifies all possible explanations and increases the risk that a child will be or remain separated from his or her family. Ratcheting refers to a tendency for the child protection processes to move in a single direction. Changing a decision or undoing its effects seems infrequent, even in circumstances where this is appropriate. It has a 'never going back' quality that may appear to protect the helper by reducing the chances of a risky decision resulting in problems or criticism.

Reason (2009) identifies four basic components in an error: the intention, the action, the outcome and the context. Errors of intention encompass whether there was an intention to act (as opposed to an involuntary action), whether the actions went as planned (absent-minded slips and lapses) and whether they achieved their intended outcome (was there a flaw in the plan of action?) (Reason 2009, p.29). Analysis of the action component raises questions such as, was the action based on a good assessment of the problem and plan of intervention; was it executed as planned; and was it adequately monitored to ensure it was going as planned? (Reason 2009, p.32). Much of the analysis in child abuse inquiries has focused on these aspects. For example, inadequacies in the assessment of the child's safety are frequently linked to flaws in communication between different professionals in contact with the family (Munro 1999; Reder and Duncan 2003). Analysing errors according to the third component – the outcome – is problematic in child protection. An adverse outcome in child protection may not, on investigation, be considered to be due to any professional error. However distressing the outcome, the blame may rest with the perpetrator alone. A good decision process can lead to a poor outcome and a poor decision process can be followed by a good outcome. The fourth component

– the context – is being increasingly recognised in other high risk services as the most useful focus for solutions. Reason (2009) contends that the situation in which errors occur is at least as important as its psychological antecedents (if not more so) in triggering its occurrence and shaping its form. 'We cannot easily change human cognition, but we can create contexts in which errors are less likely and, when they do occur, increase their likelihood of detection and correction … situations can be more or less error provoking' (Reason 2009, p.32).

There are many psychological and organisational factors that contribute to creating a blame culture. First, it offers a satisfying explanation. Those practitioners closest to the tragic outcome are readily identifiable and available to blame. Blaming someone is psychologically satisfying; it distances oneself from any responsibility and feeds the belief that errors are avoidable, not just acts of fate. One bad apple has caused the problem and everything will be fine if they are removed. The world, therefore, seems less dangerous and less beyond our control.

Second, hindsight bias distorts our judgment. Once we know the outcome, we have a tendency to overestimate what could have been anticipated with foresight (Fischhoff 1975). The significance of new information, such as an observed change, seems so clear in retrospect to those who know how important it turned out to be. They grossly overestimate how easy it was to see at the time, when it was hidden in a mass of other information. To the retrospective observer all the lines of causality home in on the bad event; but those on the spot, possessed only of foresight, do not see this convergence (Reason 2009, p.75).

Third, judgment is biased by the fundamental attribution error. We tend to explain other people's behaviour differently from our own. When analysing our own actions, we are very aware of the context, of the factors that led us to frame the situation in a particular way that then led to the choice of action. Explanations therefore tend to focus on those contextual factors. When explaining other people's actions, however, we are most aware of the behaviour itself and so focus our explanations on that rather than the context.

Fourth, organisational factors encourage blaming. To politicians and senior management, person-centred explanations have the obvious attraction of distancing themselves from the adverse outcome. It is also a simple route to take. It is usually easy to identify the people close to the tragedy who made mistakes and target them for improvement, whereas a study of the wider organisational context would take considerably more effort. Individual responsibility also fits readily into the legal system, where it is easier to ascribe individual responsibility than corporate responsibility.

The cumulative effect of blame is to create what Reason (2009) terms the 'vulnerable system syndrome'. This is characterised by three pathological entities: 'blame, denial, and the single-minded and blinkered pursuit of the wrong kind of excellence – the latter usually takes the form of seeking to achieve specific performance targets'. A vulnerable system is particularly prone to focusing only on single-loop learning – on monitoring and enforcing compliance with existing prescriptions – while double-loop learning is severely hampered by individuals' reluctance to report problems for fear of being criticised.

Janis and Mann (1977) referred to 'cognitive' or 'information' overload – suggesting that we cannot cope with a lot of information in our head at the same time. We cannot 'think straight' we cannot 'take on board' or 'work with' too many pieces of information at the same time. It is not just that, when given too much information, we fail to remember it all. It is also that when tasks get difficult we use a number of aids and devices – in research referred to as 'heuristics' – in order to help us cope (Kassin 2004). Heuristics may help us to complete a task (e.g. describing someone), but they regularly lead us to error. For example, we may have noticed that someone was old and assume, fill in or jump to the conclusion that he or she has grey hair.

Munro (2002) pointed out that to reduce human error we put psychological pressure on workers to perform better, reduce the human factor as much as possible – formalise, mechanise, proceduralise and increase surveillance to ensure compliance with instructions. What we should be encouraging instead is reflective practice which at a really basic level is about learning from our mistakes. But it can be more useful to extend this concept and use it more actively during the process of our work with service users. In other words, reflecting on what we are doing as we are doing it. It also involves reflecting back on a piece of work ideally with a colleague or supervisor and evaluating what happened and what we might have done differently.

Within the literature on reflective practice, it is possible to identify four modes of reflective practice – technical, practical, critical and process (Ruch 2000). Technical reflection is related to technical rationality and the empirical analytic level of knowing. It is decision-making about immediate behaviours or skills and it is generally associated with instrumental reflection as a means of problem solving. Technical reflection uses 'external/technical' sources of knowledge derived from formal theory and research to examine essential skills in order to resolve an identified problem. Practical reflection suggests that rather than knowledge acquisition being solely 'top-down', i.e. formal theoretical learning imposed from outside of the practice situation, it is also, and as importantly, 'bottom-up', i.e. gained from specific practice experiences. Critical reflection seeks to transform practice by challenging the existing social, political and cultural conditions that promote certain constitutive interests at the expense of others and the structural forces that distort or constrain professional practice. Process reflection focuses on the unconscious as well as the conscious aspects of practice, recognises the mirroring processes that operate in practice and emphasises the unavoidable impact on practitioners of the emotional content of interactions.

Ruch (2007) added in the notion of holistic reflective practice which she sees as having the potential to encourage thoughtful and creative practice capable of addressing the challenges of contemporary childcare practice. Findings from this research indicate that for holistic reflective practice to be facilitated, the interdependence of the practitioner, team and organisational contexts need to be recognised. Practitioners need to work within safe containing contexts characterised by: clear organisational and professional boundaries; multifaceted reflective forums; collaborative and communicative working practices; and open and contextually connected managers.

The exercise of professional judgments

Professional judgment is the magical quality which requires the interpretative use of knowledge, the use of practice wisdom, a sense of purpose, appropriateness and feasibility (adapted from Eraut 1994). Judgment making is recognised as one of the hallmarks of professional activity, requiring a demonstrable mastery of competence within the specific knowledge base as well as the ability to synthesise and analyse the information or data collected in specific circumstances. Within the social work literature it is suggested that judgment is a compilation of knowledge, skills, values and experience, a mixture of professional authority, including knowledge, experience and expertise, coupled with professional autonomy, meaning a capacity for independent thought and action (Youll and Walker 1995). Judgment in assessment involves establishing the nature of the problem and the appropriate response in the short, medium and longer term, relating to decision thresholds, determining interventions and assessing progress and consequent actions.

Problems, threats and challenges to the exercise of professional judgment

Munro (2002) organised expertise into the categories of knowledge and skills that child protection practitioners use when they are trying to analyse, make sense of situations and make decisions and judgments. These are:

- ▶ Formal knowledge: laws, policies, procedures and theories; empirical research, evidence drawn, for example, from training and reading.

- ▶ Practice wisdom: folk psychology, social norms, cultural diversity; a combination of everyday skills and wisdom with enriched skills drawn from training and practice experience.

- ▶ Values: all practice takes place in an ethical framework including, for example, consideration of the balance of rights and needs and awareness of discrimination in all its forms.

- ▶ Emotional wisdom: awareness of the emotional impact of work on oneself and others and the ability to deal with this and use it as a source of understanding about the behaviour of children, families, self and other professionals.

▶ Reasoning skills: ability to critically reflect on one's practice and reason from a basis of experience and knowledge. Ability to understand the balance between intuition and analysis in one's own decisions; and the ability to make a conscious appraisal of risks and benefits flowing from actions.

Investigating and intervening in child protection is by no means an exact science. It is less to do with verifiable facts as it is to do with descriptions of human behaviour that are open to interpretation (Munro 2005). Risk assessment tools are becoming the priority and the focus of much worker–client contact and tend to replace rather than inform professional judgment; there is little confidence in their ability to predict risk accurately (Barry 2007).

An underlying problem is that there are two different approaches to human reasoning: analytical and intuitive. Analytical reasoning is described as 'a step-by-step, conscious, logically defensible process', as opposed to intuitive reasoning which is 'a cognitive process that somehow produces an answer, solution or idea without the use of a conscious, logically defensible, step-by-step process' (Hammond 1996, p.60). In child protection practice, many professionals rely heavily on intuitive skills (Munro 1999) despite the evidence that, 'Intuition is a hazard, a process not to be trusted, not only because it is inherently flawed by "biases" but because the person who resorts to it is innocently and sometimes arrogantly overconfident when employing it' (Hammond 1996 p.88).

Stewart and Thompson (2004) summarise some of the literature on human decision-making relating to practitioners' prediction of risk. Four biases have been identified:

▶ Practitioner's tendency to under use base rates when predicting events that are uncommon (which leads to a tendency to overestimate the occurrence of an event)

▶ Confirmatory biases often prevent practitioners from considering evidence impartially (which leads to a tendency to search for evidence consistent with the conclusion they believe to be correct)

- Illusory correlations have been found to influence clinical predictions (which leads to a tendency to see two events as being related when they are not, or are related to a lesser extent)

- Practitioners tend to place too much importance on the unique characteristics of a case (which leads to a tendency to believe that similar cases are quite different and that unique characteristics are better predictors than those that are more common).

Research has shown that people are not rational thinkers who have occasional lapses; rather, they create rules that reduce difficult judgmental tasks to simpler ones by restricting the amount of information they consider (Munro 1999). These cognitive shortcuts to aid decision-making, known as heuristics, may take different forms which may be combined together in use (Vaughan and Hogg 1995). A particular example is the 'availability' heuristic, which guides decision-making about the likelihood of an event occurring according to how quickly similar instances or associations come to mind. Another is the 'false consensus effect', in which people tend to see their own behaviour as typical and assume that, under similar circumstances, others would behave in the same way (Vaughan and Hogg 1995). Such theoretical constructs, borrowed from the disciplines of cognitive and social psychology, may account for some of the observations of researchers in child protection practice.

Munro (1999) made the following observations of the way that information was used to make decisions in child protection practice. Practitioners were found to be uncritical of new information about a child or family if it supported their view of the family and, conversely, they tended to be sceptical about new information if it conflicted with their view. This led to practitioners being very slow to revise their judgments about families and to focus on a narrow range of information about a family. This phenomenon was also found by Reder *et al.* (1993), and these authors referred to this restricted consideration of information about cases as 'automatic thinking'. Along with automatic thinking, the authors also identified two categories of 'fixed views' in practitioners about families: (1) socio-political attitudes (e.g. differentiated views about how people should behave according to class status); and (2) strong personal or professional views.

Munro's (1999) research also supported the notion that facts are more memorable if they are vivid, concrete and emotive and the most recent information comes to mind more easily. For practitioners, this led to a preoccupation with what was happening now in a case, again narrowing the perspective taken of the case. This preoccupation prevented practitioners from standing back from the case and considering patterns of behaviour and cumulative factors in chronic abuse and neglect. This finding is supported by observations that the application of risk assessment tools to practice tends to minimise the effects of abuse on children and ignore cumulative harm (Goddard et al. 1999).

Dingwall et al. (1983) found that the actions and decision-making of practitioners was affected by what they termed the 'rule of optimism'. In applying this rule of optimism, practitioners tended to view the behaviour and intentions of families in the most favourable light. The rule of optimism is made up of two cognitive devices. 'Cultural relativism' refers to the tendency to try not to be judgmental about how other people live and stems from the belief that all cultures are equally valid and that all ways of rearing children may be similarly valid. 'Natural love' refers to the belief that all parents instinctively love their children and want the best for them, despite how they may go about achieving this. Support for the application of the rule of optimism and the selective ways in which practitioners recall information has been demonstrated by research that has shown that practitioners tend to underestimate the levels of violence present in the families they deal with when asked to recall such information from memory (Stanley and Goddard 2002).

Dingwall et al. (1983) expand their critique of decision-making to cases where they observed the phenomenon of 'defensible decision making'. This refers to a rationale for making a particular decision that can be promoted as the best decision, sometimes because it is presented as the only decision that could have been made. Defensible decision-making' adds a new influence to the process of decision-making in the form of accountability. Accountability and its influence on decision-making is not straightforward because there may be a tension between who or what the decision maker feels more accountable to (the client or the organisation). In an organisation that is perceived to be overloaded, the decision not to take action may be the more defensible because it means the commitment of scarce resources does not have to be justified. On a more individual level, the decision to take no action in a case where parents are likely to be very hostile means that managers do not have to justify to staff why they may be placing them in situations that pose a risk to their safety. The proposal by Stanley and Goddard (2002) that practitioners in child protection may also be behaving like hostages in the face of actual or potential violence adds another important dimension to the range of influences on decision-making in child protection services: workers may make decisions for action/inaction in order to avoid or appease their 'captor'.

Although it may be argued that the application of standardised risk assessment tools may serve to identify and counteract the flaws that arise in decision-making in child protection practice, it is argued here that these flaws exist within, and are even masked by, the application of risk assessment tools. A recent development in the way that risk assessment has been applied in child protection practice is the shift to identifying the source of protection (safety factors) for a child as well as the source of harm. A tendency to privilege safety factors has been noted in practice and has been referred to as 'risk insurance' rather than a serious attempt to predict the future behaviours of parents and carers (Parton 1997). However, approaches to child protection practice that use risk assessment to identify (and strengthen) sources of protection have emerged from strengths-based approaches, offering solutions that go beyond the monitoring of potentially abusive factors. An example of a strengths-based approach to child protection practice is Turnell and Edwards (1999) 'signs of safety' approach. This approach to child protection practice emerged as a response to concerns that practice had, in focusing almost exclusively on the deficits of parents and carers, led to adversarial and non-productive working relationships with parents (Turnell and Edwards 1999). The signs of safety approach is a development from risk assessment rather than an alternative. Turnell and Edwards (1999) state very clearly that their approach should be underpinned by sound risk assessment. The authors warn that just looking for 'signs of safety' could lead to naive practice that does not adequately protect children and they stress that the focus on safety in their approach should not be considered as '… an avoidance of the issue of danger and harm, but as a mechanism for finding a way forward that will resolve the problem' (Turnell and Edwards 1999, p.38).

Although an approach to practice that recognises the importance of working with parents to promote positive change is very welcome, practice approaches that rely on risk assessment, such as Turnell and Edwards' (1999) strengths-based approach, also rely on an idealised form of decision-making that, as demonstrated by research presented in an earlier section of the present paper, does not exist in practice. Such reliance undermines the promise of the approach to provide solutions that protect children. The new emphasis on safety factors in risk assessment can also be harmful to children because it can potentially shift the focus of practitioners away from the factors that place children at risk of harm, as evidenced in critiques of the gendered nature of child protection practice.

The literature on human reasoning and decision-making indicates that personal judgment is often influenced by contextual factors such as the representativeness of the case, the availability or vividness of information and the presumed relevance of the available information to the decision being made (Cicchinelli 1995). Munro (1999, p.754) found that most determinations of risk were based on a limited range of data, often with the most memorable cases (those that aroused emotion or were most recent) factoring into the assessment of risk more than the 'dull, abstract material in research studies, case records, letters and reports'. Subsequently, even with evidence contrary to the workers initial case disposition, revision of judgment about cases was slow or non-existent.

Decisions were also often faulty due to biased reporting or errors in communication. A critical attitude to evidence was found to correlate with whether or not the new information supported the existing view of the family. A major problem was that professionals were slow to revise their judgments despite a mounting body of evidence against them (Munro 1999). He concluded that errors in professional reasoning in child protection work are not random but predictable on the basis of research on how people intuitively simplify reasoning processes in making complex judgments. As a result, 'Analytical tools are needed to supplement intuitive skills and shift practice reasoning along the continuum towards the analytical end' (Munro, 1999, p.754). Aids to reasoning need to be developed which recognise the central role of intuitive reasoning but offer methods for checking intuitive judgments more rigorously and systematically. Hence, risk assessment instruments have the potential to improve practitioner reasoning and decision making.

Munro (2011b) says that there has been an overemphasis on individual errors of decision-making in child protection cases where a child has tragically died. She rightly highlights that there is often an underemphasis on the systemic factors which shape decision-making. However, it is still worth considering the psychological influences on decisions, as being able to identify them can enhance the quality of clinical judgments.

Study of reasoning has been divided into two forms: the prescriptive/analytic and the heuristic/intuitive. Analytic reasoning is characterised by logical, conscious and sequential steps whilst intuitive reasoning is typically unconscious and not transparent (Hammond 1996). People are not cold logic machines, and factors such as how the problem is framed can change an individual's perception of a situation, and indeed, emotion can be an important guide to decision-making (Beach and Connolly 2005). People rely on inductive processes (previous experience, intuition) when making decisions (Kahneman *et al.* 1990). Reliance on heuristic or mental shortcuts, typical of everyday decision-making can have serious implications for decision-making in child protection cases (Munro 1999).

Sutherland (1992) concisely outlines the potential pitfalls of biased thinking. First, people consistently avoid exposing themselves to evidence that might disprove their beliefs. Second, on receiving evidence against their belief, they often refuse to believe it. Third, the existence of a belief distorts people's interpretations of new evidence in such a way as to make it consistent with the belief. Fourth, people selectively remember items that are in line with their beliefs.

It is important that practitioners are aware of the problems associated with professional judgment. These problems include a lack of recognition of known risk factors, the predominance of verbal evidence over written, a focus on the immediate present or latest episode rather than considering significant historical information and a failure to revise initial assessments in the light of new information (Munro 1999).

Equally, there are a number of threats to judgment making that include ambiguity, ambivalence, task presentation, response time, environment and context, stress, mood and anticipatory regret. Practitioners also face a number of very real problems that impact on their judgment making, which include:

- ▸ Complexity: juggling many things simultaneously
- ▸ Absence of judgment: danger of reaction when there is a lack of time/resources
- ▸ Confused issues and strategies
- ▸ Judgment creep (small shifts can become entirely different decisions – no formal recognition of changed goals/direction – need to 'take stock' regularly to keep 'on track')
- ▸ Lack of evaluative mind set
- ▸ Reluctance to adjust or change judgment
- ▸ What's the problem?
- ▸ What's needed?
- ▸ How will we intervene?
- ▸ What do we look at/measure? (e.g. use scales – 'daily hassle' scale to measure progress).

Characteristics of staff able to exercise professional judgment

- ▸ A good memory
- ▸ Emotional stability
- ▸ Freedom from biases
- ▸ Knowledge of general as well as specific risk factors
- ▸ Accurate memories of personal experiences
- ▸ Memory of other people's experiences

- ▶ Ability to analyse the present
- ▶ Ability to think and reason rationally
- ▶ Decision-making knowledge, including a good intuitive decision-making base
- ▶ Problem solving knowledge and ability
- ▶ Good creative insight to aid in decisions about the future that involve foresight, perspectives, consequences, uncertainties and unknowables.

Learning involves the detection and correction of error. Responses to error can involve either single-loop or double-loop learning. When the error detected and corrected permits the organisation to carry on with its present policies or achieve its present objectives, then that error-and-correction process is single-loop learning. Single-loop learning is like a thermostat that learns when it is too hot or too cold and turns the heat on or off. The thermostat can perform this task because it can receive information (the temperature of the room) and take corrective action. Double-loop learning occurs when error is detected and corrected in ways that involve the modification of an organisation's underlying norms, policies and objectives (Argyris and Schon 1978, p.2)

Defensible and sensible decision-making

A blame culture has developed which is particularly associated with risk taking by human services professionals (Power 2004). It associates the occurrence of loss or harm from risk taking with poor decision-making. But it simply does not follow. The nature of risk taking requires that harm can, and sometimes does, occur from good decision-making. Note that the blame culture does not focus on poor risk taking which, because of good fortune, does not lead to loss. Nor does it consider all the risk decisions that ought to have been taken, but which were not. Some of those failures to take a risk will be a consequence of the fear of being blamed. The blame culture can be blamed for making risk taking more difficult. An easy way to stop harm occurring from risk taking, some foolish people think, is not to take any risks.

If harm results from a risk decision then that might be the consequence of poor risk taking. It might be – we would need to investigate. We would need to examine the total process of decision-making and risk management that went into the making of that decision. Risk taking can, and should, be judged by the quality of the decision-making and its management.

In a climate that is risk-averse, there can be a tendency to take action to, in theory or intention, avoid risk. Parton (1998) suggested that the move towards making a 'defensible decision' has become more important than making the right one.

It has become clear that the social work profession was lacking in confidence, underutilised its workers' skills, had become increasingly risk-averse, stifled autonomy and lacked appropriate support (Barry 2007). Defensible decisions are made when all reasonable steps have been taken, reliable assessment methods have been used, information is collected and thoroughly evaluated, decisions are recorded, staff work within agency policies and procedures and staff communicate with others and seek information they do not have (Monahan 1993).

Carson and Bain (2008) pointed out that a risk decision can be justified even if harm results (e.g. The surgery could have been justified even though the patient suffered harm). A risk-decision could have been unjustified even if, because of good luck, harm is avoided. 'Risk' is not synonymous with 'harm avoidance'. When we take risks we certainly hope to avoid harm occurring but because it is a risk, we have to accept that there can be no guarantee that it will not occur. Risks can be justified because their likely benefits are judged to be more important than the possible harms. If the value of the likely benefits of taking a risk outweighs the value of the likely harm, that decision can be justified. They also note that risk taking is purposive. They should identify what they are trying to achieve. Those purposes represent potential justifications. Without them it will be very difficult to justify taking, let alone imposing, a risk on another person. Professionals should not be taking risks, at least with other people, just because they are 'there' or 'for fun'.

Risk taking is a science as well as an art and a skill. There will always be more that we could know about it. By its very nature it requires us to act without perfect knowledge; it requires that decision-makers learn and practise a process which demands considerable mental agility and critical imagination; values are involved.

Decisions can only be as good as the date they are based upon. Information may be unavailable, or available but of poor quality. A risk taker may have to rely upon poor quality data when making a decision. That decision may lead to success, or at least not to harm. But the presence or absence of harm cannot determine whether or not it was a good decision.

In the prevailing blame culture we tend to assume that if the outcome was unsuccessful, if harm resulted, then there must have been fault, and there must be someone who is to blame. Sometimes the conclusion will be appropriate – blame is deserved. But it is important to appreciate that, because of the nature of risk taking, it simply does not follow automatically. If there is a 1 in 10,000 chance of death, then, assuming only that the assessment is sound, you should expect one person in 10,000 to die, even if that is a member of one's own family. That risk of death exists independently of poor quality risk taking. Of course, if there is poor quality risk taking then there may be more than 1 in 10,000 deaths. As such, each serious outcome should be investigated to discover whether it was the consequence of a poor or good risk taking decision (Carson and Bain 2008). Any risk decision-makers who deliberately failed to identify, analyse and assess the existence, potential value and likelihood of the benefits of risk taking would manifestly not have done their job properly.

Munro (2009) noted that sensible solutions are difficult to realise when we still operate in the same toxic environment that caused the problem in the first place. She expressed concern that the focus is frequently on the expertise we need in our workers rather than addressing the work context in which they need to be able to use their expertise properly.

Munro is to be commended for trying to shift child protection from its 'risk-averse' outlook to a 'risk-sensible' approach, as sensible decision-making might actually look at outcomes for children. Interestingly, however, Fitzpatrick (2011) observes that Munro herself failed to demonstrate good judgment in some aspects of her report:

Despite her criticism of the authoritarian character of some of New Labour's child welfare policies, she continues to endorse projects such as Sure Start and repeats the mantra that there is growing evidence for the effectiveness of early intervention. She references the evidence collected by politicians (Graham Allen, Frank Field) and a voluntary sector chief executive (Clare Tickell). However, this is advocacy research and propaganda, not scientific evidence. Objective assessments of Sure Start revealed equivocal evidence of any benefits. As the eminent child psychiatrist Michael Rutter, who supervised the Sure Start evaluation, observed, the government was not interested in evidence and failed to consider the adverse as well as the beneficial effects of its child welfare initiatives.

Issues frequently raised in training also include:

- Appropriate information sharing (especially in the face of barriers)
- Relevant and proportionate information
- Honesty and openness with families
- Evidence-based practice
- Being clear on the risk assessment tool and why you have used it
- Showing your working out
- Considering history after information gathering
- Adherence to policies, procedures and human rights
- Being child-centred
- Giving families opportunities and support to change and stay changed
- Accurate recording and accountability
- Management oversight of assessments and decisions (supervision and decision-making recorded)
- Adopting a non judgmental attitude
- Generating positive as well as negative hypotheses.

═══ Key messages from the chapter ═══

There are considerable contextual and contemporary challenges facing workers in the child protection field.

Some shifts have been made in relation to interprofessional communication – in that we now communicate more than previously, although we have not as yet resolved the challenge that more information does not always mean the communication has been safely received and understood.

Many of the challenges have emerged or been compounded by the organisational attempts to ration ever decreasing resources.

First-line managers act as a shock absorber for workers from the unrelenting demands of the organisational hierarchy, and they require considerably more investment if they are to reclaim reflective casework and supervision from the performance-led focus.

Workers require clarity of task and clarity of context if they are to be able to safely exercise their professional judgment and avoid errors.

The elevated expectations from the courts and others of social workers as expert witnesses require considerably more investment in nurturing and refining access to the required materials and in exercising critical thinking in their application to cases.

Emotional care and support for all staff across all agencies is an essential foundation for all practice in the child protection arena.

CHAPTER 3

Risk Unravelled

There are many professionals and just as many different interpretations of risk. There are numerous risks that professionals are asked to manage and just as many interpretations about how they should assess risk. This chapter aims to unravel the different risk foci across agencies, and definitions of the child protection process to be clear about if and how they sit together to achieve protection for children. This chapter addresses these issues and looks at how things currently sit and what needs resolution in the future.

The evolving nature of risk

Risk is everywhere: it is a normal part of everyday life. We take many risks each day, often unconsciously. We take risks for ourselves and we impose them on others, such as when we drive our cars. Many risks are choices – which form of travel is likely to be perceived as less risky? Some select those forms of transport that are in their control, with themselves as the operator, whilst others prefer a form of transport operated by others, such as the train or the plane. Few research the statistically safer option, rather making the choice intuitively. However, not all risks are within our control. We can leave for a work meeting early as we anticipate heavier traffic at peak periods, but we may never arrive if someone else hits our car when they lose control of their own vehicle through speeding or mechanical fault. Others speculate to accumulate, so the thrill of fast travel may produce the desired adrenalin rush, yet equally may turn a corner too fast and crash. Interestingly, we simultaneously embrace risk as well as rejecting it. People tend to approach risk from one of two polarised positions: their glass is seen as half full or half empty. They may operate from different positions depending whether they are making choices in their personal or their work lives. In child protection work, the consequences of a wrong decision could cause harm to a child, yet making a decision at home is often more acceptable as the consequences are more likely to be to the person themself.

Risk became a dominant preoccupation within western society towards the end of the twentieth century and, since then there has been a growing mistrust of professionals and an increased reliance by professionals on complex systems of assessment, monitoring and quality control (Barry 2007).

The increasing emphasis on risk in social work is a reflection of 'the impact of globalisation' which has 'dislocated many areas of social and economic life, giving rise to uncertainties, fears and insecurities: more importance is now attached to calculating choices of individuals' (Stalker 2003, p.216). Additionally, professionals in health and social work working in this 'risk society' have become 'increasingly reliant on complex systems of audit, monitoring and quality control' (Stalker 2003, p.217). Models of risk assessment have tended to focus on this bureaucratic approach.

Parton (1996) associates the emerging concern with risk in social work with the collapse of welfarism in the late 1970s and early 1980s, with a decline in the belief in social and collective citizenship and an increasing focus on individual risks and needs. In relation to child protection, the sense of failure was intensified by the publication of a series of highly critical reports into child protection practice during the 1980s (Smith 2008). The consistent message from the inquiries into the deaths of Jasmine Beckford, Tyra Henry and Kimberley Carlile was that social workers had not behaved with sufficient professionalism, relying instead on 'naïve and sentimental' beliefs in the positive intention of parents and carers, even in light of evidence to the contrary (Parton 2006, p.33). The inquiry reports thus made consistent recommendations to the effect that practitioners should adopt a more rational approach and that their skills in identifying the signs and symptoms of child abuse should be enhanced. As a result, the risk of harm faced by children was progressively reframed, with less weight being placed on substantiated evidence of past mistreatment within the family, and greater attention directed towards developing the capacity to predict the substance and severity of a range of future dangers.

The culture of risk taking also has to be considered. If risk taking continues primarily to be associated with the chances of harm then it will continue to be associated with damage, loss and blame. People will naturally wish to avoid risk taking because it is about possibly harming others. Second, if the primary focus is on possible harm, its seriousness and its likelihood, then decision-makers will be in a much poorer position when it comes to having to justify their decisions and actions (Carson and Bain 2008).

Davies (2008) also noted that as a specialism, child protection social work seems to be fast disappearing, and protecting children is increasingly perceived as a simple and obvious task. Media comment, at the time of the employment tribunal decision to uphold Haringey's dismissal of Lisa Arthurworrey, was that much of her role as Victoria's social worker was common sense. 'Common sense dictates that 19 pages of medical evidence have to flag serious reasons not to be cheerful about the outcome for a child' (Roberts 2004). 'These mistakes seem due to a lack of common sense rather than inadequate guidance and supervision' (Batty 2004). A view that child protection work is simple feeds into the belief that social workers can mechanistically implement managerial instructions and manage large caseloads based on sets of instructions rather than quality supervision.

Risk definitions

Definitions of concepts such as risk, dangerousness and significant harm are ambiguous and widely agreed to be determined by social, cultural and historical factors, and we know that there are trends in public and professional recognition and responses to many different public concerns (Calder 1999). Risk is 'a combination of an estimate of the probability of a target behaviour occurring with a consideration of the consequences of such occurrences' (Towl and Crighton 1996).

Risk is a course of action or inaction, taken under conditions of uncertainty, which exposes one to possible loss in order to reach a desired outcome (Kindler 1990, p.12).

Parton (1996) persuasively argued that risk was a way of thinking rather than a set of objective realities, and that social work's preoccupation with risk at that point in time reflected changes in the way social workers viewed and undertook their practice. He saw the concerns with risk as both reflecting the anxieties and uncertainties of social workers in the 'new' welfare environment, and providing a rationale for their purpose and survival in it.

Consult a dictionary on the meaning of 'risk' and you are likely to be given a definition that highlights three other concepts. These are harm, likelihood and uncertainty (Carson and Bain 2008).

Carson and Bain 2008 point out that 'risk' may be divided into its 'elements' (the features inherent in a risk proposal) and its 'dimensions' (features that may be influenced by the decision-maker). Both are important and must be considered when taking a risk decision.

The elements, the core ingredients or requirements of a risk, are particularly relevant to risk assessment. The dimensions are particularly important for risk management. Risk assessment is the stage in risk decision-making when information is collated. It is concerned with predicting the consequences of taking the risk decision and their likelihood. It focuses on the key elements of a risk. Risk management involves implementing, monitoring, influencing, controlling and reviewing the risk decision.

A risk decision can be justified even if harm results. A risk decision could have been unjustified even if, because of good luck, harm is avoided. 'Risk' is not synonymous with 'harm avoidance'. When we take risks we certainly hope to avoid harm occurring but, because it is a risk, we have to accept that there can be no guarantee that it will not occur.

Risk involves two elements: consequences and likelihood. Both of these are variable; they involve matters of degree. We do not know, because it is a risk, exactly what will occur or, exactly how likely it is.

A problem with taking risks with other people is that this snapshot quality can provide a false impression. It is much more appropriate to examine and to judge the quality of risk judgment and risk management by the sequence of risk assessments made and the risk decisions taken (or not taken). Risk takers will learn from the experience of taking a sequence of risk decisions. They will learn, for example, which sources of data may be trusted and which risk management plans work well. Although every risk decision is necessarily different, the presence of processes permits opportunities to learn (Carson and Bain 2008).

Risk taking is a science as well as an art and skill. There will always be more that we could know about it. By its very nature it requires us to act without perfect knowledge. And it requires that decision-makers learn and practice a process demanding considerable mental agility and critical imagination. Values are involved. There are plenty of opportunities for error; these are emphasised.

Risk-taking is a skill. It can be improved upon. It is not something that can be completely and exhaustively described or analysed. Equally professional judgment is insufficient on its own. Detailed knowledge of the discipline involved, and sincere empathy with the patient or client concerned is helpful but insufficient. The risk taker needs also to know how to take competent risk decisions. He or she needs to know about the findings of decision-making research, as sources of common errors have been identified by extensive research (Carson and Bain 2008).

Within social work the assessment of risk has been associated with the negativity of harm and child death (Parton 2000, p.146–7). Because of this Parton, Thorpe and Wattam (1997) argue that notions of risk are deeply embedded in cases that are categorised as 'child protection' at the point of initial assessment (p.242).

Within social work the concept of risk, although not specifically defined within the legislation is closely associated with the concept of significant harm.

Munro (2002) argued that risk has two significantly different meanings and the one you choose has a pervasive impact on your subsequent thinking. Historically, the risk of a certain outcome referred only to the probability of it happening: the term was neutral about whether the outcome was desirable or not. Indeed, some view risk as containing positive opportunities for personal development (speculate to accumulate e.g. stock exchange gambling risks some money to take the chance to improve stake) whilst others suggest that risk must be viewed as something entirely negative to be controlled and eliminated.

In more recent times risk has been associated with unwanted outcomes only. Indeed, in discussions of 'the risk society' (Beck 1992) the assumption is that we are talking about undesirable results. Ulrich Beck – risk is rarely perceived as positive – always a negative connotation. It is for this reason that risk appears to have been jettisoned from some government guidance as they want a needs-led assessment process with a focus on strengths (Calder 2003a). This does not take into account that we need to be aware of risks as well as strengths and then conduct risk-balancing exercises in which strengths that count are those which balance specific risks.

Walker and Beckett (2003) explored the implications of both the risk control and the risk management perspective that flow from care/control to strengths/risk balancing.

Characteristics of the risk control perspective:

- ▶ Definition: risk is negative – danger, threat
- ▶ Priority principles: professional responsibility and accountability
- ▶ Practice priorities: identification (assessment scales) and elimination (procedural, legalistic).

Eliminating or totally controlling risk in social work is impossible. It is undesirable to think of risk and the social work task in relation to it in this way because:

- ▶ Evidence and intuition suggests it is impossible and thus resources are wasted
- ▶ Risk is part of social life
- ▶ Social work routinely brings its practitioners into contact with dangerous people and entails professional judgments, which are potentially castigated by management, organisations and the media.

Characteristics of the risk management perspective:

- ▶ Definition: positive – risk is part of life, balancing risks and benefits is part of an individual's development, being self-determining and personally responsible
- ▶ Priority principles: self-determination, anti-oppression
- ▶ Practice priorities: solution-focused, partnership practice, empowerment.

The benefits of the risk management perspectives are that:

- ▶ They are in keeping with the values and practice of modern social work

- ▶ It emphasises the process of maximising benefits as well as minimising risks, rather than the procedures of identifying and eliminating risk

- ▶ It builds on strengths.

A risk management approach, while ensuring the safety of service users, should also be enabling in that it should celebrate the taking of risks as a way of enhancing people's lives. This sometimes creates a fundamental dilemma which staff and service users will need support in overcoming. 'Reasonable, informed and calculated risk taking plays an important part in contributing to the quality of life for young and old; this is a matter of choice, demonstrating an individual's right to self-determination and autonomy. This requires acknowledgement of users' skills and capabilities to cope with and manage risk.

Eliminating or totally controlling risk in social work is impossible

It is undesirable to think of risk and the social work task in relation to it as something that can be totally controlled because evidence and intuition suggests it is impossible, and thus resources would be wasted. Risk is part of social life and the real world of everyday experience and should not be perceived as only of interest to specific client groups. Practice, which is effective in terms of promoting individual responsibility and social competence cannot be reductionist – it must recognise the person in context and build on strengths. Social work agencies have responsibilities in law in relation to certain client groups, and practitioners need to be very aware of legislative imperatives determining the scope of their powers. Individual social workers must neither neglect these responsibilities nor accept unlimited liability – whether or not there are legal requirements.

In relation to the assessment and management of risk there is a need therefore to resist the reductionist tendency to focus exclusively on assessment of risk conceived as danger and intervention as risk control.

Ironically the danger of such practice is that in pursuing the ultimately unattainable goal of entirely risk free practice workers may:

▸ Overlook the risks attached to intervention

▸ Neglect the rights of individuals in order to control the risks they pose to themselves or others

▸ Lose sight of the individual in context, their strengths and the creative potential for development and growth

▸ Overlook the risk to the social worker.

As in other areas of practice, the skill of social work lies in intervention which is:

▸ Optimally non-intrusive

▸ Compatible with the promotion of individual potential and personal responsibility

▸ Balanced in both rights and risks, and care and control

▸ Able to recognise risks to social workers (Walker and Beckett 2010).

Calder (2002a, p.8) suggests that, in realms other than social work, a risk equation also calculates possible benefits. Risk has to be seen as a positive as well as a potentially harmful issue, which allows worker discretion to support some risk taking amongst client groups but also ensures that all efforts are made to reduce the likelihood of harmful results.

Kemshall (2008) noted that whilst risk is often seen as negative in the child care and protection field, in the areas of mental health provision and care of the elderly in particular there is much evidence to support a positive framing of risk; focusing on the empowerment of vulnerable people to take risks, make choices, and exercise personal autonomy. In this context, risk is associated with the 'right to self-determination' and the management of risk is presented as the balance between risks and rights.

If we are to accept the fact that risk has both positive as well as negative factors, then we need to construct a framework that reflects this (see Figure 3.1).

Some would argue that the potential benefits of taking a risk can always be identified *after* the event. They argue that there is no point in spending time, and other resources, to discover and to assess possible benefits until any harm has occurred. Risk takers in human services sometimes identify the potential harms of risk taking much more quickly and with greater ease than they identify potential benefits. This is part of a culture of blame and fear that has developed and been fed by litigation and inquiries.

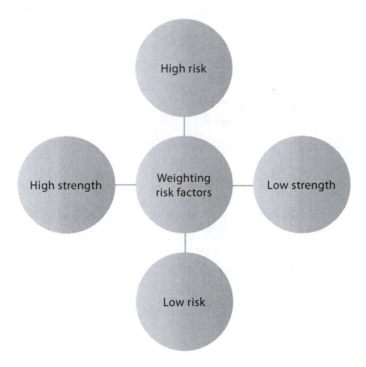

Figure 3.1 A contemporary risk matrix

Risk deletion

The first production of central assessment guidance for child protection work (DH 1988) was similarly built almost entirely on the notions of risk and dangerousness, yet these concepts have been deleted from the central procedural and assessment guidance and governing child protection (DH 1999; 2000) a decade later.

Risk has become a 'hot potato' in government. Risk equates with child protection at a time in which there is a drive to re-focus on strengths. The government has thus redefined risk as need. This is not convincing when there is repeated backtracking from needs-led assessments to a reminder that the child's safety is the primary objective of professional intervention (Calder 2000). It also represents a basic misunderstanding of what risk means. Risk is about balancing strengths and weaknesses, weighting them and then considering the type of intervention needed (Calder 2002a). Risk and need in the context of child abuse can and should be defined in terms of each other. If a child's needs are not met, there is a risk of harm. If a child is at risk of abuse, then he or she is in danger of not having some needs met (Munro 2002). Risk is thus only one component in the assessment of a child and their family's situation.

Given the tight resource situation facing local government at present, many services are now allocated according to their perceived risk, thus requiring workers to emphasise risks rather than strengths in arguing for resources for their clients. There is also a problem for workers having only materials from the strengths-loaded assessment framework to do work at the child protection end of the spectrum. In the climate of eligibility criteria, it is a restricted range of factors that define high risk, notably those associated with protection rather than the safeguarding or promoting of a child's needs. Directing services only at those identified as high risk also removes the potential benefit of preventative intervention. Social work becomes the last line of defence. The strategy is essentially reactive, allowing service reductions to create risk for some, with the deployment of resources only when a state of high risk is reached. The danger here is that 'control' replaces 'welfare' (Calder 1995). We end up dealing with an ambulance at the bottom of the cliff rather than investing in fences at the top of the cliff.

The deletion of the risk term has left many workers without an operational assessment tool and, with this, increased anxiety which disables their power of response. Many feel the baby has been thrown out with the bathwater and that they have been scrambling around for risk assessment tools that can assist them in their task. The recording forms do not allow for child protection risk assessments and indeed the associated guidance does not direct staff to the relevant literature (Calder 2003a).

Although there has been a nationally agreed framework for assessing need since 2000 (*Framework for Assessment of Children in Need and their Families* (DH 2000)), there is no equivalent agreed framework for identifying risk of harm because the underpinning philosophy is that any risk or evidence of harm will be revealed in a thorough assessment of need. Where local guidance does exist, it can quickly become out of date because of changes determined by government policy, serious case review findings and research findings. There is a perceived need among social work practitioners for clear and regularly reviewed guidance in this area, which should include updates from serious case reviews.

The Assessment Framework emphasises need and the meeting of need, whilst safeguarding and promoting the welfare of children. The notion of risk and the assessment of risk are not given any prominence. However, the threshold into child protection systems is about the risk of significant harm. How are the professionals to maintain and develop skills and attitudes consistent with an understanding of the nature of risk?

Working Together to Safeguard Children (2006) highlights the importance of considering how a combination of different factors can impact on the risk of significant harm to a child. 'Often it is the interaction between a number of factors which serve to increase the likelihood or level of significant harm' (p.156).

More commonly, risk factors interact to produce a particular outcome at a specified stage in a child's development. To complicate matters further, the same combination of risks can often produce different deficiency states in different children … the same risks may produce different manifestations at successive stages of the child's development and in different contexts (Rutter 1989 p.6).

A risk factor, however, does not mean that a consequence will automatically follow. It means that protective actions are needed to try to reduce the child's vulnerability to such consequences occurring (Adcock 2001, p.90).

The omission of risk

Warner (2003) also rejected the assessment framework for its attempt to promote a one model fits all approach. She argued that this framework provided an incomplete model of risk as it locates the difficulties within the client's ecology, thereby obscuring the contributory effects of the professional ecology. In Figure 3.2 she identifies the importance of considering the professional ecology, such as defensive practice where child protection is concerned, as such back-covering can impact extensively on the nature of the intervention.

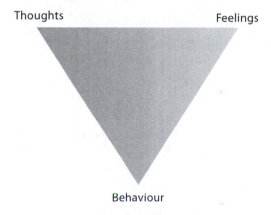

Thoughts — Feelings — Behaviour

Figure 3.2 Assessment considerations
(Warner 2003)

If we are to fully explore the processes of assessment and intervention it is necessary to elaborate the multiple relationships between behaviour, thoughts and feelings. For example, a mother may initially refuse to admit her responsibility for failing to protect her child from the father who killed him. This may not necessarily indicate her refusal to accept responsibility; her feelings of guilt may be so profound that she cannot begin to speak about them. If parents are too quickly condemned, because the meaning of their behaviour is assumed, rather than explored, poor outcomes can become a self-fulfilling prophecy. Additionally, premature condemnation of clients can act to obscure the contributory effects the style of intervention has on enabling or restricting opportunities for change within families. The communication triangle alerts people to the multiple meanings of behaviour and the different dimensions of communication. This encourages workers to think more critically about the assumptions they make about what behaviour means and how their interventions may be experienced.

Carson and Bain (2008) also point out that some politicians and journalists demonstrate sloppy reasoning. They demand that 'the risk' should be eliminated, and should never recur. They seek the impossible in a rage of ignorant indignation. The only way, for example, to stop murderers from committing further murders (i.e. to make it zero likelihood) is never to release them.

Risk in the multidisciplinary network

Risk taking with people in the human services is regularly interdisciplinary and multiprofessional. Their differences in knowledge and approach provide an opportunity for a richer understanding of each case. But that has to be managed. Different rules or understandings of the requirements of confidentiality, for example, can create problems.

Social workers' views of the language of risk are largely absent from the literature and yet they actively engage with risk on a daily basis. Differing organisational cultures, differing definitions of risk and a hierarchy of professional expertise may deter the development of a common understanding and language of risk. Calder has developed what he calls 'the Bermuda triangle of risk' to reflect the reality that professionals have a different focus when dealing with risk (see Figure 3.3).

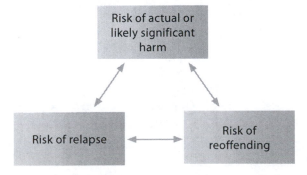

Figure 3.3 The Bermuda Triangle of risk
(Calder 2008)

Unless professionals are aware that their day-to-day task requires them to focus on different measures of risk, then the reality is that they will use the same word to discuss concerns about a family but fail to appreciate the real message being given. For example, a professional in the criminal justice field might measure the risk of an offender committing a further offence, such as domestic violence. What is not embraced is the mutation of the client's behaviour to continue the control and the harm but under a different umbrella (see Figure 3.4).

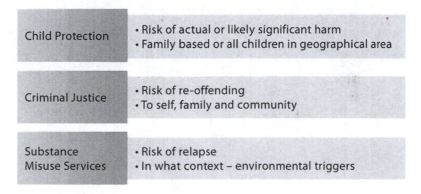

Figure 3.4 Risk remits

Calder (2008) developed the notion of a domestic abuse diamond (DAD) (see Figure 3.5) to reflect the research connection between domestic violence and animal abuse, child abuse and sexual abuse. The measure for social workers would be the actual or likely significant harm for children and young people from any presenting behaviour of concern, not simply the likelihood of whether someone will re-offend or not. In addition, we do not have clear data about the percentage of people who continue their behaviour but are never re-convicted.

There is also a lack of professional consensus as to what constitutes actual or likely significant harm, other than where it is admitted by perpetrators or is at the extreme end of the continuum. Other texts in this series will address the variety of professional interpretations of neglect, emotional abuse, sexual abuse and physical abuse. What is evident is that professionals frame likelihood at two polarised points on a continuum – with possibility at one end and probability at the other.

The threshold for a child protection response is most frequently allied with the probability point whilst the safeguarding response is set at the broader possibility that something may go wrong unless something is done about it now. What is frequently seen is a game of professional ping-pong as professionals wrestle with radically polarised perspectives that are also correlated with which agency will assume responsibility for taking the indicated work forward. Likelihood thus becomes a political ping-pong and the concern is that, in this climate, the energy is dissipated resolving the professional issues rather than engaging with the family and the problem. Likelihood can never be known with certainty, by definition.

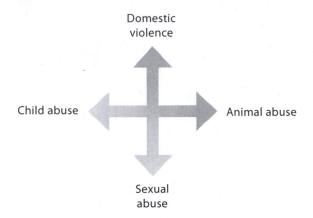

Figure 3.5 Domestic abuse diamond (DAD)
(Calder 2008)

Carson and Bain (2008) offer a very useful continuum through which we can start to unpick possibility and probability within the concept of likelihood:

- ▸ Foreseeable: in the range of 0–10 per cent likelihood
- ▸ Chance: in the range of 10–20 per cent likelihood
- ▸ Possible: in the range of 20–30 per cent likelihood
- ▸ Real possibility: in the range of 30–40 per cent likelihood
- ▸ Good possibility: by which mean in the range of 40–50 per cent likelihood

- ▶ Likely: by which mean in the range of 50–60 per cent likelihood

- ▶ Very likely: by which mean in the range of 60–70 per cent likelihood

- ▶ Probable: by which mean in the range of 70–80 per cent likelihood

- ▶ Real probability: by which mean in the range of 80–90 per cent likelihood

- ▶ Highly probable: by which mean in the range of over 90 per cent likelihood.

Risk factors

A key feature of professional risk decision-making is the use of risk factors whenever they are available. Risk factors should be based upon quality empirical research, wherever that has been undertaken. But where that is not available, risk factors may be based upon practitioners' experience. The nature of such experience deserves examination. This raises the perennial debate between actuarial and clinical factors. The core problem is that although risk factors are an exceptionally important part of risk decision-making they are also ripe for misuse. For example, double-counting.

Actuarial risk

Actuarial methods utilise statistical techniques to generate risk predictors. Some practitioners claim that uncertainty should be managed, as insurers do, by using actuarial models. This involves identifying factors associated with the expected harm and rating them according to their importance. A judgment about the likelihood of harm happening is then made on the basis of how many of these factors, or which of the most important, are present in a child's situation.

In brief, actuarial assessment predicts an individual's likely behaviour from the behaviour of others in similar circumstances. Actuarial assessment has been less developed in child protection, social care and social work where clinical judgment (often based on structured interviewing tools) tends to predominate (Kemshall 2002). Actuarial assessment establishes a baseline prediction of likely risk, and is useful in categorising high, medium and low risks of probability (for example of prison parole release or reconviction). However, the methodology does have a number of problems. These have been summarised in the research literature as:

► The limitations of extrapolating individual risk probabilities from aggregated data about groups, better known as the 'statistical fallacy'

► The limits of the research technique used to produce risk predictors, a technique known as 'meta-analysis'

► The limit of low base rates, that is, predicting general risk probabilities from low frequency behaviours (such as murder, child abduction, etc.).

The statistical fallacy refers to the problem of transferring aggregated risk factors based on group data to the individual. However, despite recent and growing criticism, actuarial assessment can be used to establish those risk factors that have a proven track record of prediction and encourage workers to focus on the 'right stuff'.

Since no single factor is sufficient to determine whether offenders will or will not re-offend, practitioners need to consider a range of relevant risk factors. There are three plausible methods by which risk factors can be combined into overall evaluations of risk, First, empirically guided clinical evaluations, which begins with the overall recidivism base rate, and then adjusts the risk level by considering factors that have been empirically associated with recidivism risk. The risk factors to be considered are explicit, but the method for weighting the importance of the risk factors is left to the judgment of the worker. Second, pure actuarial predictions, in contrast, explicitly state not only the variables to be considered, but also the precise procedure through which ratings of these variables will be translated into a risk level. In the pure actuarial sense, risk levels are estimated through mechanical, arithmetic procedures requiring a minimum of judgment. Third, clinically adjusted actuarial predictions begin with a pure actuarial prediction, but then raise or lower the risk level based on consideration of relevant factors that were not included in the actuarial method. As research develops, actuarial methods can be expected to consistently outperform clinical predictions. With the current state of knowledge, however, both actuarial and guided clinical approaches can be expected to provide risk assessments with a moderate level of accuracy.

There are a number of strengths in adopting an actuarial approach to the work:

- ▸ They are consistent with the expectation of evidence-based social care interventions

- ▸ They are useful in establishing those risk predictors which have a proven track record

- ▸ They are useful in establishing the relevant base rates for clinical assessment

- ▸ They are useful in increasing the accuracy of risk assessments

- ▸ They increase the levels of consistency and reliability (adapted from Kemshall, 2001).

Equally, there are a number of problems and potential pitfalls:

- ▸ Any tool has limitations if inappropriately used

- ▸ Statistical fallacy is the problem when seeking to transfer the information about a population to an individual user under assessment

- ▸ The use of meta-analyses (research based on the analysis of a large number of primary studies) to develop risk predictors can result in overly simple outcomes which fail to capture the complexity of the processes involved; we often require a human dimension to explain the behaviour

- ▸ A further problem relates to the predictions of risk where there is a low incidence of risky behaviour in the population as a whole; this is especially true in the case of child sexual abuse

- ▸ Collecting accurate information in cases may encourage a tick box approach

- ▸ It does not cover all permutations of situations

- ▸ It doesn't facilitate predictions in complex situations – either because of the shortage of data or through low base rate problems

▶ They only apply to specific groups such as convicted or imprisoned people

▶ They do not address the timing of the offending nor does it address any consequences

▶ They are focused on the presenting behaviour of concern and not any co-existing behaviours

▶ Acturial materials do not apply to women, young people or un-convicted men (extended from Kemshall 2001).

These models appear to offer certainty, but the appearance is misleading – and Table 3.1 clearly examines the assumptions alongside the problems with an examination of the available evidence.

TABLE 3.1 SHORTCOMINGS OF THE ACTUARIAL
APPROACH AND RELATED MODELS

Assumptions of actuarial models	Problems	Commentary
Based on evidence rather than opinion	Insecure evidence base for child maltreatment	Many of the factors have been found from establishing correlations in clinical populations. Children who are referred to services differ markedly from the wider population of maltreated children, particularly in terms of social class, ethnicity and disability. Even where factors are assessed from prevalence studies that examine this wider population, however, they are limited because little is usually known about how they related to the maltreatment.
Based on statistical tests	Correlations are not causes and there may be other reasons for the maltreatment that are not asked about	For example, it is usual to ask about family structure and to find a correlation between children who live in single parent or reconstituted families with maltreatment. However, it is not known whether the maltreatment was part of the child's life before or after the family separated.

Identify key risk factors	Factors that have been identified through the evidence base are generally too broad to be helpful	Single parenting, gender, poverty and stress are all correlated with populations of maltreated children, but they also apply to a much larger section of the population. To continue with our insurance analogy, it is helpful for insurance companies to apply broad risk factors to assess risk. For one thing they can charge more money, for another they have to deal with general populations. Social workers working with maltreated children are working with a small minority of children. They have to assess those who are most at risk of future significant harm out of that small population so the factors need to be more specific.
Maltreatment can be identified	There is a problem with the maltreatment itself	What is commonly known as child 'abuse' amounts to a vast array of behaviours and conditions that can have a number of causes, explanations and contexts. The actions depend on their context for definition. Children may fall down the stairs because they are too young to manage steps and there is no stair gate (possibly neglect) or because they throw themselves down (self-harm possibly as a result of emotional maltreatment). In addition, the range of possible injury will stretch from none to death.
Can help with prediction/ prevention	Factors identified in actuarial models to risk assessment lack the ability to deal with the complex relationships and variations between context and harm	The actuarial approach may improve as the evidence base increases, but the complexity of maltreatment makes this unlikely. The benefits are better focused on general populations (as insurance). For example, taking the whole population, what is the chance that any one child will be assaulted by their parents, sexually abused by an uncle or left unsupervised overnight under ten years of age? That information helps to develop broad prevention programmes but is of little use in assessing the chance of significant harm to a specific child reported to social services.

In practice, professionals seldom feel able to assign anything like a precise numerical value on the probability of an adverse event occurring, but if an assessment of risk is to mean anything, they should be able to say whether they think the event is more likely than not to happen, whether they think there is about a 50/50 chance and so on. However, certain models, such as the signs of safety approach, require that workers give some sort of numerical value to the risk of given events occurring.

Clinical risk, practice wisdom and intuition

Clinical methods are essentially a diagnostic assessment derived in part from the medical and mental health fields. Clinical judgment 'relies on an informal, "in the head" impressionistic, subjective conclusion reached (somehow) by a human clinical judge' (Grove and Meehl 1996). The clinical method is useful in that it provides important information on individual risky behaviours, stresses related to environmental factors, and assists in establishing appropriate management and treatment plans. Some of the reported limitations include the concern that the prediction is no better than chance, that the prediction is too influenced by experiences: workers rely primarily on their own experience, intuition and interviewing skills; that there is no evidence base, and factors typically have not been validated against outcome data. As such, they are difficult to challenge and often have a weak reliability (adapted from Kennington 2003).

Having assigned families to different bands of risk, the next difficulty for professionals is determining what an acceptable level of risk is. This is a value judgment, not fully reducible to rational analysis. In different cultures, social classes, historical epochs and even in different parts of the country, very different views exist or have existed about what constitutes an acceptable level of risk to a child and what level of risk warrants professional intervention. However, in practice, child protection agencies, individually and collectively operate various thresholds.

Traditionally based upon the subjective judgment of key professionals (such as social workers, probation officers, psychiatrists and psychologists), clinical assessment has been prone to a number of difficulties, most notably:

- ▶ Subjective bias of the assessor (for example discriminatory practice, the over-identification of vivid and unacceptable risks)

- ▶ Staff taking short cuts when under pressure

- ▶ Over identification with the subject of the assessment (for example probation officers may prioritise the rights of offenders over those of victims; social workers may prioritise the desires of parents over the needs of children)

- ▶ Over reliance on the self-report of the subject of the risk assessment (e.g. the accounts of offending behaviour provided by offenders, parental accounts of family interactions).

Whilst actuarial risk is premised upon statistical data, clinical risk highlights the importance of practice wisdom in the risk process. O'Sullivan (2005) explored practice wisdom in some detail. Once a valued if contested notion, it seems to have fallen out of favour, having been largely replaced by other ideas including competence, protocols and evidence-based practice. It has tended to be associated with unarticulated, non-codified and undocumented practice knowledge, with the most common use being to refer to social workers' personal knowledge derived from their practice experience. It is also informed from tacit knowledge obtained through practice experience, use of the theories absorbed during training and the making of intuitive judgments and decisions based on a personal body of knowledge. There are a number of definitions of practice wisdom worthy of note.

Practice wisdom as something highly personal involving the 'integration of theory, religion/philosophy and subjective experience', and how individual practitioners integrate what they know about themselves and the client 'and the present happening between the two' (Krill 1990, p.14).

Klein and Bloom (1995) looked upon this personal body of knowledge as a bridge between the limitations of scientific knowledge, what is known from practice experience, and the immediate practice situation:

> ...the accumulated knowledge social workers are able to bring to the consideration of individual cases and their practice in general.

This would appear to have three main and distinct potential sources: knowledge gained from everyday life, derived from the process of living in society and interacting with others; knowledge gained from social science, specifically research and ideas; and knowledge gained from the conduct of social work practice. (Sheppard 1995, p.279)

The value of this definition is that it recognises the varied potential sources of knowledge in social work and does not restrict practice wisdom to the knowledge gained through practice experience. Nevertheless, practice wisdom is more than stocks of knowledge. Sheppard has consistently argued that social work's professional knowledge claims are considerably bolstered by an emphasis on the processes involved in understanding, rather than the possession of stocks of knowledge whether in the form of codified or non-codified knowledge. The extension of this is that practice wisdom needs to be identified with knowledge production processes and not restricted to stocks of knowledge.

Two contrasting images of practice wisdom can be detected in this literature: practice wisdom as unreliable, personal, idiosyncratic knowledge built up through practice experience; and practice wisdom as the ability to make sound judgments in difficult, complex and uncertain situations. The former image has come to dominate, with the appropriateness and efficacy of practice wisdom as a source of knowledge being seriously questioned. Its alleged over-reliance on experiential knowledge has come to be emphasised, to the comparative neglect of its role in exercising judgment.

Practice wisdom requires a continual process of adding to, reviewing and transforming existing stocks of knowledge in the light of accumulating lifelong learning through life experience, practice experience and exposure to theoretical and empirical research. There needs to be a multiplicity of linkages between stored information if creative connections are to be made with stored ideas.

Munro (1998, p.70) maintains that social workers' current use of their practice wisdom tends to be personal and private, so making it difficult to give an account of their practice, while Hollows (2001) highlights the challenge social workers face in being able to explain their judgments in a multiprofessional arena. Although the use of practice wisdom does not preclude being explicit about reasoning, there is potential for it to form a smokescreen that obscures how particular judgments, understandings and courses of action were arrived at. Two types of reasoning can be postulated: intuitive reasoning and analytical reasoning. Both are important in social work with each being suited to different tasks. For example, Hammond *et al.* (1997) have identified 11 task characteristics, including the degree of certainty, number of cues and time available that determine whether intuition or analysis will be the most effective form of cognition.

Intuition is knowledge that stems from a gut feeling or some subconscious process. It is not to be confused with professional judgment, which is a conscious process where facts and experience are both considered to form a basis for making reasoned decisions. Intuition is usually defined as knowing or sensing something without the use of rational processes. Intuition has been described as a perception of reality not known to consciousness, in which the intuition knows, but does not know how it knows. Intuition is a rational process in which an individual reaches a conclusion on the basis of less explicit information than is ordinarily required to reach that decision. Intuition is a non-sequential information processing mode, which comprises both cognitive and affective elements and results in direct knowing without any use of conscious reasoning. Intuitive thinking and problem solving are best supported by the following skills: willingness to take risks, sense for business, ability to represent ideas, practice-minded behaviour and expertise.

Intuition is thus a contested process that often remains ill-defined. It has been defined as the use of tacit knowledge and emotions to make judgments and decisions without deliberation. It can involve sensitivity to relevant cues and the making of connections and associations with an empathic sensitivity to what people are feeling. As such it involves sensing rather than thinking. Tacit knowledge refers to implicit knowledge learnt through experience that can be inferred from action but not readily available either for internal or external scrutiny. Such routinisation is in effect the development of professional expertise but because, by definition, tacit knowledge is difficult to have under critical control, its use can result in redundant or inappropriate practice routines and be part of deficient practice as much as practice wisdom. As a consequence, not all tacit knowledge necessarily contributes to practice wisdom but tacit knowledge is important in all professions.

As intuition by most definitions bypasses deliberation, being directly based on perception, explaining the source of intuition is going to be difficult, requiring a high degree of self-awareness. Within practice wisdom, analytical reasoning involves the capacity to analyse and synthesise information into hypotheses about particular situations. This capacity to hypothesise about situations in a critical manner is likely to vary. Analysis and synthesis relate to critical appraisal and hypothesis generation. Analysing, synthesising and hypothesising in social work require conceptual frameworks that are flexible enough, rich enough and intricate enough to deal with the complexity, uncertainty and ambiguity of social situations. Knowledge is not value-free, and different forms of knowing will be valued differently from different points of view. Practice wisdom has been related to the capacity for reflective judgment, and the associated flexible and creative use of knowledge.

Intuition has been variously described as the absence of analysis, the pinnacle of expertise, or the unconscious processing of data. This means that the basis for the consequent judgment is not made explicit at the time. It can be thought of as deciding in a relatively holistic way, without separating the decision situation into its various elements. This enables it to be a quick way of deciding by making use of limited information by sensing patterns and filling in gaps. To be reliable and accurate intuition needs to be based on expertise developed over time, but it has a fundamental drawback which stems from its implicit nature. This is that the reasons behind intuitive decisions are not readily available for comment and scrutiny, which is necessary for partnership practice.

Subjective notions of risk

Allowing professionals to exercise their practice wisdom will mean that an objective measure of risk is clearly less likely, even when asked to consider risk in the same case. There is also the reality that individual workers may have a different interpretation of risk according to the day and time of the week it has to be made, and they may be influenced if they have a personal experience of a case. For example, making a judgment on risk where sexual abuse presents, may be constrained if they have an unresolved issue of sexual abuse in their background. They might under- or overestimate the risk depending on their experience, and there is also evidence that workers may be motivated to work with perpetrators as a means of retribution for their own reasons, or there are also areas where there is less urgency in terms of dealing with the risk, such as neglect with an ongoing history but no major presenting incident. The term risk is brought alive in the current legislation and safeguarding procedures through the term 'actual or likely significant harm'. Evidence from practice indicates that there is only professional consensus on risk when cases are extreme and there is massive variation when we are asked to make a judgment on the middle or lower ground – the grey areas.

Integrating not separating

In order to assess and manage risk effectively, reliable methods are necessary. Since there are two different approaches to risk prediction, it is important to consider how to weight the use of the actuarial and clinical approaches so they work with each other rather than against each other. Calder (2011) suggested that the use of actuarial materials are useful when attempting to wade through the large numbers of referrals with a request for a response, as they offer an objective rather than a subjective consistency to decision-making. In a similar vein, an objective measure of risk is needed to review the progress made in relation to any original risk measurement and the actuarial approach can offer a lot in this scenario. However, the difficulties of attempting to simplify complex, often multiple problems into a statistical framework doesn't sit easily, especially when we are frequently attempting to move from the specific risk at referral to the broader more holistic context. He suggested a sequence that allows the differing concepts to fuse into a single process that sees judgment as the sandwich filler nestled in between the actuarial doorstops (see Figure 3.6).

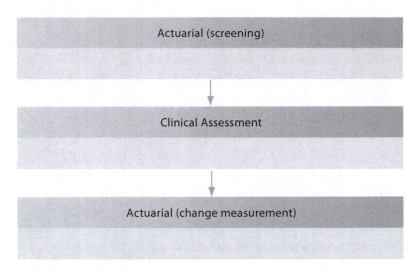

Figure 3.6 Risk sandwich
(Calder 2011)

Static, stable and dynamic risk factors

Carson and Bain (2008) introduced the notion of 'risk periods' as an aid to considering how long a shelf life a risk decision might hold for. The key point to appreciate is that each of these risks decisions is taken for a period of time. Each decision, except the last in the sequence, is designed – at least implicitly – to last until it is reviewed and another (risk) decision is taken. Decision-makers should only include those risks whose outcomes could occur, and only to the extent that they might occur, within the risk period for the decision they are contemplating.

We know that future behaviour can never be predicted with certainty. Nevertheless, a growing body of research indicates that well-informed practitioners can predict sexual recidivism with at least moderate accuracy. Hanson (1998; 1999) argued that risk assessments consider two distinct concepts: enduring propensities, or potentials to re-offend; and factors that indicate the onset of new offences. These offence triggers are not random, but can be expected to be organised into predictable patterns (offence cycles), some unique to the individual and some common to most sexual offenders.

Different evaluation questions require the consideration of different types of risk factors. Static, historical variables (e.g. prior offences, childhood maladjustment) can indicate deviant developmental trajectories and, as such, enduring propensities to sexually offend. Evaluating changes in risk levels (e.g. treatment outcome), however, requires the consideration of dynamic, changeable risk factors (e.g. co-operation with supervision, deviant sexual preferences). The relatively low recidivism rates of sexual offenders make it difficult to detect dynamic risk factors. Over a four to five year period, approximately 10–15 per cent of sexual offenders will be detected committing a new sexual offence (Hanson and Bussiere 1998). Although age is sometimes considered a dynamic factor, the most important dynamic factors are those that respond to treatment. Dynamic factors can further be classified as stable or acute. Stable factors have the potential to change, but typically endure for months or years (e.g. personality disorder) and, as such, represent ongoing risk potential. In contrast, acute factors (e.g. negative mood) may be present for a short duration (minutes, days) and can signal the timing of offending. Most risk decisions require consideration of both static and dynamic risk factors. Calder (2000) has reviewed these concepts in detail as they relate to adult male sex offenders.

Prentky *et al.* (2000) and Ryan (2000) have started to consider the concept of dynamic and static risk factors with young people who sexually abuse (see Figure 3.7). Ryan has argued that the more research that becomes available with this group the more it shows that they are not noticeably different from other groups of young offenders, such as those who self-harm or commit violent offences. She has provided us with a useful embryonic, and at this stage, hypothetical framework for considering factors relevant to abusive functioning. The usefulness of her framework is considerable as she has extended the concept of risk factors to include assets. This is an important extension of the concepts developed in the adult field and is consistent with the view that risk assessment is about balancing risks and assets, weighting them within the presenting situation and then coming to an informed conclusion. Jane Gilgun in her work with children exhibiting sexual behaviour problems developed a framework that also embraces assets alongside risks. She argued that it is important to have a framework that explores assets as well as risks (see Table 3.2 below). The ideal is that we protect children from risks. However, the power of risks can be moderated by creating an imbalance with greater assets. The child with high risks and high assets may be less dysfunctional than the child with few risks but few assets. The most dysfunctional outcome is likely to be the child with high risks and low assets.

FIGURE 3.2 BALANCING RISKS AND ASSETS (GILGUN 1999)

LOW ASSET LOW RISK	HIGH ASSET LOW RISK
LOW ASSET HIGH RISK	HIGH ASSET HIGH RISK

STATIC RISK FACTORS AND ASSETS

RISKS	ASSETS
Prenatal insults	Prenatal care
Premature/traumatic birth	Normative birth
Unempathic care	Empathic care
Caregiver loss/disruption	Consistent caregiver(s)
Trust failure	Trustworthy relationship
Disordered attachment	Secure attachment
Dysfunctional modelling	Normal growth/development
Witness to domestic violence	Functional modelling
Abuse, neglect, failure to thrive, trauma	Nurturance and protection

Stable risk factors and assets

Stable risk factors are those that remain somewhat constant across the life-span. They are less changeable although they may be moderated.

RISKS	ASSETS
Difficult temperament	Easy/adaptive temperament
Low functioning	Average-high intelligence (IQ)
Learning disability	Positive internal working model (self and others)
Heritable psychiatric disorders	
Chronic PTSD reactivity	Normative physical and neurological functioning

Dynamic risk factors and assets

Dynamic risk factors are constantly changing, either purposefully or by chance. They are clearly changeable.

GLOBAL (foreseeable in life span)	CIRCUMSTANTIAL (specific/ fluctuating daily)
Constant/expected stressors	Current/unexpected stressors (conflict or emotional trigger)
Unresolved emotional issues	
Unsafe environment/persons	Perceived threat vulnerability
Injury/illness	Lowered self-esteem/efficacy
Temporary disabilities	Negative expectations
Lack of opportunity/support	Isolation/lack of support
Change/loss	Mood dysregulation: anger, depression, anxiety
Sexual drive/arousal	
Abusive memories	Projection/misattributions
Failed relationships	Limited options/skill deficits
Access to vulnerable persons	Abusive memory/fantasy
	Sexual arousal/thought
	Lowered inhibitions
	Access to vulnerable persons

Dynamic assets

Ryan also sets out the following observable outcomes of evidence of change relevant to decreased risk:

- Consistently defines all abuse (self, others, property)

- Acknowledges risk (foresight and safety planning)

- Consistently recognises/interrupts cycle (no later than the first thought of an abusive solution)

- Demonstrates new coping skills (when stressed)

- Demonstrates empathy (sees cues of others and responds)

- Accurate attributions of responsibility (takes responsibility for own behaviour and doesn't try to control the behaviour of others)

- Rejects abusive thoughts as dissonant (incongruent with self-image).

It is important that we simultaneously consider the outcomes related to increased health:

- Pro-social relationship skills (closeness, trust and trustworthiness)

- Positive self-image (able to be separate, independent and competent)

- Able to resolve conflicts and make decisions (assertive, tolerant, forgiving, co-operative; able to negotiate and compromise)

- Celebrates good and experiences pleasure (able to relax and play)

- Able to manage frustration and unfavourable events (anger management and self-protection)

- Works/struggles to achieve delayed gratification (persistent pursuit of goals; able to concentrate)

- Able to think and communicate effectively (rational cognitive processing, adequate verbal skills)

- Adaptive sense of purpose and future.

Rotational Risk (Calder 2007)

Perry and Sheldon (1995) concluded that there is no such thing as a risk free assessment and neither are there any criteria which enable us to place individuals into sharply defined, once-and-for-all categories of 'dangerous' or 'not dangerous'. Rather, there is a continuum of statistical risk with uncomfortably limited predictive capacity. Calder (2007) coined the term rotational risk to reflect the concerns he identified when examining whether UK-developed frameworks for assessing the risk in cases of domestic violence were transferable to ethnic communities that are both growing as well as extending. In a literature review of the risk and protective factors in three ethnic communities he identified that there were at least 42 additional risk and protective factors that did not feature in the existing frameworks. More concerning, however, was the finding that strengths in existing frameworks might actually represent risks in the three additional ethnic communities. This raises the need to not only accept that risk is both about positive and negative elements, but that risks and strengths in one family or community might be the opposite of what is safe or evidence-based.

Interestingly, Calder referred to the earlier work of Jane Gilgun (1999) in developing materials designed to gauge risks from children presenting with sexual behaviour problems. *The Clinical Assessment Package for Client Risks and Strengths* (CASPARS) brings strength perspectives to practice. Not only do these instruments direct attention to positives, but they also contribute to treatment plans, help estimate progress in treatment, and provide measures of outcome. Short, easy to administer and score, and based on research and theory on risk and resilience, the CASPARS are ecological in scope. They cover five domains that are central to child and family wellbeing. These domains are emotional expressiveness, sexuality, peer relationships, family relationships, and family embeddedness in the community (see Figure 3.7 for example).

Emotional Expressiveness
Jane F. Gilgun, Ph.D., LICSW

The following are streamlined items for assessing emotional expressiveness. Based on open-ended interviews with the individual, informal conversations with the individual, and any other information you have, score the individual on the following items. Your score requires your clinical judgment on where the individual falls on each of the items.

1. The individual shows a range of feelings.

5	4	3	2	1	2	3	4	5
Absolutely Yes				Mixed				Absolutely No

2. The individual can articulate how s/he is feeling.

5	4	3	2	1	2	3	4	5
Absolutely Yes				Mixed				Absolutely No

3. The individual can articulate how others feel.

5	4	3	2	1	2	3	4	5
Absolutely Yes				Mixed				Absolutely No

4 The individual expresses his/her feelings directly, without being aggressive or passive.

5	4	3	2	1	2	3	4	5
Absolutely Yes				Mixed				Absolutely No

5. The individual consciously emulates others who manage their emotions well.

5	4	3	2	1	2	3	4	5
Absolutely Yes				Mixed				Absolutely No

6. Others in the individual's life recognize when s/he demonstrates appropriate expression of emotion.

5	4	3	2	1	2	3	4	5
Absolutely Yes				Mixed				Absolutely No

7. In general, the individual manages his or her emotions well.

| 5 | 4 | 3 | 2 | 1 | 2 | 3 | 4 | 5 |

Absolutely Yes   Mixed   Absolutely No

8. In general, the individual is respectful of the emotions of others.

| 5 | 4 | 3 | 2 | 1 | 2 | 3 | 4 | 5 |

Absolutely Yes   Mixed   Absolutely No

Scoring: add scores in each column. If you want to score the individual as both yes and no on a item, score him/her "mixed" and give the individual a 1 for both yes and no. You will then have scored for strengths & risks on emotional expressiveness.

Yes Score_____   **No Score**_____

Figure 3.7 CASPAR Domain Detail Example

Atomistic or holistic approaches

Munro in her review of child protection advocated a holistic approach to assessment (Table 3.3).

TABLE 3.3 ATOMISTIC AND HOLISTIC APPROACHES
TO CHILD PROTECTION (MUNRO 2011c)

	Atomistic approach to child protection	**Holistic approach to child protection**
Nature	► Narrow: tending to concentrate on individual parts or elements	► Broad: elements seen as standing in relation to each other
Perspective	► Isolated problems	► Whole system
Cause and effect	► Looking only at immediate and/or proximal effects ► Short chains of causality	► Separated in space and time ► Long chains of causality, ripple effects, unintended consequences, feedback effects

cont.

	Atomistic approach to child protection	Holistic approach to child protection
Style of recommendations	▶ Regulation and compliance ▶ Technocratic	▶ Strengthening professionalism ▶ Socio-technical
Results (observed and sought)	▶ Narrow range of responses to children's and young people's needs ▶ Defensive management of risk ▶ Command and control management, frameworks and procedures, squeezing out professional discretion ▶ Compliance culture ▶ Focus on standardised processes, frameworks and procedures	▶ Requisite variety in responses to meeting children's and young people's needs ▶ Acceptance of irreducible risk ▶ Supportive and enabling of management ▶ Learning culture ▶ Focus on children, their needs, appropriate pathways beneficial outcomes

When applying the different approaches to risk we find that both have a place. When a referral is made it is clear that time, and frequently, access to information are limited and so attention is focused on the presenting concern and a decision made on any action taken. Such an approach clearly lacks a broader context and it has the potential for workers to miss many other parallel problems – snapshots are intrinsically limited and not necessarily representative. That said, a more holistic approach is not a practical starting point although as a fuller assessment is conducted, we would expect to see a more holistic approach to identify all of the presenting problems and any correlation or a context to the original presenting concern.

Practice struggles to use a singular definition of holistic and we have to guard against it being a buzzword that lacks integrity or understanding. A holistic approach to risk assessment entails analysing situational factors alongside the research-based factors. Risk and need are both fundamentally based on the quality of information. Where information is lacking, risk can be assessed as being very high, when the situation may not present a negative risk to a child at all. Assessing risk and decision-making depends significantly on the quality of the information available. Making judgments about whether harm will occur in the future to an individual child involves decision-making about specific information. In the absence of certainties, or clearly defined risk factors, it is important to guard against faulty professional judgment and unsound decision-making.

Time and risk

Time is needed if a risk is to be carefully analysed and assessed. Delays may be unavoidable if necessary information is to be collected and people consulted and involved. But if the risk is also a dilemma then that time can only be obtained by imposing, or causing extra harm. Dilemmas involve more pressurised decision-making than risks. The fact that harm or loss may occur if additional time is taken over making the decision is a defining characteristic of a dilemma. It is a feature of the kind of decision involved rather than the decision-makers.

Carson and Bain (2008) noted that time is exceptionally important to risk taking in a number of different ways. First, there is the time during which a risk decision is being taken. It is the outcome, beneficial or harmful, which could occur during the risk period, the time for which the risk will last, that matters. It is what may go right or wrong and how likely during this treatment, this flight, or from this decision to the next time that it is reviewed or renewed, that matters should be assessed. It is inappropriate to make professional risk predictions many years in advance; the science rarely justifies it. Second is the amount of time that is available to make a risk decision. The absence of time to make a fully considered decision is one of the factors that make it a dilemma. It is a resource in short supply. The absence of time in which to obtain more information, get more or better resources, to think about it and so on and the requirement to take action to reduce harms such as continuing pain and loss of blood puts it at a premium. Those who face up to a dilemma deserve to have that reality taken into account with the result that they are judged by lower standards that would apply if there was not a dilemma or emergency. Third, there is the time available to intervene in the implementation of a risk decision. This is the meaning most readily associated with risk managements. What time is there, for example, to intervene in a risk decision to stop it from failing?

It is also important to differentiate between short- and long-term risks. Short-term risk relates to the immediate danger to the child and, where none exists, the danger is that no services are provided. This can potentially contribute to the detrimental effects on development in the longer term through parenting deficits. It is for this reason that a more objective measure of care is required to standardise the measurement of likely or actual harm in the non-crisis orientated cases such as neglect and emotional abuse. The practice of focusing on assessing immediate harm can skew practice so that the longer-term risks are ignored or undervalued. We know from Utting (1997) that children in long-term care placements may well be the cases that become unallocated but then the risk is that we do not pick up on changing circumstances and harm ensues.

Risk to staff

An interesting aspect of the moral panic about risk is that the risk to social workers from dangerous people and the adverse attention of politicians and the media has not been of such concern. In terms of its frequency, the risk of abuse and physical threat or attack for social workers is far more prevalent than similar risks to their service users. Social workers – particularly in residential settings – are among those who share the highest risk of assault at work. The recognition of this risk should be a primary consideration for all social workers, their managers and the organisations within which they work. Littlechild (2008) noted that families who are subject to child protection inquiries from statutory agencies are more often than not involuntary clients. One implication of this, from a small minority of clients, is the use of aggression and violence against social workers.

Such aggression has been shown to significantly affect workers' wellbeing, and their commitment to that work. Lord Laming, in his child abuse death inquiry report into the death of Victoria Climbié, stated:

> I recognise that those who take on the work of protecting children at risk of deliberate harm face a tough and challenging task. Staff doing this work need a combination of professional skills and personal qualities, not least of which are persistence and courage. Adults who deliberately exploit the vulnerability of children can behave in devious and menacing ways. Staff often have to cope with the unpredictable behaviour of people in the parental role. (Laming 2003, p.3)

Social workers in child protection work have a dual role; not only do they have to try to engage with families to help improve the health and wellbeing of the children involved in an abusive situation, but also have to act as agents of social control if the abuse is so severe that action has to be taken, immediately in the most severe situations, or in the longer term if there is neglect or abuse which is continuing after intervention. Howe states that the, 'welter of procedures and guidelines' has led to the social worker becoming an 'investigator, reporter and "gatherer" of evidence' (Howe 1992, p.502).

This dual role, or double mandate, in social work, appears to have a significant bearing on the causes of such violence. Social workers are expected to support, but then also control and judge, parents in the area of child protection. This then relates to effects of power, authority, and control in the social work role, and parents' use and experience of that role in relation to their children and the workers involved. This role ambiguity is one of the reasons for aggression towards workers from parents when carrying out the dual role which contains supportive and investigative functions; an element of the work which official guidance tends to ignore – see section later in this chapter on official government agency guidance. Stanley and Goddard (1997) suggest that abusive families can use tactics to draw the worker into the role of victim. One particularly severe form of such dynamics, they suggest, is the Stockholm syndrome (Wardlaw 1982), concerning the relationship which can develop between hostages and terrorists, which may also apply to relationships in and surrounding abusing families – including the relationship with the child protection worker. They suggest that this complex set of dynamics can draw the worker into becoming a victim of these abusing/controlling dynamics, which means they are unable to challenge the abuse, or utilise procedures properly. They also suggest that at times, workers appear to indulge in self-deception and denial of violence.

Young people's perceptions of risk

Risk taking is a developmentally critical phase for young people but there are some risks that are more manageable than others. It is expected that the transition from childhood to adolescence will be characterised by the search for a greater level of independence, but the consequences may expose them to a broader range of risks within their peer, family and wider networks – many of which may be outside of their control. Many young people are driven by the need for immediate gratification and in so doing do not take into account or consider the short-or long-term consequences. This is associated with their rather immature stage of brain development when they haven't yet learned to apply the brakes. Many young people have a sense of invulnerability which raises exposure to risks. The social context of young people growing up continues to change and their perception of normal can be quite extreme to others growing up in earlier times. A regular case example includes sexualised behaviours as the virtual world allows them access to extreme literature, videos, music and games. The advent of sexting, posting of materials on Snapchat and Facebook are alarming, frequent and invite copy or extension. Peer acceptance becomes one of the most powerful drivers for young people as parents and family significance recedes. A growing number of young people may be convicted of a range of sexual crimes, not simply because of the gratification driver, but because of peer 'dares' to retain group acceptance. The experimentation with alcohol and substances is similarly concerning.

It is interesting to note the low level availability of research that has sought to elicit young people's versions of how they comprehend their own risk worlds and risk-taking behaviour. Most of our views on risk have been shaped by adult views of what is 'risky' for young people and not enough attention has been paid to the views and agendas of young people themselves. Ward and Bayley (2009) addressed this and identified several useful points worthy of note. They asked two different age groups (10 to 12-year-olds and 16 to 17-year-olds) what they associated with the word 'risk'. The groups gave quite sophisticated understandings of the concept, although not unexpectedly responses differed by age. The notion of 'harm' linked to an action was pervasive. The younger age framed risk as 'something you shouldn't be doing', compared to the 16–17 year olds who did consider this but also considered the consequences of their actions. Other factors cited included uncertainty, individual choice and responsibility (suggesting some element of control) as well as considering the odds against the potential outcomes. Many young people framed risk as a predominantly negative concept, although it could inform future positives when becoming aware of the consequences of the original action. Clearly risk changes over time as experiences are processed and lessons learned to inform their next behaviours. Some situations that could be construed as risky were therefore presented as positive challenges that were part of learning how to negotiate the way through life and sifting out right from wrong. Young people rationalised the outcomes of their decisions to engage in something risky as helping to shape them into the person they were becoming and to develop confidence to confront the unfamiliar arenas into which they were moving.

Young people's perceptions of risk are clearly influenced by their local community and networks and many can identify specific crime 'hotspot' areas that were perceived as 'risky' should they be out in such places.

Risk and gender

Ward and Bayley (2009) also found that risk is a gendered experience, mirroring the gender-role stereotypes that exist in society. They found that girls were more likely than boys to associate risk with accidents at home and personal safety. Boys more often described outdoor and electrical-related incidents and sport and skill mastery.

Males typically constructed their risk worlds around physicality, while girls' accounts were constructed in more emotive terms. These were around romance relationships, body image and appearance and empathised with parental concerns such as financial issues and family arguments.

Male risk activity was also associated with achieving status, highlighting the importance of an audience being more important than the behaviour itself. It would follow therefore that young people may actively seek out, and connect with, like-minded people.

Young women framed risk more as relating to issues such as physical appearance and clothing or not looking the right way and connected risk to being scrutinised by other young people prior to embarking on any kind of friendship.

This could be linked both to different perceptions about body image and attitudes toward and engagement in sexual activity.

One area where further work is needed relates to the changing demographic profile such as how young people respond to the parents' cultural expectations and how young people negotiate their dual identities.

═══════════ **Key messages from the chapter** ═══════════

Risk is both positive and negative although in the field of child protection it is often framed as negative. This is both self-protective for professionals and alienating for families. It is a purposeful slant for professionals to manipulate thresholds that are getting harder to cross and as always are a passport to prioritisation and resources.

Professionals measure the risks of different things depending upon their primary remit and the unfortunate consequences of this can be that professionals using the same word may actually be talking at cross purposes about something completely different.

Different professionals use different forms of evidence in calculating the risk that they talk to each other about: actuarial or clinical. Both have their strengths and weaknesses and the emerging middle ground is a risk sandwich that is more professionally referred to as a clinically adjusted actuarial risk approach.

Risk is subjective and this allows flexibility but it also often means that the same case is managed very differently by different staff. This can be misused on occasions as cases can be allocated to a worker whose decision-making is known to be either interventionist or diversionist.

Whilst the best predictor of future risk is previous risk, this can alienate families who perceive that the outcome of the assessment is pre-determined. The potential for change has to be embraced and the notions of static, stable and dynamic risk allows for this.

Risk is a natural part of development and so the normality of risk taking in certain circumstances has to be acknowledged whilst also factoring in the consequences of the actions taken.

CHAPTER 4

Risk Assessment

What is assessment?

There are a number of definitions of assessment, but Milner and O'Byrne's five stage definition is useful because it follows process.

- ▶ Preparation: deciding who to see, what data will be relevant, what the purpose is and what the limits of the task are.

- ▶ Data collection: people are met and engaged with, different gaps are addressed, and empowerment and choice are safeguarded as we come to the task with respectful uncertainty and a research mentality.

- ▶ Weighing the data: current social and psychological theory and research findings that are part of every social worker's learning are drawn on to answer the questions, 'Is there a problem?' and 'How serious is it?'.

- ▶ Analysing the data: one or more of the analytic maps are used to understand and interpret the data in order to develop ideas for intervention.

- ▶ Utilising the analysis: this is the stage in which judgments are finalised.

This definition makes clear that throughout the assessment process – from determining which data are relevant at the preparation stage, through to making a final decision based on analysis – research is used to inform every decision. Having a 'research mentality' is an integral part of conducting meaningful and accurate assessments. Of course, because assessment is an active and fluid process, informed by a research mentality, demarcation between the stages is not always clear-cut; stages of the process inevitably merge into one another.

Taylor (2010) argued that '…the aim of assessment is to gather and order information for analysis so as to inform professional judgment and decision processes about care [and protection].' No assessment framework or tool will automatically provide practitioners with the right answers with regard to identifying the needs of children. Many of the questions linked to the frameworks and tools are dependent on practitioners assessing and making professional judgments regarding acceptable parenting standards, strengths and deficits. But professional judgments involve the *interpretative* use of knowledge, practical wisdom, a sense of purpose, appropriateness and feasibility (Eraut 1994, p.49).

'Good assessment is fundamental to good practice: for all potential service users, regardless of age. It is an analytical process that requires intelligence, logic, flexibility, open mindedness and creativity, and it should be experienced by the consumer as a positive contribution to their life…' (Middleton 1997).

Samra-Tibbets and Raynes (1999) provided a very useful model for approaching joint investigations and the comprehensive assessment (see Figure 4.1). The framework offers us a clear and structured approach that generates a solid basis for decision-making. The assessment is built upon thorough planning, and the concerns identified through the investigation and conference stages of the process.

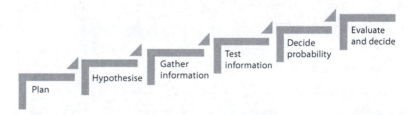

Figure 4.1 A stepwise model of assessment
(Samra-Tibbets and Raynes 1999)

In the first block, planning is essential. This is often left out by the professionals as they feel pressured to get on with the task. This may be safe where they work together on a regular basis, but is more concerning where they have never worked together beforehand. There needs to be a careful look at the information held already, and what still needs to be gathered. There needs to be some agreement on channels of communication, as it is unrealistic for the social worker to expect to know everything at every stage of the process.

The second block attends to issues of hypotheses. This is defined in the dictionary as 'a starting point for an investigation'. There is evidence to show that workers sometimes begin the assessment with one particular hypothesis and gather evidence to support this. This can be dangerous as it actually forms a conclusion before the assessment has begun. The workers should consider all possible hypotheses, be open-minded in gathering evidence, and prioritise hypotheses only where there is clear evidence to do so. They need to take a step back from the early intervention in order to generate the maximum number of possibilities, so as not to shut down any avenue prematurely. Gawlinski *et al.* (1987) offered the following characteristics of a hypothesis:

- ▶ It is stated in specific rather than vague terms
- ▶ The statements within the hypothesis are logically connected
- ▶ It is comprehensive and so takes account of most available significant information
- ▶ It contains statements about predisposing and precipitating factors
- ▶ It identifies factors which continue to place the family at risk for further child abuse
- ▶ It points to a clear action plan and also suggests courses of action that should be avoided (p.29).

The initial hypothesis is necessarily speculative and is used as the basis for gathering more information that will either confirm or refute it.

In the third block, there is a need to gather information. Nothing is more sterile than information collecting for the purpose of information collecting. The kind and amount of information collected will be dictated by the defined problem for work and the preliminary goals that are established. It is difficult to deal with areas of data collection concretely because the specific areas to be explored depend on the situation.

There are, however, some principles that should be considered. It is a joint process and the client should be involved in helping to determine the areas to be explored. The client should be aware of the sources being used for data collection although they may not always be asked for their permission.

There should be a connection between the problems identified and the data collected, and the client should be aware of any connection as well as helping them to understand the areas the worker seeks to explore. Data collection goes on all the time, but it is critical to the problem identification, goal setting, and assessment stages of work. It is crucial that the worker understand the client's view of all areas of data collection – their thinking, feelings and actions (Compton and Galaway 1989).

There is a tendency to gather too much information, and we need to guard against this as well as irrelevant information. We may modify our original hypothesis many times as new information is gathered from the family. It is not necessary to wait for a definitive hypothesis before intervening, as many times only the interventions themselves produce crucial information. Since the major purpose of a hypothesis is to make connections, how information is gathered is extremely important. The worker must take a neutral position and try not to imply any moral judgments or to align themselves with any one faction of the family. Change often comes about through the worker's ability to stand outside the family and gain a holistic view. The intervention is then geared at the most relevant of the presenting problems. In gathering information, it is helpful to keep the following questions in mind. What function does the symptom serve in stabilising the family? How does the family function in stabilising the symptom? What is the central theme around which the problem is organised? What will be the consequences of change?

The fourth step requires that the information collected is tested out. Different professionals will come together with information around levels of risk and potential, and targets for change, and there needs to be some analysis about what evidence there is to either support or refute their views. Strategies for achieving change or the management of risk in the interim do need to be agreed, as do areas where gaps exist and further information may need to be gathered. The following risk assessment checklist is helpful in identifying areas for testing out the information, and which lead us into the next block around deciding on the probability of future harm:

▶ What is the nature of the concern?

▶ What is the category of abuse?

▶ Check out how your own attitudes and values will affect your responses

▶ Are there racial, cultural, linguistic or other issues that need consideration?

▶ Are the injuries/incidents acute/cumulative/episodic?

▶ When and how is the child at risk?

▶ Did the injuries/incidents result from spontaneous actions, neglect or intent?

▶ What are the parents'/carers' attitudes and responses to your concerns?

▶ Is their explanation consistent with the injury/incident?

▶ What does the child mean to the family?

▶ What are the child's views/needs/wishes?

▶ What is the potential for change in the family?

▶ Are incidents/injuries likely to re-occur?

▶ How safe is the child? What are the possibilities? What is the probability? How imminent is the likely risk? How grave are the likely consequences?

In the decision block, the professional group is being asked to make recommendations for the longer-term child protection plan, through the child protection review. The professionals may have to make recommendations for the future protection of children in contact with the perpetrator. This may be to the civil or criminal courts or child protection conference. In the final step, there is a need to review the way forward. This may well include the potential for change within both the perpetrator and their family; the viability and focus of the necessary work; any mandate needed; any relaxation of contact restrictions; and any family reconstitution. The assessment needs to move beyond the changes required, to identifying whether change is possible, and what motivation exists for change. In many senses, the client will have to experience some element of discomfort with their current situation for them to be motivated to change. Accompanying this must be some hope of reaching the goal, an ability to consider what has gone wrong and some opportunity for change in the situation (Compton and Galaway 1989).

The stepwise model to the framework for assessment

The assessment framework repeats the mistakes of earlier assessment systems by focusing on information gathering and not on the process of assessments, the route from referral to care plan. The stepwise model illustrates the steps which workers need to follow to produce an effective assessment and, more importantly, a care plan. At the planning stage, where a group of professionals, particularly those who do not regularly work together, are to jointly undertake an assessment, they need to agree not just how they will assess the family but also how they will work together effectively. Many workers tend to concentrate on the tasks they need to undertake in respect of the child and the family, but spend little time considering how they will maximise the groups' combined skills and knowledge, and support and complement one another's work. In addition, consideration should be given to developing strategies for resolving difficulties and differences of opinion. The assessment framework does provide some compatible guidance with the stepwise model.

Setting up and beginning:

▶ What questions require answering through the assessment, what are the issues and what are the likely consequences for the child's health and development of the present situation?

▶ Is/are the child(ren) safe, now? Has there been or is there risk of significant harm?

▶ Who is most worried about this child or family – does anyone else have concerns? Are they the same? Who is requesting this assessment?

▶ Who is involved – which children, family members, workers, agencies, court?

▶ Has the family been assessed before and for what purpose(s)?

▶ Are there any special considerations?

▶ What is the family's first language, culture, religion or identity?

▶ Are any family members disabled? What is their main communication method?

▶ Is there a need for an interpreter?

▶ Who can help best understand and work with this family?

▶ Are there any likely or possible barriers to carrying out this assessment?

▶ Is there agreement with the family and between family members about the need for and purpose of the assessment?

▶ Is there agreement within the professional group about the need for and purpose of an assessment?

▶ Is there agreement about respective professional roles and responsibilities, what information will be shared and who has lead responsibility?

▶ Are other types of assessment concurrent?

▶ Are there adequate resources to carry out the assessment?

▶ Is the worker competent and does he/she possess the necessary knowledge and experience to carry out the assessment working to the framework?

In the hypothesising stage, workers often remain narrowly focused on proving or disproving whether the immediate risk still exists and fail to consider the broader picture. The assessment team should consider all the possibilities regarding the harm that the child could be suffering, both within their family and the wider community. Each hypothesis should be addressed and only discounted when there is clear evidence to do so. Explicitly hypothesising about all possibilities ensures that every possibility is considered, assessment team members' attitudes and biases are addressed and the family can clearly understand what concerns the workers may have. While this stage has been placed at the beginning of the assessment process in stepwise, it is important to recognise that this process should be repeated when any new evidence comes to light, which may challenge previously held views.

In the next stage, information for the assessment should be gathered from all adults who are significant to the child, plus, of course, from the child. The assessment team will need to be clear about their reasons for approaching people. Members of the extended family, people who are not relatives but act as carers e.g. childminders or friends, workers in voluntary community organisations and other professionals can all provide valuable information. However, parents need to be aware that they are being asked to contribute and issues of confidentiality will need to be addressed. There is a range of tools available to assist workers in gathering information, and these include genograms, ecomaps and critical incident charts. The testing and evaluating stage of an assessment is particularly important, but often given limited attention.

Workers frequently use most of the time allotted to the assessment to gather information and produce a report, which details this but fails to evaluate the information or draw conclusions. Those involved in evaluating information will need tools to assist them. The risk assessment checklist can be used by individuals in their assessment work and as a basis for joint discussion within the assessment team. The checklist asks a series of questions which will assist workers to consider the type and level of harm a child may be suffering, the possible effects of that harm, the likely outcomes of intervention, the safety factors in the child's environment and the potential for change within the family.

The assessment framework has a further checklist for the analytical stage. It is worthwhile checking this out at the beginning of the analytical step as it informs the work that needs doing.

- ▶ Is the assessment providing adequate evidence to analyse before making judgments leading to decisions about future actions?

- ▶ Is the worker distinguishing between fact and opinion?

- ▶ Is there reasonable cause to suspect that a child is suffering, or is likely to suffer, from significant harm?

▶ Has the assessment revealed significant unmet needs for support and services?

▶ If the decision is not to provide services, this is itself a decision. What is the next step?

▶ Is the worker able to evaluate evidence drawing on his/her understanding of theory, for example, child development?

▶ Is the worker drawing on knowledge of research?

▶ Is the worker informing the family (including the children) of the outcome and recommendations arising from the assessment?

▶ Is the supervisor ensuring that rigour and challenge form part of their supervision?

▶ Is the supervisor able to ask questions, to challenge and probe where necessary? This may mean asking obvious or unpopular questions.

▶ Is the supervisor encouraging both factual analysis and reflective practice?

▶ Is the supervisor able to address the areas of potential impact on the worker?

▶ Is there a supervisory agreement in place that allows for constructive challenge and feedback?

▶ Is the supervisor evaluating how the worker is currently making judgments?

▶ What is given priority and why?

▶ Which factors are marginalised and why?

▶ Which factors are causing most discussion and debate in terms of determining priority and why?

▶ What is this saying about their current practice?

The final pages of the assessment framework core assessment forms contain tables which relate to care planning. The problem with this part of the framework's process is that, having sub-divided the situation into 20 dimensions these pages fail to bring everything back together again.

The linear nature of the design implies that there is one outcome per objective whereas this is not the case; one objective can have a number of desired outcomes and one outcome can measure a number of objectives. Also, objectives cannot be limited to one domain. Take, for example, 'to improve the relationship between parents and child', this must be a fairly common objective. Which dimensions should it be in? Basic care? Ensuring safety? Emotional warmth? Stimulation? Guidance and boundaries? Stability? Family's social integration? Wider family? Family history and functioning? Emotional and behavioural development? Identity? Family and social relationships? Social presentation? It would be easier to list, which dimensions it wouldn't be covered in.

A good care plan will differentiate between high and low level objectives, will set measurements against these objectives, will list tasks and who will carry them out and identify systems for monitoring success. Our care plan format allows the assessment team to pool the information gleaned from the assessment, consider the situation as a whole and identify, via the care planning process described above, objectives, tasks, targets and monitoring arrangements.

One of the challenges for staff is to resist the requirement to allow the timescales accompanying the assessment framework to drive all assessment practice. The most obvious danger for staff is that they respond to the clock starting to tick by collecting information without first having attended to the planning process and also developing hypotheses. The consequences of accelerating through the initial assessment stages is that workers will collect information for the sake of doing so, without relating the task of information collection to that of testing hypotheses. Such practice is routinely identified in inquiry reports which commend a worker's capacity to collect information but criticise the random and unconnected nature in which it is collected and then remains unharnessed in developing plans to address the originating concerns.

There are also serious side effects of such a contracted assessment process. If workers do not attend to the planning and the hypothesising process it not only means that various professionals may remain confused or harbour different ideas about the assessment task but it also acts as a barrier to engaging parents. This can have potentially enduring and sometimes irreplaceable consequences in that parents feel alienated or done to and this is correlated with poor outcomes.

The stepwise model can serve two essential functions for assessors. First, it can offer a generic template for all assessment practice that offers some format for standardisation. This mirrors the intention of the assessment framework. However, it can offer an additional dimension in encouraging the worker to apply case or harm-specific evidence to the generic framework and this allows realistic hypotheses to be formulated according to the specific circumstances of the case rather than assuming one structure is applicable across all types of assessment.

There are differences and similarities between the assessment of risk and the assessment of need within child protection in terms of how comprehensively situations are assessed, the methods of undertaking the assessment and how the information is aggregated. Dalgleish (2003) highlights the significant similarity between the two types of assessment, in that they are both forms of assessment, and contends that, 'both are essentially linked. One should not do one without the other' (p.88). The children and families involved with child protection services are multifaceted and bring a variety of problems. To engage in a discourse which focuses on either risk or harm is likely to reduce the possibilities of working effectively with these multifaceted and multiproblem families.

Changing the framework for social work assessment in itself is not enough to change the practice. The discourse of risk versus need fails to understand adequately the possibility of assessment as a means of building and developing understanding about children, families and their functioning. Focusing upon risk and need lends itself to a tendency to focus almost exclusively upon the objective and outcome of the assessment, to the exclusion of what goes on in between. What goes on in between is crucial if assessment is to be located within wider social work practice, and within an ecological model of understanding the child and family.

Structured decision-making

Structured decision-making is a general term for carefully organised analysis of problems in order to reach decisions that are focused clearly on achieving fundamental objectives. It encompasses a simple set of concepts and helpful steps, rather than a rigidly prescribed approach for problem solving. Key concepts include: making decisions based on clearly articulated fundamental objectives, dealing explicitly with uncertainty and responding transparently to legal mandates and public preferences or values in decision-making. Structured decision-making methods spend more time at the start of a decision-making process, working with stakeholders to bound the problem and to develop a comprehensive set of concerns. Both tangible and intangible concerns are considered – a level playing field for analysis.

This approach represents a way of guiding social workers through a decision-making process, utilising both risk assessment tools as well as clinical judgment. This reflects the reality that it is workers rather than tools that make the decisions: the tools simply guide us.

Case formulation

Case formulation refers to an integrative process that synthesises how one understands the complex, interacting factors implicated in the development of a client's presenting problems. It takes into account the child and family's strengths and capacities that may help to identify potentially effective intervention approaches. Workers should strive to keep the formulation as simple as possible as well as keeping an open mind – allowing the conceptualisation to change, based on either disconfirmed hypotheses or new data.

Other benefits of formulation include:

- ▶ Theory, empirical knowledge and specialist experience merge with the understanding of an individual/family/system
- ▶ It allows us to understand why a difficulty exists rather than simply describing a set of symptoms/problems
- ▶ It fills the gap between describing and intervening
- ▶ It helps organise often complex and contradictory information
- ▶ It guides intervention
- ▶ It is individually sensitive and specific

▶ It allows us to understand complexity/co-morbidity.

Calder (2015) developed the 11 Ps of case formulation in Table 4.1.

TABLE 4.1 THE 11 Ps OF CASE INFORMATION

Presenting issues	▶ Incident or process ▶ Referral route: civil or criminal ▶ Victim, abuser or both ▶ Accepted or denied ▶ Family supportive, causal or both ▶ Assessment or intervention
Pattern onset and course	▶ Isolated or accumulative ▶ Spontaneous or planned ▶ Episodic or persistent
Predisposing factors	▶ Factors in their background – such as experiences or personality – which make an undesirable outcome more likely ▶ It is something that creates vulnerability
Precipitating factors	▶ Factors that are happening which are specific to the client and their family at this time and which have an immediate effect directly related to the concern ▶ Such events or circumstances that may trigger the behaviour or disinhibit usual behavioural controls (motivators, disinhibitors) ▶ They are usually amenable to influence and are frequently the focus of targets for change
Perpetuating factors	▶ These factors may contribute to prolonging the existence of the risk factors and include unresolved vulnerabilities
Potential problems	▶ There are three potential levels of problem that require attention: the incident, patterns and processes as well as underlying values, beliefs and attitudes ▶ Multiplicity and co-morbidity require exploration as they indicate poorer prognosis, greater risk of relapse and a higher risk of harm
Protective factors	Protective factors can be understood as circumstances that moderate the effects of risk in a positive direction
Prognosis	The likelihood of change, whether the change is likely to be maintained and whether it can be achieved within the child's timeframe

Provisional conceptualization/ plan	This needs to be consistent with any other plans in existence, is outcome focused, measurable, can be negotiated with the family and is adjusted when there is a significant change of circumstances
Prescribed interventions	▸ Match the problem with the effective intervention – not simply that which is available or preferred ▸ Offence or young person focused ▸ Cost vs. consequences (enhanced risk in short term) ▸ Duration ▸ Mandate ▸ Sequencing of interventions ▸ Client attitude to intervention
Partnership between worker and client	Treatment outcomes are driven by three interrelated elements: the establishment of a bond of mutual respect between worker and client, identifying goals which are important to the client and the negotiation of manageable tasks to accomplish these goals Yatchmenoff (2008) identified some helpful factors to consider in this process: ▸ Receptivity: openness to receiving help, characterised by recognition of problems or circumstances that resulted in agency intervention and by a perceived need for help ▸ Expectancy: the perception of benefit; a sense of being helped or the expectation of receiving help through the agency's involvement; a feeling that things are changing (or will change) for the better ▸ Investment: commitment to the helping process, characterised by active participation in planning or services, goal ownership, and initiative in seeking and utilising help ▸ Working relationship: interpersonal relationship with caseworker, characterised by a sense of reciprocity or mutuality and good communication ▸ Mistrust: a negatively related factor, defined as the belief that the agency and/or worker is manipulative, malicious or capricious, with intent to harm

The assessment framework – risk-averse and perpetrator friendly

The UK Assessment of Children in Need and their Families (DH 2000) adopts a needs-led approach with the assessment process focusing on the child's developmental needs, parental capacity, and family and environmental factors. Its fundamental principles, including child-centeredness, an ecological approach, strengths-based and partnership are all very laudable. However, it has completely sidestepped the concept of 'risk'. By so doing, the government has, in effect, thrown the baby out with the bathwater (Calder 2003). Harrison (2009a) points out that engaging in the business of child protection without the application of risk assessment is like trying to make omelettes without eggs. The whole point is to weigh up risks and opportunities and to make a plan based on the best interest of the child. Clearly, the framework reflects a noble attempt to re-balance child protection and family support. However, this relegation of risk creates a huge operational problem because, with the use of thresholds, the primary focus of intervention falls under the child protection agenda. This results in managers having to provide front-line staff with supplementary frameworks that are specific to particular presenting situations (Calder 2007).

The assessment framework might well seem to encapsulate an ethos of management and scrutiny, but the Department of Health has claimed that it can provide the basis for therapeutic encounters between social workers and service users. This idea that social work assessments can have intrinsic, 'therapeutic' benefits beyond the goal of gathering information en route to the allocation of resources or to judgments of risk, is not entirely new.

Millar and Corby (2006) examined the therapeutic potential of the assessment framework, measuring it against:

- ▶ Gaining trust: A prerequisite of a therapeutic encounter, arguably, is that of engaging with service users and developing a sense of trust. A key element in this process is that of listening to and validating feelings and concerns.

- ▶ Sharing concerns, creating openness: It was evident that in some cases the use of the assessment framework facilitated open and clear communication between social workers and service users. The framework itself provided a useful tool for this. Parents and social workers were required to work together in producing a document that was explicit about concerns and identified what should be done to address them. Many parents (though certainly not all) were given copies of the assessment decisions and plans, and this practice was seen by some as a clear and open way of communicating.

▶ Influence and confidence: In several cases, use of the new assessment framework created conditions for involving parents so that they felt genuinely influential and more confident. Some social workers managed to sit down with parents and work through parts of the assessment framework in a positive way, resulting in parents feeling that they had made an important contribution to the process.

▶ Bringing about change: One goal of a therapeutic intervention can be to bring about change.

What is a risk assessment?

Investigating and intervening in child protection is by no means an exact science. It is less to do with verifiable facts as it is to do with descriptions of human behaviour that are open to interpretation (Munro 2005).

The term risk assessment is used to define a number of different assessment and decision-making processes in various agencies. It is the systematic collection of information to identify if risks are involved, and if so, what these are: identifying the likelihood of their future occurrence (prediction); whether there is a need for further work; and what form this should take. It can also be used to predict the escalation of the presenting behaviour as well as the client's motivation for change (Calder 2002a).

Carson and Bain (2008) rightly identified that the meaning of 'risk' must, obviously, partially determine the meaning of 'risk assessment'. Risk assessment involves collecting and assessing the quality and significance of information about a perceived risk. It does not include making a decision on that information. It is true that we often run the two together in our daily life. Risk assessment and risk management are interactive and iterative. Risk assessment provides information for a possible decision. Risk management suggests ways in which that decision may best be implemented.

Calder (2000) reminds us that there is no Holy Grail for undertaking a risk assessment – there is no definitive text or framework. Yet it would constitute reckless management not to install as robust as possible a system for the identification of risk. At the same time it needs to be recognised and acknowledged that no assessment tool will predict with certainty which situations are dangerous and which are not. Risk factors do assist to generally suggest what kind of situation may result in abuse, but none should be seen as an inevitable, or even probable, cause of abuse (Beckett 2003).

Risk assessment in child protection is seen by practitioners and commentators as focusing too much on the process and not enough on the outcome of assessing risk. Risk assessment tools in child protection are criticised in the literature for being overly actuarial and time-consuming to complete, and little is known about the related risk factors. Culpability in child protection is also focused on the family (rather than external factors such as poverty in terms of child neglect, for example) and/or on the practitioner, and there is little evidence of corporate responsibility for child protection issues. This often results in practitioners working defensively and applying objective and often compulsory measures *to* families rather than building trusting relationships *with* families (Barry 2007).

Assessment in child protection generally involves two distinct processes: assessing the level of risk of future harm for particular children and a contextual assessment of child and family functioning to inform casework decisions and service planning (Shlonsky and Wagner 2005a). However, these processes are also related. Effective risk assessment is dependent on workers gaining a holistic, ecological and empirically based assessment of the family. This includes an understanding of the conditions that brought the family into the child protection system, each individual family member's history, the systems of which the family is a part, and the strengths and resources the family already possesses (Cash 2001).

The primary objective of risk assessment processes is to identify, from cases referred to child welfare authorities, the subgroup of children at high risk of future abuse or neglect so that action may be taken to prevent it. A second identification relates to the likely severity of subsequent maltreatment (Morton and Salovitz 2006).

The most extensive application of risk assessment in child maltreatment cases has been in the first context, estimating the likelihood of maltreatment recurrence. Since child protection agencies are not resourced to serve all children and families in which a report is substantiated, risk assessment has been suggested as a rational way to triage those families and children most in need of a service intervention. Current risk decision-making predominantly relies on theoretical instruments, with protocols containing items presumed to relate to future serious harm, but mostly without established validity. It seems unlikely that statistical models for predicting serious harm from re-maltreatment will achieve sufficient sensitivity and specificity due to the comparatively low base rate of serious harm.

Up to now, risk assessment has been concerned with classifying a child as safe or unsafe. To move safety assessment and decision-making forward it is important to view safety as a dynamic and changing quality, influenced by dynamic variables rather than simply as a dichotomous status or condition.

Holder and Morton (1999) offered six considerations in developing a safety model. Safe and unsafe were defined as:

▶ A child may be considered safe when there are no threats of harm present or when the protective capacities in the family can adequately manage foreseeable threats of harm.

▶ A child is unsafe when the present or emerging threats of harm that exist cannot be managed by the family's protective capacities, in which case agency intervention is needed to supplement those protective capacities.

▶ Their definition suggested that safety was a function of two spheres of influence, threats of harm and protective capacities.

In addition, Holder and Morton (1999) proposed six necessary elements of a safety model: threats (of harm); harm; severity; vulnerability of the child; imminence (time); and protective capacities. The work by Holder and Morton (1999) offered several enhancements to safety decision-making. First, it distinguished the threat of harm from the harm itself (the maltreatment). The threat of harm is the dynamic or condition that leads to the maltreatment and its related harm or potential for harm. Second, their framework suggested a specific consideration of child vulnerability as an element of safety assessment. Finally, it included a specific separate consideration of protective capacities as an integral component of safety decision-making. While all protective capacities might be thought of as family strengths, not all family strengths are protective capacities, meaning that they have the potential to negate serious harm due to maltreatment. Holder and Morton (1999) also suggested categories of threats. These included: situations (e.g. unsafe home, criminal activity); behaviours (e.g. impulsive actions, assaults); emotions (e.g. immobilising depression); motives (e.g. intention to hurt the child); perceptions (e.g. viewing child as a devil); and capacities (e.g. physical disability). Morton and Salovitz (2003) proposed a dynamic model that proposes that the degree of safety is explained by the interaction of three categories of variables: threats of serious harm, family protective capacities, and child vulnerability.

Child vulnerability can be divided into two categories. The first category includes characteristics of the child that make the child more vulnerable to serious harm. The second are those that serve as an interactive stimulus for dangerous caregiver responses.

In reviewing a number of fatality cases, the authors have frequently noticed a distinct pattern of escalating 'danger-loaded' risk elements (e.g. increasingly negative perceptions of a child, elevating caregiver stress because of the child's behaviour, increased frequency and amount of alcohol or drug use, or increased externalising behaviour of a child) and/or diminishing protective capacities. Danger-loaded risk elements might be viewed as a select set of concurrently operating risk dynamics within the family system that, if they worsen, could lead to serious harm. The complicating factor in understanding child safety outside of the context of a current incident is that the perceived severity of the next incident may be influenced heavily by the perceived severity of the previous incident. If the previous incident was not severe, there may be a tendency to underestimate the severity of the next.

Likelihood

Risk assessment involves collecting and assessing information about both elements of risk taking: the outcomes and their possibility. Whose likelihood? Measuring outcomes involves value judgments. Assessing likelihood does not. We need to know how likely it is that the offender will reoffend, the patient will experience side effects or not return to the ward. The likelihood of the outcome is given, even if we do not know it to any exact degree. But we could not, and professionals cannot, give up at the first sight of a little local difficulty. The risk assessor's duty to identify the likelihood should be based upon the best knowledge available, applied to the particular risk proposed and the surrounding circumstances.

Risk management is concerned with how the risk decision is implemented. Risk judgments and the decisions taken should consider risk management as well as risk assessment. Risk assessment provides the setting and key information for risk management to focus upon. Kirk Heilbrun (1997) developed the distinction between risk assessment and risk management, with particular reference to forensic risk decision. He emphasised how risk management has received much less attention, both in empirical research and policy analysis, than risk assessment. And yet risk management provides more powerful tools for controlling risk taking. His approach may be affected by his therapeutic concerns and assumption that risk only relates to negative outcomes.

Risk management has a major contribution to make to the decision-making process and with more situational factors where the emphasis would be on altering the 'setting' (rather than the client), such as arranging and supporting employment.

Poor risk management can lead to harm, inquiries and litigation. Good risk management, because it comes after the assessment could prevent a poor risk assessment from causing harm. It is that important. But good risk assessment cannot prevent poor risk management from causing harm. A risk assessment might have demonstrated, consistent with contemporary professional standards, that it was appropriate to return a child from his or her foster parents to the natural parents. But the way in which that decision was implemented may have been inappropriate, or been the cause of the problems. There can be liability for poor risk management as well as for negligent risk assessment.

Professional risk assessment should be undertaken with an eye to the possibilities for risk management. The resources available for risk management could suggest what the risk period should be. That would then be used in the risk assessment. It is a potentially creative process. The availability of particular risk management resources in one country could, quite properly, lead to a different risk proposal being assessed from that in another country that does not have those resources.

People are another major resource for risk management. It is not just the number of people but their qualities. The number of people able to visit to check on how a risk decision is going will be important. But having those people will be of little advantage if they are not sufficiently knowledgeable, skilled, or both, to identify problems and opportunities, and to make appropriate interventions. Before making their decision, professional risk takers should consider what they know, its quality, plus what they do not know, and its significance (Moore 1996). A risk assessment may have been prepared on the information to hand, but is there more information which could, and perhaps should, be obtained? There will always be incomplete information, that is a central characteristic of risk. It is not suggested that there should be a constant search for more information and a continuing dread of decision-making. It has to be proper, because it is risk taking, to make decisions with incomplete information. The issues are the nature and value of the missing information, the time and other costs there would be in obtaining it. The risk decision-makers have to make preliminary risk decisions about (a) whether further information is likely to make a significant difference to their assessment or management plan and (b) whether – presuming is not an emergency or dilemma – it is appropriate to wait until they can obtain more and/or better information.

Knowledge is a form of power which, in turn, enables degrees of control. Risk management concerns the implementation of risk decisions. People and knowledge are ways of exercising control but there can be others. An important source can be the law.

Risk management is fundamentally about resources and, therefore, about politics. Even if a good risk assessment can be made on limited resources (there must be some, such as a professional knowledge base), a good risk management plan presupposes adequate resources for carrying it out. Improving risk assessment may, substantially, be achieved by improving skills and knowledge. The costs of doing that may be hidden in a general or other's budget, for example, in general education rather than for a particular service. But, quite simply, risk management can be improved with more money, with better resources – and that requires funds from the services concerned. So risk assessment can be portrayed – simplistically – as purely professional, but risk management is political. However, it is totally artificial, and contrary to good practice, to separate risk assessment and risk management in this way (Carson and Bain 2008).

The difficulties involved in making clinical decisions about the risk of future harm in specific cases has led to the development of formal risk assessment measures or instruments to overcome the shortfalls of unassisted clinical judgment. Cicchinelli (1995) notes that among the most salient deficiencies, which encouraged the development of risk assessment models in child welfare were:

- ▸ The lack of a rational basis for making decisions regarding the future of abused and neglected children and their families
- ▸ Subjective and inconsistent decision-making across cases
- ▸ Ineffective intervention options and inefficient resource allocation
- ▸ A lack of agency accountability
- ▸ Insufficient worker training and on-the-job support.

Macdonald and Macdonald (2001) argue that the assessment of risk is related to the probabilistic component of our knowledge base, therefore the assessment of risk necessarily involves the weighing up of both positive and negative outcomes for children and families. Caddick and Watson (2001) discuss the individual's right to choose to take risks and the need for an understanding of risk in order to also understand the consequences of those decisions for society and others. Macdonald and Macdonald (2001) highlight that clients are not passive within risk assessment, and that consequently 'interventions to reduce adverse risk may have the opposite or no effect'. The client may choose to take greater risks as their perception of the current risk reduces.

Strengths-based approaches

> To assess the power of the individual to create change,
> it is necessary to focus on their strengths as well as
> the problems. This focus can lead to interpretations of
> behaviour as coping abilities or survival strategies.
>
> (Rodwell and Blankebaker 1992, p.159)

Any deficit-based assessment targets the individual as the problem and this often leads to reinforcement for the client of their powerlessness as well as reinforcing the social structures that generate unequal power. It often acts as a self-fulfilling prophecy.

The strengths perspective focuses on the capacities and potentialities of service users. It concentrates on enabling individuals and communities to articulate, and work towards, their hopes for the future, rather than seeking to remedy the problems of the past or even the present. According to Saleebey (1996, p.4), the strengths perspective formula is simple: 'Mobilise clients' strengths (talent, knowledge, capacities) in the service achieving their goals and visions and the clients will have a better quality of life on their terms'. The strengths perspective requires practitioners to adopt an optimistic attitude towards the individuals and communities with whom they work.

The strengths perspective draws also on empirical research about psychological resilience. Saleebey (1996) pointed to research demonstrating that adverse life events are not strong predictors of future capacities. Reviewing research on childhood trauma and adversity, Saleebey contended that the majority of people do not reproduce the problems to which they were exposed as children (see Saleebey, 1992). The resilience research also suggests that people can actually benefit from difficult life events: this is particularly true for adults' acute experiences of adversity, such as surviving a life-threatening illness or natural disaster. Drawing on the work of Saleebey (1992) and

Weick *et al.* (1989), we can identify the following key assumptions of the strengths perspective:

▶ All people have strengths, capacities and resources

▶ People usually demonstrate resilience, rather than pathology, in the face of adverse life events; this is because, according to strengths perspective theorists, 'all human organisms have an inclination for healing' (Saleebey 1996)

▶ Service users have the capacity to determine what is best for them and they do not need human service workers to define their best interests

▶ Human service professionals, including social workers, tend to focus on perceptions of clients' problems and deficits while ignoring their strengths and resources; Saleebey (1996, p.297) warns that, 'Pursuing a practice based on ideas of resilience, rebound, possibility, and transformation is difficult because, oddly enough, it is not natural to the world of helping and service'

▶ Collaborative partnerships between workers and service users reflect and build service users' capacities; yet human service professionals, including social workers, are reluctant to collaborate with service users in a spirit of mutual learning and genuine partnership, preferring instead to protect their professional power.

The increasing popularity of the approach is premised on the principles of empowerment, hope, resilience and self-determination. However, whilst offering an optimistic therapeutic approach, where change is possible, it has to be balanced against a misplaced optimism that is dangerous and can end in tragedy where vulnerable children are involved. Strengths based approaches that demote or exclude risk often result in the 'rule of optimism' to explain how health and social workers reduced, minimised, or removed concerns for a child's welfare or safety, achieved through taking an overly positive interpretation of the family. Dingwall *et al.* suggested that the rule of optimism was only discounted when parents refused to co-operate with workers and rejected help, or when there was a 'failure of containment' where a number of workers became involved with the case and the pressure for statutory action became too great. The operation of such biases was supported by Munro's (1999) assessment of errors of reasoning in child protection work. Munro reported that professionals were slow to revise their judgments of families, even in the face of contradictory evidence. They also tended to rely too much on the family's outward appearance and circumstances to determine risk of harm to the child. Thus, outwardly respectable parents appeared able to resist statutory intervention, despite the risk to the child of significant harm, because they didn't seem like 'abusers'.

Thus, in adopting a strengths-based approach there is some potential to create a therapeutic environment where a desire to engage with clients overrides evidence that a child is at risk of harm. The danger is in focusing too much on ensuring that parents remain co-operative, looking for strengths too early (and failing to work on family risks), or in overemphasising strengths that may have little to do with parenting capacity at the expense of addressing the underlying causes or deficits that led to child abuse. Furlong (1989, p.215) states that there are good reasons for being positive, and while this is preferable most of the time, such an approach can become an obstacle: '[Our] preferred language can encourage habits that de-emphasise or even disqualify gritty and often unpleasant practicalities ... thus making it impossible to be explicit about the breach of major social norms.'

What is interesting is the idea of individual responsibility for actions being new – it is one that child protection workers have generally subscribed to for some time. Put simply, the premise is that in order for change to occur, responsibility must be taken for abusive behaviour (Jenkins 1990). In contrast, Scott and O'Neil (1996) state that the strengths-based approach is not necessarily about owning responsibility for past actions, but owning responsibility for solutions. This presents a dilemma for those wanting to adopt a primarily strengths-based approach. An invitation to accept responsibility involves looking at what has led to the abusive incident, and holds that one cannot move forward until this has occurred.

Working with strengths has considerable advantages, not least that it is consistent with the values underpinning the social work profession.

Other advantages include:

▸ It takes cognisance of the power relationship between social workers and clients. Clients enter into the relationship in a vulnerable position and with comparatively little power. A strengths perspective reinforces client competence and thus mitigates the significance of unequal power between the client and the worker.

▸ It provides a structure and content for an examination of realisable alternatives, for the mobilisation of competencies that can make things different, and for the building of self-confidence that stimulates hope.

▸ By combining personal and environmental resources it creates situations for goal achievement (adapted from Cowger 1994).

The strength approach is one model, which has proved useful in engaging resistant families. Maluccio (1979) found that social workers repeatedly underestimate client strengths and view clients as reactive organisms with continuing problems, underlying weaknesses, and limited potential. He also found that social workers had more negative perceptions of clients than clients had of themselves. If this is true then one must look to a cause. One possibility is that workers do not have a guidebook to help them understand and then deploy strengths-based thinking.

The strengths approach cannot be adopted on a blanket basis without reference to individual circumstances. The social worker doesn't change people, but aims to act as a catalyst for clients discovering and using their resources to accomplish their goals (Saleebey 1992). This makes it less likely that workers will 'rescue' clients and be more likely to reinforce their strengths, even in a crisis.

Any proactive approach to child protection focuses on family strengths and capability in a way that supports and strengthens family functioning. All families have strengths and capabilities. If we take the time to identify these qualities and build on them rather than focusing on correcting deficits or weaknesses, families are not only more likely to respond favourably to interventions, but the chances of making a significant impact on the family unit will be enhanced considerably.

A major consideration as part of strengthening families, is promoting their abilities to use existing strengths for meeting needs in a way that produces positive changes in family functioning. This can be achieved by using empathy or attempting to promote some mutual agreement between each other.

There are a number of documented benefits of adopting the strengths approach, which include:

- ▶ An emphasis on strengths as well as on risks increases the opportunity for developing a helping alliance – a crucial element in achieving positive treatment outcome and risk reduction.

- ▶ Positive reinforcement for positive conditions and behaviours is more effective than trying to convince or coerce individuals to alter negative conditions or behaviours.

- ▶ Cultivating strengths offers the opportunity for more permanent change.

- ▶ Emphasising strengths helps family members build successes in their lives, which in turn should help them more effectively manage crises and stress.

- ▶ Helping families through short-term positive steps empowers families to take control of their lives.

- ▶ Celebrating successes changes the tone of treatment, for both client and helper.

- ▶ Communicating a true belief that a family can change destructive patterns helps to promote more long-lasting change.

(DePanfalis and Wilson 1996)

Leung, Monit Cheung and Stevenson (1994) identified a set of guiding values for workers within the strength perspective: children should grow up in their own families, people can change, people can do their best when empowered and instilling hope is a central part of the child protection remit. There are several components of a strength approach: developing positive attitudes towards clients, focusing on family strengths and not problems, encouraging them to engage in effective behaviour, challenging clients to appreciate their own ethnic and cultural backgrounds and encouraging clients to locate their own resources (e.g. family group conferences).

The strengths model may be perceived by professionals as taking risks by focusing on strengths at the expense of overlooking the child and the dangers. We do need to note that we can uncover strengths when assessing for risks. A good assessment identifies the silent issues and difficulties facing the family, which all concerned agree need to be addressed, as well as identifying the major strengths and resources the family bring to bear on the issues.

Empowerment represents recognition of client strengths. Child protection, based on anti-oppressive premises, needs to believe that families have the ability to define their own problems, set their own goals and take their own action for change – a commitment to basing this change on a broader social analysis than is commonly the case, with most professional intervention, and a style of working in partnership with people which facilitates and empowers them to move in the direction they choose (Ward and Mullender 1991, p.12). Boushel and Lebacq (1992) identified certain elements required of a model of empowerment for child protection work:

▶ Supports the right of service users to choose the social roles they wish to fulfil (e.g. mother, daughter, carer, or partner)

▶ Supports the right of service users to undertake those roles in ways that do not jeopardise the welfare of others

▶ Facilitates an awareness of the ways in which the dynamics of structural and interpersonal oppression operate in the service user's situation

▶ Acknowledges, and where possible, builds upon a service user's previous attempts to protect themselves and/or others from child protection work

▶ Provides information on the range of resources and options available to service users and their possible consequences

▶ Supports and facilitates service users in their expression of equivocal feelings about interventions, issues and problems

▶ Generates an awareness in service users of the power exercised by welfare professionals on behalf of the state and their rights of redress

▸ Facilitates service users in challenging paternalistic or discriminatory welfare provision (pp.45–6).

The strengths perspective argues that client empowerment is central to social work practice and client strengths provide the fuel and energy for that empowerment. Client empowerment is characterised by two interdependent and interactive dynamics: personal empowerment and social empowerment. The personal empowerment dynamic is where clients give direction to the helping process, take charge and control of their personal lives, get their 'heads straight', learn new ways to think about their situations, and adopt new behaviours that give them more satisfying and rewarding outcomes. The social empowerment dynamic recognises that client definitions and characteristics cannot be separated from their context and that personal empowerment is related to opportunity.

Social work practice based on empowerment assumes that client power is achieved when clients make choices that give them more control over their presenting problem situations and, in turn, their own lives. In addition, it has to assume that people have choices available to them. This leads workers to attend to the dynamics of personal power, the social power endemic to the client's environment, and the relationship between the two. For workers, promoting empowerment means believing that people are capable of making their own choices and decisions. Their role is 'to nourish, encourage, assist, enable, support, stimulate, and unleash the strengths within people ... [by helping] clients articulate the nature of their situations, identify what they want, explore alternatives for achieving those wants, and achieve them' (Cowger 1994, p.264). The role of the social worker is not, however, to empower people. They do not possess power that they can distribute at will. They are resources for enabling client empowerment.

Forensic not therapeutic

A typical forensics investigation consists of two main phases, exploration and evidence. During the exploration phase, investigators attempt to identify the nature of the problem and what exactly happened or is expected to happen at the crime scene. The evidence phase takes place after the exploration has been concluded. It consists of accumulating all documentation which will be acceptable to the court. From a data viewpoint, this two-phase procedure can be broken down into six stages: preparation, incident response, data collection, data analysis, presentation of findings, and incident closure. Some of these stages may be so complex in certain circumstances that they are divided into sub-stages. The most time consuming tasks in digital forensics investigation are searching, extracting, and analysing. Therefore, there is a need for a forensics model that allows formalisation of the digital forensics process, innovative data mining techniques for the forensics process, and a dedicated infrastructure for digital forensics.

Profile of an effective detective

- ▶ Personal qualities: Intelligence, common sense, initiative, inquisitiveness, independence of thought, commitment, persistence, ability to talk to people, flexibility, ability to learn, reflexivity, lateral thinking, creative thinking, patience, empathy, tolerance, interpreting uncertain and conflicting information, ability to work away from family and home, interpreting feelings, ideas and facts, honesty and integrity.

- ▶ Legal knowledge: Knowledge of the law referring to police powers, procedure, criminal justice process, a good grounding in criminal law, awareness of changes to legislation, courtroom protocol, rules of disclosure, use of evidence, format of case file and awareness of defence arguments.

- ▶ Practical knowledge: Technology available to detectives and used by criminals, understanding the context in which crime is committed and awareness of investigative roles of different functions of the police organisation and specialist advisors. Recognition that crime changes with time and place and may require police responses that are tailored to specific context. Forensic awareness and practical expertise (e.g. crime scene preservation and packaging of evidence).

- ▶ Generic knowledge: Recognition that knowledge changes, awareness of developments in practice will allow the detective to remain up to date.

- ▶ Theoretical knowledge: Understanding of theoretical approaches to investigative reasoning and theories of crime.

- ▶ Management skills: The management and control of case information, implementing investigative action, formulating investigative strategies, verifing expert advice, prioritising lines of inquiry, formulating media strategies, awareness of resource availability and knowledge of roles of personnel available to the investigation, managing knowledge and learning through the use of research skills to enable the detective to remain up to date.

- ▶ Investigative skills: Good interviewing technique, presenting evidence, cultivating informants, extracting core information (from files, reports, victims and witnesses), file construction, appraising and evaluating information, ability to absorb and manage large volumes of information, statement taking, problem-solving, formulating lines of inquiry, creating slow time, assimilating information from a crime scene, continually reviewing lines of inquiry, questioning and challenging legal parties.

- ▶ Interpersonal skills: Ability to communicate and establish a rapport with a range of people, remaining open minded, having awareness of consequences of actions and avoiding speculation.

The five most important characteristics of a good detective are:

- ▶ Good empathic communication (skill style): Detective should be a 'people person' or else he/she will not be able to get the most valuable information out of a person (witness, victim, suspect, etc.), however, at the same time he or she must know and follow the law in detail so that the acquired information is applicable in court.

- ▶ Open-minded curiosity (skill style, and perhaps a bit of risk style): Detective should have a mind that is curious about things, which is open to new ways of doing things to not only discover information by making connections through being curious, but also to be open enough to avoid tunnel vision and conforming to stereotypical ideas.

▶ Creative thinking (risk style): Detective should be able to think creatively about the information/evidence by putting it together in different ways or looking at it from different perspectives. This outlook forms the basis for further creative thought in how to go about getting other information/evidence needed to solve a case. Creative thinking also correlates highly with curiosity and being open-minded (second characteristic).

▶ Logical, methodical reasoning (method style): Detective should be able to logically derive what piece of evidence is available and useful in a particular case/situation and how legally to get hold of it. Hence, a detective must think things through in a methodical manner without jumping to unwarranted conclusions or developing tunnel vision about a situation or person that cannot be supported with legal and logical inferences.

▶ Dogged determination, persistence (challenge style): Detective should be able to hang in for the long haul on a difficult and protracted investigation as persistence can often crack a case. However, the reason it is the last characteristic is that just being determined will not of itself necessarily find the information or evidence needed in an investigation, hence, the reason for listing the other characteristics in priority order. If a detective has enough of the other characteristics, then determination is more likely to pass off in the long run.

Kemshall (2008) argued that to carry out a vulnerability assessment, workers should focus on:

▶ The accurate identification of the risks to which the person is exposed and why

▶ The likely impact or consequences of the risks to the person

▶ Whether the risks are externally posed, or are endemic to the person and their circumstances

▶ Whether the risks are acceptable – those externally posed by others (such as adult offenders to children) are usually less acceptable

▶ Where the risks arise from the person and their situation, a key question is whether the risk should be run. What are the costs and benefits of the risk? What are the costs and benefits of putting in place protective measures?

▶ Balancing the desirability of reducing the risk against the likely reduction of choice, independence and autonomy of the individual; for example the reduction of risk for older persons through the use of residential care

▶ Risk management strategies are usually characterised by a desire to achieve this balance and to resolve where possible tensions between autonomy, quality of life, rights and risks.

Checklist of risk assessment information required

The following checklist provides the information to carry out the risk assessment in a way which provides reliable decision-making:

▶ What is the risk? Write down the risk decision to be taken. If there are several risks you may need to consider each separately. If you are not clear what the risk decision is, then write down what you think it is – you can alter it later in the light of further analysis. Make sure the risk decision is specific so it is clear what is in focus. Remember the key risk questions to apply to the child are: Does this child need protection and if so what? What are the specific risks involved? What needs to be done and how soon to ensure the child has the protection needed from this risk of harm?

▶ Risk time period. What is the time period covered by the risk decision if it is not so great that immediate removal from the risk is the aim? The risk decision is only for the time period until it will be reviewed, or until the conditions are triggered which put into operation the contingency plan. So do not include factors which are outside this time period – they will be taken into account at the review, if necessary.

▸ Risk or dilemma? A dilemma is a risk where (a) there are no harm-free options and (b) a rapid decision is needed to prevent harm. A dilemma-based decision may not be as thought through as a full risk analysis decision. However, think whether the dilemma could reasonably have been foreseen.

▸ Outcomes. List all the positive consequences (outcomes) – you may want to group them under beneficial (positive) or harmful (negative) headings – whether major or minor. This gives rise to questions such as: Why is this risk decision being proposed? What is the intended result? What justifies the proposed action? What might happen? Why are people anxious? If it goes wrong, what might others say? Should I have realised? Who would benefit and who could be harmed? Is inaction an option? What would be the result of doing nothing differently from now? Will the outcomes lead to a new situation? If so, what are the knock-on effects and for whom? Will new opportunities or dangers arise? Very significant possible outcomes (positive or negative) are worth highlighting for explicit assessment.

▸ Resources. Some possible courses of action may not be possible due to a lack of resources. Work first on including all that seems relevant. If necessary, list separately what appears realistic within the required resources. It may be that the decision is made to make the resources needed available. If not, then at least it is clear what is available and what is not. Lack of resources is not an automatic justification for not pursuing a course of action. If the result of using lack of resources as an excuse not to pursue a course of action is to add to the harm (risk), then the decision could be open to challenge. Furthermore, a review of resource use could show they were not being used efficiently enough.

▸ Relevance check. Are any of the outcomes listed ones which could not occur within the time period? If so, delete them. Are any of the outcomes as likely to occur whether the risk decision is made or not? If so, delete them, as they could not be as a result of the risk decision.

A model for risk assessment (Brearley 1982)

For each stage of the analysis, try to answer the question WHY?

- ► List the dangers in this case. A 'danger' is something you want to avoid, so what possible events would you fear in these circumstances? Rank these dangers in order of their significance. Consider not only the 'effect' of the danger if it occurs but the 'chance' of it happening.

- ► List the hazards in the case. A 'hazard', in this context, is something which might result in a danger being realised – something that helps to bring about the circumstances you want to avoid.

- ► Divide the list of hazards into two: predisposing hazards and situational hazards. A 'predisposing hazard' makes the danger more likely. It is something that creates vulnerability, though it may need to be activated by something else, perhaps a situational hazard. A 'situational hazard' is something that happens, and which has an immediate effect directly related to the danger.

- ► List what you consider to be the strengths in this case. Strengths are those factors whose effects counteract the danger, and make it less likely to become a reality.

- ► Identify the additional information which you believe to be necessary. Evaluating the information you already have may indicate that there are some important gaps in your knowledge, gaps which should be filled before a final assessment.

- ► Indicate the decisions you feel should be taken.

Chronology construction

Chronologies provide a key link in the chain of understanding needs/ risks, including the need for protection from harm. Setting out key events in sequential date order, gives a summary timeline of child and family circumstances, patterns of behaviour, and trends in lifestyle that may greatly assist any assessment and analysis. They are a logical, methodical and systematic means of organising, merging and helping make sense of information. They also help to highlight gaps and omitted details that require further exploration, investigation and assessment.

They can, and should, also be used to promote engagement with the service user/s. The content of chronologies is, however, determined by individual/collective professional judgments as to what is in fact significant in a child's and family's lives. They should not replicate or attempt to substitute for case recording, but should rather provide a clear outline of the most important elements of individual or family circumstances. For this reason, they must be:

▸ Succinct, if too detailed and capture every issue or contact, they lose their value

▸ Simple, ensuring that information can be effectively and efficiently combined and sorted

▸ Standardised in a format to capture core details.

A good chronology is a critical tool in helping make sense of the complexity of a child and family's life and circumstances. It also establishes a sound foundation for future understandings and analysis where professional staff change, or new staff, or services come on board. Chronologies are, however, not an end in and of themselves, rather they constitute one significant element of the suite of tools provided in facilitating analysis of needs/risks in assessments and interventions.

As dynamic tools, chronologies require consistent attention to ensure they are kept accurate, informative and up-to-date.

Interagency chronology

It is widely recognised that children and young people are most effectively safeguarded if professionals work together and share information. Single factors in themselves are often perceived to be relatively harmless; however, if they multiply and compound one another the consequences can be serious and, on occasions, devastating. A multi-agency child protection chronology (MACPC):

▸ Provides a mechanism through which information can be systematically shared and merged

▸ Enables agencies to identify the history of a family

▸ Provides invaluable information about a child's life experience

- ▶ Can reveal risks, concerns, patterns and themes, and strengths and weaknesses within a family
- ▶ Identify previous periods of professional involvement/support and the effectiveness/failure of previous intervention
- ▶ Informs the overall assessment regarding the caregivers' ability and motivation to change.

Chronologies are not only a means of organising and merging information, they enable practitioners to gain a more accurate picture of the whole case and highlight gaps and missing details that require further assessment and identification.

The chronology provides a skeleton of key incidents and events that inform the assessment of children and young people who are considered to be at risk of significant harm and are the subject of child protection plans.

The purpose of the MACPC is to inform assessment. It is therefore essential that the chronology is owned by the core group and used as a tool in assessing progress and the level of concern regarding significant harm. The chronology is only one means of collating information and will need supplementing by reports that draw out messages from the chronology. Getting the facts agreed and seeing the overall pattern is crucial and can often be informative and revealing.

The formatting of shared information will be done in a simple, agreed format:

- ▶ Date – the date the episode event is said to have taken place (not the date of recording)
- ▶ Name – of the individual involved in the episode (e.g. the child or caregiver)
- ▶ Source – the agency or individual sharing the information
- ▶ Episode/event – the significant piece of information (e.g. police log of reported incidence of domestic violence; report from school that child arrives from home hungry, unkempt and tired; missed medical appointments; allegation of non-accidental injury (NAI); anonymous referral regarding child left unsupervised; Section 47 inquiry, etc.)

▶ Comment – Basic info to add to the above. That is, the comment should inform the reader of any action taken in response to the event or episode.

Significant information/events

A significant event is an incident that impacts on the child's safety and welfare, circumstances or home environment. This will inevitably involve a professional decision and/or judgment based upon the child and family's individual circumstances. A chronology provides a sequential story of significant events in a family's history whilst interweaving information about emotional and/or relationship difficulties. It contributes to an emerging picture based on fact and interactions of a case – current information is understood in the context of previous information–informing professional assessment. The key purpose of the chronology of significant events is early indication of an emerging pattern of concern. This may be evident by gradual and persistent withdrawal from protective factors such as non-attendance at health appointments and non-attendance at nursery/school alongside frequent attendance at A&E or GP on-call services. Events such as domestic abuse referrals should also be recorded.

Each professional or agency are responsible for recording any such event as and when they become aware of them. Chronological history of events should be completed for every child on a caseload. It should be updated contemporaneously for every child on the chronology page specifically for that child within the family. It should include any event that may potentially impact negatively on the welfare of the child though not necessarily involving them (e.g. domestic abuse incidents). It is only necessary to record a brief description of the event on this page as detail will be recorded in the assessment, care plan or progress notes for the child or parent where appropriate. All agency referrals, such as any specialist service should be recorded. There are a number of core incidents, which should be recorded. Dependent upon the nature of the harm, these may differ from case to case. Examples of core incidents:

▶ Contacts or referrals about the child and/or family

▶ Assessments (e.g. family support)

- Strategy discussions/meetings
- Section 47 investigations
- House moves
- School exclusions
- School attendance/major incidents (e.g. bullying racism)
- Attendance/admittance to hospital
- Criminal proceedings
- Change in school
- Change in GP (e.g. this could be particularly significant in cases of fabricated and induced illness)
- Referrals to other agencies/teams
- Enquires to the Chid Protection Register
- Child absconded/missing
- Child becomes looked after/child is discharged from local authority care
- Death in the family
- Parent/carer has new partner
- Another person moves into the family home
- Birth of a new baby
- Person moves out of the family home
- Attempted suicide or overdose
- Police logs detailing pertinent info re: family members/family home (e.g. reported incident of domestic violence, drunken behaviour of carers, etc.)

There are also a number of other incidents, which may be significant to the child and family, depending on their circumstances. Examples include:

- A significant observation during home visits (e.g. the frequent presence of unknown adults, evidence of damage to the property)

▶ If chronologies are to accurately reflect family circumstances, positive factors should also be recorded; examples include:

» Evidence of the family's engagement with professionals

» Parents self-referral for help/guidance support with relevant agencies

» The child's presentation in school significantly improves.

The chronology should not replace existing case notes or records which will include much more detailed and sensitive information which is owned by the child and or family and a clear distinction must be made between the two. This brief and summarised account of events provides accumulative evidence of emerging needs and risks and flags up when a multi-agency response might be necessary or when a reduction in intervention might be in the best interests of the child. The chronology should be factually based and it should be clear what the source of the information is.

Resurrecting social histories

The lack of a thorough social history on which to base a more coherent and developmentally informed analysis (rather than description) has been identified as a particular weakness of many cases in which a child died or suffered serious injury or neglect (Brandon *et al.* 2008). The 1993 and 1999 studies of serious case reviews by Reder, Duncan and colleagues argued for better assessments of the relationship between accumulating risks. They also valued clearer links being established between research and practice, and more developmentally informed analyses.

Assessments should be based on a set of theoretical constructs that guide the type of information needed and the sense that can be made of it. The theoretical framework should be the central reference point for selecting the observations to be made, formulating appropriate questions and giving meaning to the responses. Otherwise, the assessment is directionless and generates a mass of discrete pieces of information that cannot be organised or understood...in our view, the most useful theoretical principles are those within an interactional framework that portray individuals as existing in relation to other people and functioning within a social and relational context. Their history helps to describe who they are and further evidence can be found in the pattern of their current relationships with significant others. In practice, this framework guides professionals to integrate historical and contemporary information about the family, its functioning, problems and relationships. (Reder and Duncan 1999, pp.98–101)

A good social history is a synthetic form of history not limited to the statement of so called historical fact but willing to analyse historical data in a more systematic manner. It attempts to view historical evidence from the point of view of developing social trends. It is an attempt to organise information in a coherent and structured way that enhances analysis potential and should tell the reader a story.

Protective Factors

It is essential, in predicting risk, to consider protective factors. Protective factors are defined as those factors or processes that, in combination with the risk element, seem to modify, ameliorate, or alter the likelihood of future harm for the child. The literature on protective factors groups them into three general categories: individual characteristics, family characteristics, and supportive significant others. Individual characteristics include attributes such as self-sufficiency, high self-esteem, and altruism. Family characteristics include supportive relationships with adult family members, harmonious family relationships, expressions of warmth between family members and mobilisation of supports in times of stress. Community support refers to supportive relationships with people and/or organisations external to the family. These external supports provide positive and supportive feedback to the child and reinforce and reward the child's positive coping abilities.

The following information provides a more detailed description of each of these areas:

INDIVIDUAL CHARACTERISTICS

This category of protective factors refers to factors that are innate (birth order, age, gender) as well as those that are learned (self-care and interpersonal attributes). Individual attributes include:

- Birth order: first born
- Health status: healthy during infancy and childhood
- Activity level: multiple interests and hobbies, participation and competence
- Disposition: good-natured, precocious, mature, inquisitive, willing to take risks, optimistic, hopeful, altruistic, personable, independent
- Developmental milestones: meets or exceeds age-appropriate expectations
- Self-concept: high self-esteem, internal locus of control, ability to give and receive love and affection
- Perceptive: quickly assesses dangerous situations and avoids harm
- Interpersonal skills: able to create, develop, nurture and maintain supportive relationships with others, assertive, good social skills, ability to relate to both children and adults, articulate
- Cognitive skills: able to focus on positive attributes and ignore negative
- Intellectual abilities: high academic achievement.

FAMILY CHARACTERISTICS

Family characteristics that offer protective qualities include attributes that apply to the entire family unit as well as personal relationships with parental figures. Family characteristics include:

- Structure: rules and household responsibilities for all members
- Family relational factors: coherence and attachment, open exchange and expression of feelings and emotions
- Parental factors: supervision and monitoring of children, a strong bond to at least one parent figure, a warm and supportive

relationship, abundant attention during the first year of life, parental agreement on family values and morals

- ▶ Family size: four or fewer children spaced at least two years apart
- ▶ Socioeconomic status: financial security
- ▶ Extended family: nurturing relationships with substitute caregivers such as aunts, uncles and grandparents.

COMMUNITY CHARACTERISTICS

Community characteristics include individuals and institutions, external to the family, that provide educational, emotional, and general supportive ties with the family unit as a whole or with individual family members. These protective factors include:

- ▶ Positive peer relationships
- ▶ Extended family in close proximity
- ▶ Schools: academic and extra-curricular participation and achievements, closer relationship with a teacher(s)
- ▶ Reliance on informal network of family, friends and community leaders for advice.

This brief overview of the individual, family, and community protective factors that serve as a buffer to some children in stressful and/or abusive situations is presented generically.

However, given the differences in family structure, child rearing practices and relationship to community, the degree to which the above factors apply to cross-cultural situations is unclear. Certainly some of the characteristics are universal across ethnic and class background. However, other factors may have a greater or lesser impact on families depending on their ethno-cultural orientation. In fact, some characteristics that apply specifically to some families may not be represented in the above discussion. The following list of protective factors may have special relevance to cross-cultural situations:

- ▶ Active extended family: relatives that are active in the child's life, provide material resources, child care, supervision, parenting, emotional support to the child

- Religious affiliation: belongs to and actively participates in a group religious experience, faith and prayer.

- Strong racial identity: exhibits racial pride, strongly identifies with ethnic group through clubs, organisations, political and social change movements

- Close attachment to the ethnic community: resides in the ethnic community, easy access to ethnic resources including social services, merchants, media (newspaper), demonstrates a commitment to the ethnic community

- Dispositional attributes: activity level, sociability, intelligence, competence in communication (oral and written), locus of control

- Personal attributes: high self-esteem, academic achievement, assertiveness

- Supportive family milieu: cohesiveness, extensive kinship network, non-conflictual relations

- External support system: involvement or non-involvement of fathers, male role models, supportive social environment.

Assessing risk therefore requires a careful balance between the facts which aggravate risk and those which mitigate against risk in a given situation. It is incorrect to suggest that risk assessment is a process which deals with negative issues only, in fact, the worker's judgment with respect to each rating is informed by information related to positive and negative aspects of the individual's and family's functioning. It is extremely important to clarify the family's perception of the issues identified by the risk factors. Issues the child protection worker may assume are positive mitigators of risk may in fact be the opposite. For example, the daily visit of a grandparent can be a support or it can be experienced as a stressor. What is crucial to the accurate assessment of risk is how the factor operates in that family's situation. At any time, when a risk assessment is completed, the child protection worker may not have complete knowledge of the child and family's functioning, but, is at all times required to assess risk on the basis of the facts that are available (assumes thorough and ongoing information gathering).

Reassessment of risk

Risks are rarely fixed, they are open to change and often require a highly flexible approach to their management. One of the key flaws of recent risk assessment tools has been their tendency to engender a static response to risk, and despite good practice advice to review assessments regularly, one-off assessments and fixed responses have become the norm (Kemshall 2003). Changes in individual functioning, family circumstances, or family dynamics can result in an increase or decrease of risk to a child. The worker needs to be alert to changes impacting the child and family, and especially to changes having the potential to increase the risk of harm to a child. Some examples of important changes include:

▶ Caregiver influence

  » Changes regarding alcohol/drug use

  » Changes in physical capacity to care for a child

  » Changes in emotional capacity to care for a child

▶ Child influence

  » Changes in the child's development/behaviour which may trigger an abusive caregiver response

  » Changes in the child's mental health

  » Changes in the child's physical health

▶ Family influence

  » Changes related to living arrangements/environment

  » Loss of relationships or support systems

  » Changes in employment

  » Changes related to income security/stability

  » Changes in the marital relationship

  » Changes related to who is living with the family

▶ Intervention influence

  » Sudden or major changes in the client's relationship with the worker or other service providers

» Sudden or significant changes in motivation and co-operation regarding services

» Premature withdrawal from services

» Unavailable for access by the social worker.

How to judge whether a risk assessment tool is fit for purpose

A key challenge in child protection services is the identification of effective tools and models that assist caseworkers, managers and organisations to ensure that such decisions are based on the current state of knowledge and research, not only surrounding child protection practice, but of human decision-making processes. A particular concern is the identification of common human errors in decision-making and ways that these may be avoided – especially as such errors in a child protection context can prove fatal.

It is helpful to their acceptability if risk assessment tools have the following features: user friendly, resource lean and easy to train staff to use appropriately. The process of use is transparent and accountable (particularly important in those cases where assessment decisions are subsequently challenged). Staff also need to be convinced about the reliability, integrity, and usefulness of the tool – in essence they need to be convinced about how it was developed, what it can do, and how accurate it is. These issues are particularly important if the tool is imposed from the 'centre' with little practitioner consultation or input. Research has indicated that the following criteria are essential in judging the fitness for purpose of a risk assessment tool: validated for use against a relevant population, the risk factors used in the tool have a proven track record of reliability and predictability, the tool must be able to differentiate between low, medium and high risk, the tools must have inter-rater reliability (e.g. consistency across users) and they must assist workers to make relevant risk management plans (Kemshall 2008).

Essential ingredients of a risk assessment tool

▶ Guidance – questions to ask

▶ Child and family friendly – jargon free

- ▸ Tailored for the specific risk and agency
- ▸ Balance of risk
- ▸ Evidence-based
- ▸ Offers a clear outcome
- ▸ Worker friendly
- ▸ Clear and easy to understand
- ▸ Incorporates a multi-agency perspective and information
- ▸ Relevant and proportionate to specific risk
- ▸ To identify motivation and capacity to make changes and measure sustained change
- ▸ Allows worker to plan, gather information, test information and analyse
- ▸ Child-focused assessment tool
- ▸ Allows cultural difference and norms to be accurately considered
- ▸ Encourages an enquiring mind
- ▸ Identifies triggers to risk
- ▸ Embraces presenting incident, background and triggering factors and anything that might impede or block changes.

Evidence-based assessment

As indicated in the earlier chapter addressing the challenges of professional judgment and evidence-based assessment, workers draw a great deal upon practice wisdom – gut feelings – intuition, and this section is an attempt to help validate it is a defensible arm of structured decision-making.

Analytic thinking is 'a conscious and controlled process using formal reasoning and explicit data and rules to deliberate and compute a conclusion' (Munro 2007). Analysis should be seen as acting like a good secretary keeping a check on the products of intuition, checking them for known biases, developing explanatory theories and testing them rigorously. Intuitive thinking is an unconscious process that allows the integration of a large amount of information to produce a judgment in an effortless way. Gut feelings 'take advantage of the evolved capacity of the brain and are based on rules of thumb that enable us to act fast and with astonishing accuracy' (Gigerenzer 2002).

Intuition is knowledge that stems from a gut feeling or some subconscious process. It is not to be confused with professional judgment, which is a conscious process where facts and experience are both considered to form a basis for making reasoned decisions. Workers drawing upon intuitive (clinical) prediction call upon issues arising from their own life experience as a child, their own life experience as an adult, relevant similar cases in their working life, an understanding of research as well as their understanding of theories (e.g. stigma, attachment, bonding, loss and bereavement) and their relevance.

It is the combination of intuitive and analytic modes that produces the kind of evidence-based practice by which social work knowledge establishes its relevance, expertise and authority (Morrison 2009b).

Dhami and Thomson (2012) noted that contemporary research on judgment and decision-making has focused on the strengths of analytic cognition and the limitations of intuition. However, there is an emerging trend towards acknowledging the benefits of intuitive thought. Although it is now recognised that intuition is both an important and necessary cognitive tool for managing an organisation, they also recognise that it is not sufficient. Effective workers have to employ a combination of intuition and analysis, as appropriate to particular situations. Unfortunately, research has tended to focus on one or the other of these modes of cognition and there is a dearth of research directed at their shared use or the middle ground between intuition and analysis (i.e. 'quasirationality' (Hammond 1996; 2000)). Quasirationality is defined as the combination of intuitive and analytic thought and is increasingly considered to be widespread and beneficial. There are many situations where either analysis or intuition cannot be easily employed (Hammond 1996), and indeed there are many obstacles and challenges to the use of pure analysis and pure intuition. Therefore, on observing the characteristics of management tasks, it is clear that intuition and analysis alone cannot explain how managers perform these tasks.

One of the most important recent developments in the field of judgment and decision-making is the recognition that analysis and intuition can be integrated into one coherent theoretical framework.

Cognitive continuum theory states that there are modes of cognition which can be arranged along a continuum ranging from pure intuition at one pole to pure analysis at the other. The modes of cognition that lie in between these poles include a variable combination of both intuition and analysis, and are referred to as quasirationality. Most judgments involve some mix of both intuition and analysis. In addition, cognitive tasks can also be arranged along a continuum in terms of their ability to induce intuition, quasirationality, or analysis. When performing a task, cognitive activity moves back and forth along the continuum. Success on a task inhibits movement (or change in cognitive mode) while failure stimulates it. Movement along the cognitive continuum is oscillatory or alternating, thus allowing compromise between intuition and analysis (i.e. quasirationality). See Table 4.2 for the defining properties of intuition and analysis.

TABLE 4.2 SOME DEFINING PROPERTIES OF INTUITION AND ANALYSIS (ADAPTED FROM DOHERTY AND KURZ 1996)

Property	Intuition	Analysis
Area of brain activity	Mostly right hemisphere	Mostly left hemisphere
Consistency/reliability of judgments or cognitive control	Low	High
Awareness of cognitive activity	Low	High
Speed of cognitive activity	High	Low
Memory	Little encoding	Complex encoding
Metaphors used	Pictorial, qualitative	Verbal, quantitative
Information use	Flexible	Consistent
Confidence in judgments	Low	High
Errors in judgment	Many but small and normally distributed	Few but large and non-normally distributed

See also Table 4.3 for the benefits and disadvantages of the intuitive mode.

TABLE 4.3 BENEFITS AND DISADVANTAGES OF THE INTUITIVE MODE

Benefits of intuitive mode	Disadvantages of intuitive mode
Can process speedily especially in conditions of urgency	Over-confidence in gut feeling leads to poor judgments
Better for immediate/short-term decisions	Relies on personal experience
Validates emotions and hunches as important information	Limited by information capacity of short-term memory
Values contribution regardless of status or experience	Short-term focus results in lack of contingency plans
Can be very accurate for modest effort	Generates low-level theory with limited application
Value life experience and practice wisdom	We seek to confirm own beliefs despite the evidence
Ensures systematic data collection and analysis	Requires training
Maximises options and alternatives	Can be perceived as cold and mechanical
Based on formal probability theory	Can be hard to engage busy practitioners and managers
Can generate higher level theory with wider application	Can be used to bolster expert attitudes
Support public explanation of decision	Can be manipulated to justify decisions as scientific or objective

Analysis

The principal purpose of a risk assessment is to come up with sufficient information to develop a plan, which in many cases will involve the collecting of further information.

To analyse something is to break it down into its components and, by identifying the constituent parts and exploring the relationship between them, find out what it is made of or how it is constructed. Analysis is presented as a largely objective process undertaken in order to gain a better understanding or to draw conclusions about the thing or issue under review. The strength of analytical thinking is that, used properly, it is rigorous, systematic and methodical. In the social work literature, it is generally discussed in the context of analysing information or situations and involves working carefully and logically through a mass of often complex, confusing or incomplete information, such as might be gathered in the course of an assessment.

Analysis is often contrasted with intuition, and the two are presented as opposite poles or ways of thinking. Typically, analytical thinking is portrayed as precise, objective and rational while intuition is woolly, imprecise and prone to bias and individual idiosyncrasy. These pictures of the different modes of thinking may well contain some truth but are oversimplified. So while the strengths of analytical thinking should be acknowledged, it is also worth noting that it has some limitations, and that intuitive thinking may also have something to offer on its own terms. There are arguments to support the considered use of intuition in social work – for example that it is a basic mode of thinking and one that we all draw on so it does not have to be taught (which is not to say that its use cannot be developed and improved). It is quick, can be used in establishing rapport and to demonstrate empathy and it draws on the practitioner's life experience and (sometimes tacit) practice knowledge as well as formal research knowledge. So rather than seeing analysis and intuition as either/or modes of thought, it may be more constructive to consider how skilled social workers make use of both, and to understand the trade-offs or strengths and limitations of each way of thinking. The importance of formal analysis should not be overlooked but it is not the only way of thinking in social work. Other elements have been identified – for example, analytical thinking is often discussed alongside another concept – critical thinking.

Some of the enduring issues with assessments have included the need for them to be more focused, transparent and collaborative, with a better focus on the child's development and environment. Too much analysis is descriptive/static, not interactive, focusing on events not patterns, with an over focus on behaviour, not explanation. Early impressions dominate, often presenting as higher on intuition and lower on analysis, with a resistance to revising the original analysis. There has also been an enduring concern about parents' explanations overriding children's views.

A good analysis is linked to the purpose of the assessment, is based on a clear theoretical framework and the best possible information from different sources. It is clear about missing information, context and value base. It identifies themes and underlying patterns about needs, risks and strengths. It generates/tests different ways of understanding the situation and includes the service user's explanation. It gives meaning to the themes, using knowledge based on experience and research which leads to a formulation of the problem and possible solutions. It uses supervision to assist reflection, hypothesising and objectivity, is collaborative with service users and other agencies, is able to explain its conclusions and provides a foundation for planning.

The *Framework for Assessment of Children in Need and their Families* (DH 2000) states that the conclusion of an assessment should result in:

▶ An analysis of the needs of the child and the parenting capacity to respond appropriately to those needs within their family context

▶ Identification of whether and, if so, where intervention will be required to secure the wellbeing of the child or young person

▶ A realistic plan of action (including services to be provided), detailing who has responsibility for action, a timetable and a process for review.

Research and experience has shown that there is usually lots of information available about the child and family. However, reviews of practice often find that there was insufficient shared analysis to form a good plan.

Analysis is:

▶ A step-by-step, conscious, logically defensible process

▶ Deliberation over the different elements in a situation in a systematic, precise and organised way

▶ In contrasts with intuition in that the latter is imprecise and rarely defensible.

The strength of analysis is that it encourages openness about reasoning and so potentially holds your work open to scrutiny. The disadvantage in this approach is that it can induce misplaced faith in the ability to make predictions, particularly in the increasing social work field of risk assessment.

Risk analysis enables a risk assessment to be made, on which decisions about action for risk management can be made and implemented. Risk analysis should thus provide information on:

▶ The nature of the risks and dangers these give

▶ The frequency of such risks arising

▶ The degree of seriousness of the dangers

▶ The personal characteristics of those involved and how far these add to or minimise the risks

▶ The relevant wider knowledge base on which to draw

▶ The timescales for a risk decision

▶ How a plan will be monitored in practice, and what feedback will indicate a change to the fall-back plan to further reduce the risk if it escalates.

What are the current problems facing us in relation to analysis?

▶ Piling up: This is where negative statements are just aggregated on the basis that more negative attributes must mean there are problems. But knowing that there are problems doesn't tell us very much: we need to know the relative weight, connection and importance of the problems in respect of the child's needs and the parent's capacity.

▶ Winding up: This is not only where negative features are aggregated. There is a suggestion that each is acting as a multiplier and hence the result is almost as if the effects are growing exponentially. Maybe they are but evidence would need to be adduced to demonstrate how this was thought to be operating.

▶ Setting up: Inevitably, 'piling-up' and 'winding-up' can lead quickly to a family being 'set-up' to fail. Then, a well-known phenomenon soon develops, whereby only new information, which confirms the original assumptions and hypotheses, is taken account of, that which disconfirms them tends to be ignored. Hence a process of misinformation grows iteratively.

Some of the widely reported concerns include:

- No guidance on analysis

- Immensely subjective and personal analysis

- Lack of freedom to express what you want

- Lack of prognosis and treatability criteria.

Factors that workers should take into account when approaching any assessment include reference to:

TABLE 4.4 FRAMEWORKS FOR ANALYSIS

Presenting situation	The circumstances of the current referral – is it an incident or a culmination of a process accumulating numerous smaller concerns?
Predisposing factors	These are factors in the person's background – such as their experiences and personality – which make an undesirable outcome more likely. It is something that creates vulnerability
Precipitating factors	These are factors which are specific to the family at this time and which has an immediate effect directly related to the concern. Generally, these are factors that the worker can seek to influence and may be considered the area of focus for change
Perpetuating factors	Those factors which may contribute to prolonging the existence of the risk factors

The framework also needs to be holistic and thus will address four key domains shown in Figure 4.2.

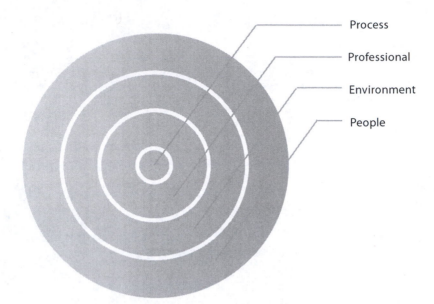

Figure 4.2 Four key domains of a holistic framework for analysis

These areas are defined below to guide workers.

TABLE 4.5 DOMAIN DESCRIPTION

People	What do we know about the players in the abuse situation – currently and historically?
Environment	What do we know about the environment – is it contributing to the harmful situation or ameliorating it?
Professional	Are there any contributing professional factors including risk to staff, resource limitations, etc.
Process	Will the intervention aggravate any identified risks? Were there any errors in the previous case management?

A blank template encapsulating these elements for worker completion may look like:

TABLE 4.6

	People	Environment	Professional	Process
Presenting situation				
Predisposing factors				
Precipitating factors				
Perpetuating factors				

Risk management

No decision in life, let alone social work or management can be made on the absolute certainty that that decision will be right. Decision-makers, whether expressly, or by implication, decide on a greater probability or likelihood that the decision will be right. Probability, rather than certainty, is the principle that insurance companies use to calculate the risk that the insured-for event will occur. There is a greater probability, based on data collected over time, that a young male driver will crash his car than a mature female driver. On this basis, the higher probability of an accident will lead to higher insurance premiums for young male drivers, regardless of the driving ability of a particular young man. Society, as reflected by politicians and the press, expect that social work decisions on child protection or the detention or otherwise of the mentally ill, will always be correct. In essence, there is an expectation that social work decision-makers will be infallible, acting on the basis of perfect knowledge of the past, present and future.

Experienced social work decision-makers, with in-depth knowledge of the case in hand, have a greater probability of making informed decisions which are more often right than wrong. However, there may be incorrect and wrong elements that cause hurt and, in some cases, harm to the individuals, families and communities involved. Social work decision-making, and the latitude given to decision-makers by law and policy, depends to a large extent on the willingness of society to accept risk and the reality of a probability that any decision will be wrong.

In a climate that is risk averse, there can be a tendency to take action, in theory or intention, to avoid risk. A decision may be made to take a child into care, not risking the possibility that his/her mother and partner will neglect him/her despite a range of support offered or provided. That intervention is not necessarily benign, as the care system in which the child is placed contains a risk of abuse and poor outcomes. Social work decision-makers work in a field of constantly altering realities. The basis upon which decisions will be made – the individual, the family, the community, its socioeconomic context – alters, producing a kaleidoscope of risk scenarios (Rose 2008).

Risk assessment and risk management are now key tasks for practitioners in social care, social work and criminal justice. Broadly speaking the implications for workers have been:

- The rationing of services on the basis of risk

- Emphasis on regulating risky behaviours rather than on ameliorating need

- An increasingly compulsory element to service use

- Risks outweigh rights

(Kemshall 2008)

Key messages from the chapter

Risk assessment requires a detailed approach that embraces strengths and risks.

A number of different options exist which guide workers to a more holistic approach.

This balanced approach makes it more likely that workers will engage with parents and that agencies' anxieties about an interventionist approach from social care will be reduced.

Risk assessment has to be resurrected within the current operating frameworks as, despite the drive from Munro to reclaim the use of the word, it has not been accompanied by any frameworks that are specific and manage subjectivity sufficiently.

Good risk assessment requires collecting the relevant information to assess the risk, rather than collecting information that is available or indicated on assessment templates.

A more forensic approach is required that promotes honesty, efficiency, transparency and focus. This does not deflect from the need for partnership working with families and across professionals: it is integral to it.

CHAPTER 5

Risk Restoration

Frameworks for Practice

Having set out the issues relating to the ever-changing but serially unhelpful context for social work practice, it is alarming for workers that they have not been furnished with a full risk assessment framework to guide this ever more complex area of work. Against a backdrop of blame and anticipated blame, workers are disabled in the exercise of their professional judgment and this is most evident in the inquisition they receive from the judiciary every time they get into the court arena.

As a safeguarding manager I accepted that it was unhelpful to leave workers with a blank piece of paper as a guide to risk assessments and I set up developing my prototype template for risk assessments in 2000 after the full deficits of the assessment framework were being recognised. Risk Assessment, Analysis And Management Model (RASSAMM) (Calder 2003c) was conceived as not only offering a framework to guide risk assessments, but also trying to redress some of the concerns repeatedly highlighted in the serious case review findings – principally the need to have a greater correlation between the risk assessment and the subsequent analysis and management of the risk plans. This derived from the available research in relation to risk factors and also drew upon my significant experience as a child protection worker and manager.

One of the important starting points is to find a way of resurrecting risk within the assessment framework and as a means of achieving this I developed the risk diamond (see Figure 5.1). This framework acknowledges that the triangle has to be helped to work as opposed to being replaced, not least since its principal authors were non-social workers and operated in a therapeutic as opposed to an adversarial context with families.

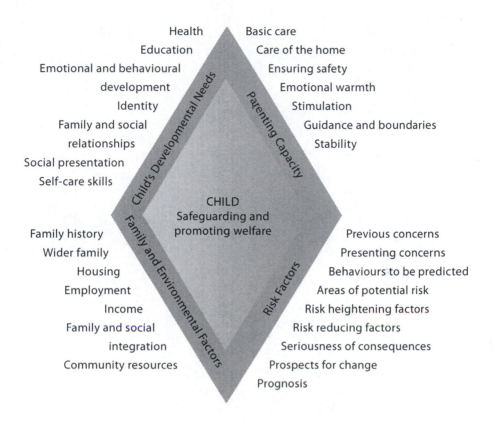

Health — Basic care
Education — Care of the home
Emotional and behavioural — Ensuring safety
development — Emotional warmth
Identity — Stimulation
Family and social — Guidance and boundaries
relationships — Stability
Social presentation
Self-care skills

Child's Developmental Needs — Parenting Capacity

CHILD
Safeguarding and
promoting welfare

Family and Environmental Factors — Risk Factors

Family history — Previous concerns
Wider family — Presenting concerns
Housing — Behaviours to be predicted
Employment — Areas of potential risk
Income — Risk heightening factors
Family and social — Risk reducing factors
integration — Seriousness of consequences
Community resources — Prospects for change
Prognosis

Figure 5.1 Risk diamond

RASSAMM was developed to:

- ► Assist in the structuring of child protection decision-making

- ► Allow the professionals, and those caring for the children, to be clearer about what they are worried about and how worried they are that abuse or neglect will continue or recur

- ► Inform the child protection plan or prescribing courses of action to protect children

- ► Help evaluation by drawing together and summarising the professionals' previously prepared assessments of the child and family's situation.

Calder (2002a) offered the following framework for conducting risk assessments by identifying areas where risk questions should be considered. They do not all have to be answered all of the time but the more gaps there are the less reliable the conclusions that can be drawn.

Risk questions to guide information collection:

- ▶ Assess all areas of identified risk: Write them each down and ensure each is considered separately (e.g. child, parent, family, surrounding environment, type and nature of maltreatment, intervention issues).

- ▶ Define the behaviour to be predicted: Rather than focus on the 'dangerous' individual, assess each behaviour individually as each is likely to involve different risk factors.

- ▶ Grade the risks, and be alert for especially serious risk factors: (e.g. previous corroborated or uncorroborated concerns, unwillingness or inability to protect) While numerical weighting is hard to give, some weighting has to be given to significance. A less likely event with a serious outcome if it occurred, would need to be weighted, (e.g. injury, death, traumatic emotional impact). A more likely event with a high frequency, even though a not too serious outcome, would need to be weighted. Who is affected could add to the gravity (e.g. the harm to a child is often greater than if to an adult).

- ▶ Be aware of risk factors that may interact in a dangerous manner: (e.g. a case of physical injury and the abuser is heavily drinking at present) Take into account both internal and external factors – almost all behaviour is the result of interaction between characteristics of the individual (e.g. attitudes, skills, controls) and those of the environment (demands, constraints, stressors, etc.).

- ▶ Examine the nature of the risk factors: How long have they been operating for? How severe are they? Risk factors that are long-term and relatively uncontrollable generally signal a higher level of risk.

- Avoid focusing exclusively on the severity of the abuse: We need to consider other factors that point to future risk, not just commissioned harm. Distinguish between the probability and the cost of the behaviour – we need to distinguish between the likelihood of the behaviour occurring from the seriousness of it if it does. Failure to do so makes any decision-making more problematic.

- Assess family strengths and resources: While risk assessment is essentially a negative process, workers should be examining family strengths and resources that may be used to counteract the risk factors present. For example, good bonding and supportive networks. It is argued that the assessment process is incomplete in the absence of this dimension.

- Use specific and descriptive terms to document the risk factors: Do not rely on terms such as 'multi-problem family'.

- Gather real and direct evidence whenever possible: Do not relay on hunches, hearsay or circumstantial information.

- Check whether all necessary information has been gathered: As in some cases, few sources of data may be needed to develop a strong understanding of the behaviour, whereas in others we may need to qualify any predictions made due to the entirely inadequate or irrelevant material.

- Identify if/when specialists or other outsiders need to be involved: Predictive accuracy is often improved when we utilise the combined skills across agencies and sometimes beyond. Where this is lacking, workers should explicitly state how their recommendations have been affected by such omissions.

- Awareness of probable sources of error: Which may come from the person being assessed (e.g. their poor reliability as an informant), the assessor (a difficulty in suspending personal values), or the context (such as an agency bias in favour of one or other party involved).

> ▶ Plan key intervention: Because a sound assessment of risk will be based on the formulation of the mechanisms underlying the behaviour. It will automatically identify those processes, which appear to be key elements in increasing or reducing such risk (e.g. within the individual or the couple).

Calder (2003a) extended this to include:

> ▶ Previous incidents of abuse or neglect: Detail any previous incident of abuse or neglect (type and frequency) in this family OR any record of the current caretakers having abused or neglected other children. Is there a pattern of abuse (such as physical abuse being repeated) or is it changing (such as the concerns spanning a range of categories of child abuse)? There is widespread research evidence that suggests children are more at risk in the care of those who have previously abused or neglected children. Do they accept any of the previous concerns? Do they have any insight into their previous behaviour? If so why the lapse? Do they accept or reject themselves as a continuing risk?

> ▶ Taking a detailed social history and producing a detailed chronology.

From information collection to risk analysis

Research and experience have shown that there is usually lots of information available about the child and family. However, reviews of practice often find that there was insufficient shared analysis to form a good plan. The strength of analysis is that it encourages openness about reasoning and so potentially holds one's work open to scrutiny. The disadvantage in this approach is that it can induce misplaced faith in the ability to make predictions particularly in the increasing social work field of risk assessment.

Risk analysis enables a risk assessment to be made on which decisions about action for risk management can be made and implemented. Risk analysis should thus provide information on:

> ▶ The nature of the risks and dangers these give

> ▶ The frequency of such risks arising

- The degree of seriousness of the dangers

- The personal characteristics of those involved and how far these add to or minimise the risks

- The relevant wider knowledge base on which to draw

- The timescales for a risk decision

- How a plan will be monitored in practice, and what feedback will indicate a change to the fall-back plan to further reduce the risk if it escalates.

Calder (2002a; 2003c) argued that the risk analysis stage should consider the following questions:

- **What are the weaknesses in the situation being analysed?** What are the factors in the situation being analysed that make the occurrence or continuance of abuse more likely – what are the weaknesses or vulnerabilities in the arrangements for the care and protection of the child? These are usually inadequacies in the care provided by the child's family or in the protection afforded to the child. There may also be weaknesses in the services available to the family or their willingness to co-operate with them. The emphasis should be on the situation being assessed and the physical and emotional care that can be provided for the child. However, consideration should also be given to factors from the past where there is evidence that these are making current coping more difficult. For example, the fact of parent(s), themselves having been abused or neglected in childhood would be included if it was thought to be having an effect on their capacity to care for and provide for their children. The responsibility of the parents/ caretakers for previous abuse or neglect to this child or other children should be given particular consideration.

- **What are the strengths in the situation being analysed?** Understanding how to assess strengths and intervene in ways that strengthen and support family functioning is of particular importance in child protection work. It can help us work effectively with families in a way that protects the child, but does not oppress the family. A wide view should be taken of possible strengths including extended family and community supports but they should be related to the abuse or neglect under consideration. A supportive extended family will be a strength where parents need to share some of their burden of child care, they will normally be of little use in protecting a child from a devious sex abuser. Here, too, the emphasis is on the situation being assessed but consideration should also be given to factors from the caretaker's past where there is evidence that these are strengthening current coping capacity. For example, a parent who has coped for a number of years prior to the current concerns, this shows the capacity under other circumstances to provide good enough care for the children. Further guidance is found in Calder (1999).

▶ **What are the risk-reducing factors that also need to be taken into account?** An admission by a parent of the problem and a willingness to co-operate with a treatment and intervention programme would reduce risk. The use of interventions known to bring benefits, for example, appropriate, regular medication for a mental illness, would also reduce risk. It is always difficult to know which questions to ask, although the following predictive questions might be of assistance:

» Parenting skills and the capacity to learn – can methods of teaching and imparting parenting skills matched to the parent(s) methods of learning be improved?

» Health care and safety – poor parents are as concerned as any to maintain health and treat illness or injury. The problem is they are often slower in responding to emergencies, such as choking, thus allowing the problems to get worse.

» Decision-making – is often high on rapidity and low on thoughtfulness, with poor quality decisions made as a result.

» Parent and child interaction – emotionally, is often as warm, attached and committed as for most parents. Multiple deprivations can reinforce a tendency to a more restricted, punitive response. Research indications are that this may be due to not knowing what standards to set, what behaviour to reinforce, and non-punitive ways to ignore or reprimand undesirable behaviour. The danger of filling the gaps with middle-class family norms, and patterns as goals, then has to be avoided.

» The capacity to generalise learning to adapt it to new situations.

▶ **What are the prospects for change and growth in the situation?** Is there evidence of growth and positive change in the circumstances that have surrounded the abuse or given rise to the concern, or is there evidence of deterioration and negative change in the situation? A risk assessment should attempt to forecast how a situation will develop in the future, clearly the capacity for improvement or deterioration in the current conditions is central to any such assessment. A key indicator of the likelihood of change is the parent's attitude to the abuse or concerns – an acknowledgement of the difficulties and a preparedness to work towards change would normally be seen as lessening the risk and the denial of the problem as increasing it. However, care needs to be taken not to discriminate against parents solely on the basis of their taking a different view of the abuse or alleged abuse from the social worker or other professionals. Co-operation also needs to be viewed in the context of the seriousness of the abuse or neglect. Some incidents are so serious that compulsory protective action may need to be taken despite evidence of co-operation from parents.

▶ **What can be offered to build on strengths and combat weaknesses?** At all stages in the process it is important to see help and support as running alongside assessment, so even at an early stage it would be important to comment on the availability of help and the likelihood of it being used. There is much research evidence that the majority of child abuse investigations are trigged by poor or inadequate parenting rather than deliberate acts of abuse or neglect. Offering support services will be an outcome of many child protection investigations. Clearly a positive response from parents to such services is helpful but we need to be aware of the danger of discriminating against parents solely on the basis of their not co-operating with services and the danger of superficial co-operation hiding deeper resistance.

▶ **What is the risk associated with intervention?** We need to consider whether the benefits of intervention outweigh the problems of separation if we are considering removal from home – the inability to place siblings together in substitute care, the location of the placement may be some distance and can thus disrupt the child's peer networks, schooling and social life.

▶ **What is the family's motivation, and capacity, for change?** A key indicator of the likelihood of change is the parent's attitude to the abuse or concerns – an acknowledgement of the difficulties and a preparedness to work towards change would normally be seen as lessening the risk and the denial of the problem as increasing it. However, care needs to be taken not to discriminate against parents solely on the basis of their taking a different view of the abuse or alleged abuse from the social worker or other professionals.

▶ **What is the likelihood of abuse occurring or recurring? What is the level of risk?** Determining the level of risk is a complex decision-making process where the worker considers the following conditions or criteria:

   » Number of risk factors (how pervasive are they?)

   » Severity of risk factors (how severe?)

   » Duration of risk factors (how long have they been present?)

   » Parent or child's ability to control risk factors

   » Family strengths and resources

   » Ability of worker or agency to provide necessary services.

▶ **Distinguish between the probability and the cost of the behaviour.** We need to distinguish between the likelihood of the behaviour occurring from the seriousness of it if it does. Failure to do so makes any decision-making more problematic. For example, a repeat physical injury from a smack may be more likely to occur but the outcome of this may be considered to be significantly less serious than a repeat fatality! In the light of the information collected a judgment of the level of risk in the current situation may be made. The level of risk is a compound of two elements: how serious is the abuse or neglect that it is feared might occur or reoccur and how likely is its occurrence or reoccurrence?

Framework for analysis

In Chapter 4, I identified the need for an organising framework for risk analysis that reflected the need to balance risks and strengths to offer a more balanced view (see Figure 5.2).

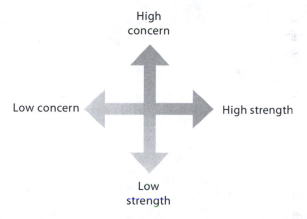

Figure 5.2 Organising analysis framework (OAF)

Workers are asked to plot the information collected on the risk identification factor matrix (see Table 5.1) to provide an indication about the level of risk and the indicated risk management options. Evidence-based indicators were identified in each section, recognising that many of the strengths are the product of practice experience as opposed to research. Little has focused on the strengths in abusing families, and in many respects the definition of strengths is the absence of risks. The worker is asked not to simply use the numbers to offer a mathematical formulation of risk but to use it is the basis of reflective supervision which should assist the need to exercise professional judgment. For example, we may have a baby who has sustained a serious physical injury believed to be inflicted but not admitted.

TABLE 5.1 RISK IDENTIFICATION FACTOR MATRIX
(CALDER, SNEDDON AND MCKINNON 2012)

High concern	Low concern
Current injury/harm is severe	No history of significant trauma or abuse
Pattern of harm is continuing or escalating	Recognition of the problem
Parent has indicated repeat behaviour is likely	Perpetrator demonstrates remorse/empathy
Access to vulnerable persons	Perpetrator accepts responsibility for their behaviour
Diagnosis of untreatable mental health and substance misuse	Children are able to protect themselves if the need arises
A history of interpersonal conflict and violence – power problems/poor negotiation and lack of autonomy/recent separation or reconciliation	Healthy peer relationships
Uncontrolled contact between perpetrator and children	No documented school problems
The parent is unwilling or unable to protect the children	No history of behavioural/emotional problems
High levels of trauma in parent's childhood not recognised as a problem	Parental mental health and/or substance problem responsive to treatment
Previous child protection concerns with no significant changes effected or sustained	Empathy for the child
Parents do not accept their behaviour is a concern and not willing to work with professionals	Parental competence in some areas
Children are too young to be able to take any action to protect themselves and require rapid parental change	Risk reactive to circumstances and identified capacity for change
Child presents as fearful of parents or other household member	Social support and access to child care facilities and networks
Children engaging in self-harm, substance misuse, dangerous sexual behavior or other 'at risk' behaviours	Temporary disabilities
Parent is young – under 21 years of age	Constant/expected stressors
Social isolation/lack of social support	
Violent, unsupportive neighbourhood	
Parent is experiencing high levels of stress	
Physical and social environment is chaotic, hazardous and unsafe	
Inability to predict timing and severity of risk recurring or changing	

High strength	Low strength
Parents demonstrate good protective attitudes and behaviours	Parents and young person appear not to care what happens
Family has clear, positive boundaries in place	Young person has poor communication skills
Family demonstrates good communication	Young person has no support/is rejected by parents/carers
Family demonstrates ability to positively process emotional issues	Young person is excluded from school
Family is positive about receiving help	Isolated family
Young person lives in supportive environment	Absence of supportive/structured living environment
Network of support and supervision available to young person	Parents/carers unable to supervise
Young person has positive plans and goals	Family enmeshed in unhealthy social network
Young person has positive relationship with school/work	Family has high levels of stress
Young person has experienced consistent, positive care	History of unresolved significant abuse in family
Young person has at least one emotional confidant	Family unable to understand the consequences of their behaviour
Young person has good problem solving and negotiation skills	Family refuses to engage with professionals
Demonstrates new coping skills (when stressed)	No or inappropriate professional resources available
Demonstrates empathy (sees cues of others and responds)	Limited options/skill deficit
Accurate attributions of responsibility (takes responsibility for own behaviour, doesn't try to control behaviour of others)	Perceived threat/vulnerability
Able to manage frustration and unfavourable events (anger management and self-protection)	Lowered self-esteem/efficacy
Able to resolve conflicts and make decisions (assertive, tolerant, forgiving, co-operative, able to negotiate and compromise)	Negative expectations
	Isolation/lack of support
	Lowered inhibitions
Able to think and communicate effectively (rational cognitive processing, adequate verbal skills, able to concentrate)	
Pro-social peers	

Background assessment indicates that there are no other concerns and significant strengths across the family. The presence of one risk and multiple strengths does not indicate that the latter is weighted as more significant if the injury and the likelihood of repetition is real. Workers have to show how they made their decision and why they weighted the recommendation in one particular way. This is an integral judicial requirement and reflects open and transparent decision-making

Once the matrix and framework has been completed and judgment exercised in relation to the quadrant most reflective of the information received and analysed, there is a need to examine what action and/or intervention is most reflective of the risk identified. Table 5.2 highlights the indicated response and next steps. The aim is to ensure a match between the risk and the plans for intervention.

TABLE 5.2 RISK MANAGEMENT PATHWAYS

Low strength/high concern	High concern/high strength
Parents are likely to be at the pre-contemplative stage and unlikely to move from this position Families assessed to be in this category are the most worrying The children are likely to need looking after, probably long term The length of time in care will be dependent on the parent's ability to change, however their own upbringing may have left them too damaged to change	Parents may be more willing to change at this level. There will be parents at different stages of change There could be worries about children living in these families and alternative placement may be an option however this depends on the parent's ability to change There is more scope for working with families in this group and less need to separate
Low concern/low strengths	**Low concern/high strengths**
Families in this grouping are highly unlikely to need care These are the referrals that are likely to be referred on a number of occasions before they are willing to change Community resources are the best outcome, use of family in need (FIN) model These young people should not come into care as generally there are no issues to put the child at risk at home	Network of support and supervision is available to young persons Families in this group are generally of little worry and would probably benefit from standard support systems, school, GP, etc. Generally these families should not be referred to social services as their needs are similar to the standard population They may need advice and guidance from standard services

Risk and resistance

Having developed a framework for risk assessment it became clear that there is little point in this if the plans are those of the professionals alone, and the resistance from the family prohibits any sharing of the identified work. Families have to work as least as hard as the professionals if progress is to be made. This led to the need to develop a parallel framework to help identify, assess and successfully navigate client resistance. In doing so, it became clear that there was an important correlation between motivation, resistance and change (see Figure 5.3).

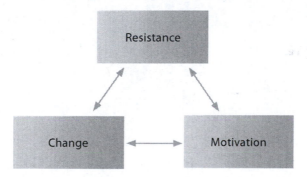

Figure 5.3 A framework for approaching client resistance

Resistance

CONTINUUM OF CONFRONTATION

There can be a wide range of unco-operative behaviour by families towards professionals.

> ▸ **Hostile and threatening behaviour**: This involves behaviour which has a damaging effect, physically or emotionally, on other people. This includes a range of behaviour such as violence – being physically, verbally or emotionally aggressive, threatening or intimidatory. The impact of such behaviour on individual staff will vary but the fear of violence and aggression is recognised as impacting on judgments, interpretation and intervention. Threatening behaviour can consist of:

» The deliberate use of silence

» Using written threats

» Bombarding professionals with emails and phone calls

» Using intimidating or derogatory language

» Racist attitudes and remarks

» Homophobic attitudes and comments

» Using domineering body language

» Using dogs or other animals as a threat

» Deliberately damaging property of an organisation or its workers

» Swearing

» Shouting

» Throwing things

» Physical violence

» Knowledge of a previous conviction that suggests they present a threat (e.g. for serious assault or gun crime).

▶ **Non-compliant/uncooperative behaviour**: This involves proactively sabotaging efforts to effect change or alternatively passively disengaging. This includes a wide range of behaviours and attitudes such as passive non-compliance with plans of work, failure to keep appointments, refusal to allow access to the child(ren) or to the home, paying lip service to co-operation.

▶ **Disguised compliance (apparent co-operation)**: This involves parents or carers not admitting to their lack of commitment to change but working subversively to undermine the process. Examples of this could include:

» Agreeing to keep appointments or to undertake individual action but never carrying them out or putting little effort into making changes work

» Co-operating with some services but not making important changes

» Change does occur but as a result of input of agencies: not as a result of the parent/carer actions.

It is important to be clear about what level of behaviour the parents are displaying and, therefore, what level of risk this poses to both children and workers. Uncooperative responses may include:

▶ **Ambivalence,** which may, understandably, be present in many parents in the safeguarding arena. This may be seen when people miss a number of appointments or avoid discussing difficult areas.

▶ **Avoidance,** which is also very common and will include such behaviours as regularly avoiding appointments, visits and meetings – using distracting techniques to avoid discussing difficult areas.

▶ **Confrontation** includes direct challenge to workers, either based on verbal, sometimes written, exchange, or extreme avoidance (such as not answering the door as opposed to not being in). Some comments can be covertly intimidating over a period of time.

▶ **Violence,** which includes either threatened or actual violence. Threats may be explicit or implicit and may involve threats of actual violence, use of threatening dogs or other adults. This represents the minority of uncooperative behaviour but can be the most difficult for workers to engage with and presents the highest risk to both children, the non-violent parent and workers.

Disguised compliance

Disguised compliance involves a parent or carer giving the appearance of co-operating with child welfare agencies to avoid raising suspicions, to allay professional concerns and ultimately to diffuse professional intervention (Reder *et al.* 1993). Examples of disguised compliance would be a sudden increase in school attendance, attending a run of appointments, engaging with professionals such as health workers for a limited period of time, or cleaning the house before a visit from a professional.

Disguised compliance occurs when parents want to draw the professional's attention away from allegations of harm. It is often highlighted as a theme in serious case reviews: 'Apparent or disguised co-operation from parents often prevented or delayed understanding of the severity of harm to the child, and cases drifted. Where parents ... engineered the focus away from allegations of harm, children went unseen and unheard' (Brandon *et al.* 2008). Parents' behaviour can thus mislead us about the progress they are making and about the true nature of the lived experience of the child. The worker needs to be mindful of the impact the hostility to outsiders may be having on the day-to-day life of the child/young person. They may have become desensitised to violence, have learnt to appease and/or be simply too frightened to tell.

Reder *et al.* (1993) identified patterns of 'closure' or 'flight' when families needed to reduce their contact with the external world in an attempt to 'regain control by shutting out professionals' (p.99). Often when professionals took a more controlling stance, this was defused by apparent co-operation of the family, the effect of which was to 'neutralise the professional's authority and return the relationship to closure and the previous status quo' (Reder *et al.* 1993, p.106).

Workers may believe they have engaged in a positive way with parents/carers in addressing risk and working towards change. However, this may not be the case. As a consequence the following may happen: cases can drift, risks are not reduced or may actually be increased and workers may fail to recognise significant issues of concern, misinterpret vital information and lose interagency communication. The child, therefore, remains in a high risk, unprotected environment (Stoke-on-Trent Safeguarding Children Board 2015 *Guidance on Resistant Families*).

In many cases parents were hostile to helping agencies, and workers were often frightened to visit family homes. These circumstances could have a paralysing effect on practitioners, hampering their ability to reflect, make judgments, to act clearly and to follow through with referrals, assessments or plans.

Sometimes parents may be hostile to specific agencies or individuals and if the hostility is not universal, then agencies should seek to understand why this might be and learn from each other. Hostility towards most agencies may result in everyone backing off, leaving the child unprotected, the family is punished by withholding of services as everyone 'sees it as a fight', at the expense of assessing and resolving the situation for the child and there is a divide between those who want to appease and those who want to oppose – or everyone colludes. The risk of a breakdown in interagency collaboration is probably at its greatest when there is selective hostility to specific agencies. Any pre-existing tensions between professionals and agencies or misunderstandings about different roles are likely to surface.

Differentiating between challenging service users and dangerous service users

Professionals should be alert to the threats posed to them yet at the same time need to differentiate between those who challenge and those who are dangerous.

Challenging service users	Potentially dangerous service users
▸ Constant challenge, no threat ▸ Critical of staff, making complaints ▸ Constant requests to change staff ▸ Restricts access to child(ren) ▸ Subverts attempts to engage with child(ren) ▸ Deflecting role and function ▸ Misses arranged appointments ▸ Distracted during meetings.	▸ A record of violence ▸ A consistent pattern to offences ▸ History of concern from other workers ▸ Evidence of threats being enacted ▸ Legitimises use of violence ▸ A past history of mental health issues ▸ Substance misuse ▸ Collusion with others.

The key to dealing with these behaviours is to understand why they might be occurring and the reasons may include: boredom, fear, frustration, immaturity, previous negative experiences, confusion, individual issues such as learning disabilities, mental health issues, family factors such as domestic violence or substance misuse, community factors such as isolation, lack of community resources, lack of recreational activities and opportunities, and societal factors such as poor housing, lack of support and funding for appropriate interventions, and a lack of education.

Situations associated with resistance and non-compliance include:

- Child protection inquiries
- Removal of child into care
- Domestic abuse
- Previous threats of violence
- Presence of weapons
- Potentially dangerous animals (snakes/dogs)
- Research showed that 'high levels of parental mental illness, alcohol and drug misuse and domestic abuse feature, significantly in families where children become involved in the child protection system' and these factors need to inform any assessment and ongoing work (Stoke-on-Trent Safeguarding Children Board 2015 *Guidance on Resistant Families*).

Additional factors may include the fact that they:

- Do not want their privacy invaded
- Have something to hide
- Refuse to believe they have a problem
- Resent outside interference
- Have cultural differences
- Lack understanding about what is being expected of them
- Have poor previous experience of professional involvement
- Resent staff changes
- Dislike/fear or distrust authority figures
- Fear their children will be taken away

- Fear being judged to be poor parents because of substance misuse or mental health problems

- Feel they have nothing to lose (e.g. where the children have already been removed)

- Hold a distrust of professionals

- Are frightened of the consequences (e.g. removal of child)

- Are frightened of change/premature change efforts requested by professionals

- Have a different understanding of the problem to the professionals

- Adopt a natural defence mechanism

Recognition of non-effective compliance

Factors, which may indicate and evidence non-effective compliance:

- No significant change at reviews despite significant input

- Parents/carers agreeing with professionals regarding required changes but put little effort into making changes work

- Change does occur but as a result of external agencies/resources not the parental/carers efforts

- Change in one area of functioning is not matched by change in other areas

- Parents/carers will engage with certain aspects of a plan only

- Parents/carers align themselves with certain professionals.

(Stoke-on-Trent Safeguarding Children Board 2015)

Engaging males

There is evidence from research and from inquiry reports that professionals focus primarily on mothers in families and pay much less attention to father figures – whether they are biological fathers, stepfathers or partners. Most of this research is about children in families where there have been child protection concerns – physical, sexual and emotional abuse as well as neglect.

The Challenge of Partnership in Child Protection, (DoH 1995a) identified that it is routine practice to see a child's mother. It should be equally standard practice to see relevant male adults, both those in the household and those living elsewhere who have parental responsibility. This is essential because they are part of a child's life and are significant either for positive or negative reasons. If professionals aspire to partnership with parents and carers it is a poor beginning to undervalue the contributions of men known to the child. Such an approach may be based on assumptions of guilt or insignificance which prove unfounded when the situation is explored properly. It may also be dangerous for the child if the social worker makes only a second-hand assessment of a man's potential to protect of abuse the child in the future.

Operational difficulties include fathers distancing themselves from the process and from practitioners. Workers may collude because they are more comfortable with working with mothers, and fathers who show hostility or violent behaviour may undermine a mother's ability to co-operate.

A key point is professionals' avoidance of working with men. This may be because of fear of violence and aggression, which may be a very real and sensible fear. However, there is a general assumption that male workers will be less intimidated by other men than women will be – hence the reaction of some managers to 'make sure a male worker goes with her'. In fact, men may feel just as vulnerable and may be forced to conceal their own fear and anxiety. In fact, research has shown that the principal source of violence against child protection workers is not men but women (i.e. the mothers of children with whom the agency has become involved). What is needed is a careful assessment of the risk to the worker and strategies to ensure safety – not avoidance. Workers may avoid coming into contact with men, for example, visiting when they know they are not going to be there or, if they come into contact with them, intentionally avoid any meaningful interaction or communication with them (e.g. not engaging them in the conversation, colluding with them watching TV/reading the paper, etc). What is not helpful is avoidance of engaging men and the father figures in the child's life, which prevents a thorough understanding of the relationship between the man, the mother and the child.

Failure to adequately involve men leaves mothers even more vulnerable. It may mean that women are dealing with the professionals alone and then having to explain what is going on to the men who may vent their anxieties and frustrations out on the women. This may increase the man's power over the woman, he may then try to influence the situation through the woman. Most importantly, father figures may be vital protective factors for children, which may be ignored.

The concept of 'shadowy men' developed as a result of serious case reviews in which workers failed to gather information about certain men in the child's life and failed to appreciate the important roles these men had in the family, either as protective factors (where concerns should have been heightened as these men were effectively pushed out of the child's life, thus reducing their opportunities to monitor and protect) or as sources of risk (where workers were not aware how much contact the child was having with this person or the level of influence the adult had on the family home). In some cases the 'shadowy men' were biological parents but they could also be new partners of the mother or members of the extended family.

Messages from research

Seminal research in the 1990s into the operation of the child protection system identified some key points that relate to the issue of engaging families in the identified assessment and intervention work:

▸ Doing 'to' families does not create an environment conducive to engagement or change

▸ Excluding families from the decision-making process heightens resistance, lowers motivation and creates a 'them and us scenario'

▸ Families will not sign up to or implement plans they have not been party to constructing or with which they fundamentally disagree

▸ Involving families in plans enhances ownership and this is correlated with greater and more sustained change

▸ Working together successfully requires the integration of formal and informal systems

- The roles and responsibilities of professionals are often unclear and this impedes the construction and implementation of the child protection plans

- Task allocation is idealistic rather than realistic

- The focus on registration deflects us from planning and risk assessment.

The four categories of resistance

Resistance can take a variety of forms, and there are a number of different categorisations to draw from:

- Hostile resistance: shown through overt anger, threats, physical intimidation and shouting

- Passive–aggressive resistance: conveyed under a guise of niceness or obsequiousness, with overt compliance on top of covert antagonism, anger and the suppression of explosive behaviours

- Passive–hopeless resistance: a more overt presentation demonstrated by tearfulness, immobility, and an attitude of despair towards any help that is offered

- Challenging resistance: which is manipulative behaviour along the lines of 'cure me if you can'.

(Dale *et al.* 1986)

Categories of client resistant behaviour

Arguing: the client contests the accuracy, expertise or integrity of the worker by:

- Challenging: they directly challenge the accuracy of what the worker has said

- Discounting: they question the worker's personal authority and expertise

- Exhibiting hostility: the client expresses direct hostility towards the worker.

Interrupting: the client breaks in and interrupts the worker in a defensive manner by:

- Talking over: the client speaks whilst the worker is still talking without waiting for an appropriate pause or silence

- Cutting off: they break in with words obviously intended to cut the worker off.

Denying: the client expresses an unwillingness to recognise the problems, co-operate, accept responsibility or take advice by:

- Blaming: the client blames other people for their problems

- Disagreeing: the client disagrees with what is said without offering any constructive alternative

- Excusing their own behaviour

- Claiming impunity from any danger caused by the presenting behaviours of concern

- Minimising the risks and dangers, by claiming they are exaggerated and that things aren't really that bad

- Pessimism: where they make general statements about self or others that are pessimistic, defeatist or negative in tone

- Reluctance: the client expresses reservations and reluctance about information or advice given

- Unwillingness to change: they express a lack of desire or an unwillingness to change, or express a clear intention not to change.

Ignoring: the client shows evidence of not following or ignoring the worker:

- Inattention: where the client's response indicates that they have not been following or attending to the worker

- No answer: where they respond to a query in a way that doesn't answer the question

- No response: the client gives no audible, or a non-verbal reply to a worker's query

> ▶ Sidetracking: the client changes the direction of the conversation that the worker has been pursuing.

Chronology of compliance

All agencies should be asked to review their files and pull out any indications of compliance and non-compliance. Once integrated this can provide a clear overview about the family behaviour towards professionals as well as providing a roadmap of potential engagement opportunities.

Change

The model of change is a widely used template to help track changes and examine any blocks that may exist (see Figure 5.4). In order to start the engagement process, workers need to consider where the client is starting from, as there is frequently a discrepancy between professional and client starting points, which contributes to the problem, rather than serving to address and resolve it. This point can be made more clearly when looking at the model of change. This model is very useful for setting out realistic plans of work at the outset, for setting attainable targets, and for reviewing what progress, if any, has been made. The model of change shows just how important it is for the professional to allow the client to move from pre-contemplation through to action if there is to be any professional–family congruence about what needs to happen. Any failure to allow for this (and this is a very real issue with the timescales set down) sets the worker and the family up to fail. Given the worker should allow sufficient time in their assessment schedule to negotiate and hopefully create the necessary conditions for the client to engage in the work and effect some of the mutually agreed areas requiring change, workers do need to have some understanding of the important initial steps in the model of change. These are described in Figure 5.4.

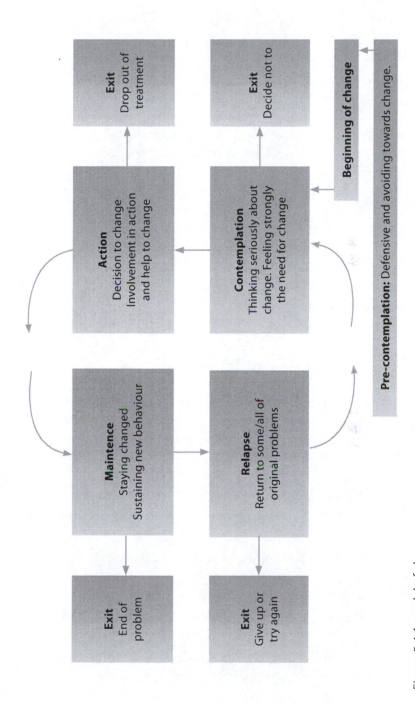

Figure 5.4 A model of change
(Prochaska and DiClemente 1982; 1986)

The model follows a logical and sequential process as follows.

Pre-contemplation

This is where the individual is considering change far less than the professionals, who are often reacting to the presenting situation. Morrison (1995) pointed out that this phase is characterised by blaming others, denying responsibility, or simply being unaware of the need to change (e.g. depression). Whilst in this stage no change is possible. Individuals thus require information and feedback in order that they can raise their awareness of the problem and the possibility of change (Miller and Rollnick 1991, p.16).

Families who fall into this area are unlikely to comply with any agreement as they often see the worker as their problem. It is therefore important for workers to assess the driver behind the resistance, to offer a means of trying to challenge it, and invite change. There are four categories of pre-contemplator:

- ▶ Reluctant: inertia or lack of knowledge. This features heavily in cases such as sexual abuse where a mother may be told about her partner or someone significant posing a sexual risk to the children. This rarely accords with their view of the alleged abuser and so they are unlikely to truly believe that contact between the two needs to be limited. If they are provided with information about the specifics of his behaviour coupled with the modus operandi of offenders then this may induce a change of position as she moves to prioritise the safety of the children. If they change and wish to engage in work then a family safety policy may be indicated, but conversely no shift would render one dangerously optimistic.

- ▶ Rebellious: heavy investment in the behaviour which needs to change or in making their own decisions. This may relate to adults dependent on alcohol or drugs or could relate to the fact that they see nothing wrong with physically chastising their children and have no intention of exploring the possibility of alternatives.

- ▶ Resigned: overwhelmed by problems and has given up hope of changing. These people may have experienced prior contact with agencies and not achieved their outcome, and as such may not work with anyone, or if they do it is with a deep sense of pessimism and lack of motivation or drive to stick with an agreed plan. They see a pre-determined (and often negative) outcome awaiting them.

▶ Rationalising: will explain away the problem and why no change is required. People in this category may argue that their behaviour is acceptable or argue that whilst unacceptable it doesn't expose the children to any harm and therefore fails to meet their criteria for social work involvement and planning.

Contemplation

People in this phase may be more open to considering the possibility of change but may be ambivalent. They may be open to receiving, feedback, observations, information and even confrontation and they may respond to 'consciousness raising' or to emphasising the gains or giving examples of past successes. Morrison (1991) identified six stages of contemplation which offer workers some reference point to judge whether they may be approaching a willingness to accept the need for a plan. They are:

▶ 'I accept that there is a problem.'

▶ 'I have some responsibility for the problem.'

▶ 'I have some discomfort about the problem and my part in it.'

▶ 'I believe that things must change.'

▶ 'I can see that I can be part of the solution.'

▶ 'I can see the first steps towards change.'

It is important to separate out their motivation (how willing and ready is the parent to change and what is the evidence for this) with their capacity (how able is the parent to change)? The capacity to change and sustain change can be scaled:

▶ Absolute refusal to change or denial of the need to change

▶ Had had support and/or learning opportunities to help to change

▶ Has demonstrated by their actions some understanding of the need to change

- ▶ Achieving basic changes with support
- ▶ Sustaining basic changes with support
- ▶ Demonstrating building on changes made and making progress with reduced support
- ▶ Sustaining changes made without support
- ▶ Sustaining changes and using own initiatives to improve parenting

(Archer 2002).

In this stage, the client may now accept that something has to change although they may be unsure how it can be achieved. The task for workers is to remove any barriers to change, and create an environment where change is a realistic possibility. Change remains a very painful process.

Action

This is when the adults start to work in a structured way on change to which they are committed. Change is stressful and may fail or people may feel they have failed. The worker should focus on success and reaffirming the client's decision to change and look out for signs of relapse. There may also be disengagement and this should not be underestimated either. It may signal the need to review the originating plan.

Action is a potentially stressful stage of change as actions can fail and clients feel that they have failed or been rejected. We need to plan for relapse and involve the wider family and the community networks, for it is they who are most likely both to spot the early signs of lapse, and who will provide the most day-to-day support (Morrison 1995). This stage is where the individual is seen 'in action', implementing the plan. It is where they feel able to make a public commitment to action; to get some external confirmation of the plan; to seek support; to gain greater self-efficacy; and finally to create artificial, external monitors of their activity (DiClemente 1991, p.198–9). For the worker, they should focus on successful activity and reaffirm the client's decisions. They should point out that change is predictable where a person adheres to advice and the plan. The focus should be on learning, exploring and rehearsing ways of relating, thinking, behaving and feeling. All change is essentially a combination of these four basic human processes. This stage may take several months as new behaviour takes time to become established. At the end of the initial planning stage, the aim is to produce a longer-term plan of work.

Maintenance

Maintenance is about sustaining and consolidating change and preventing relapse. This is the real test. It occurs when the new ways of relating and behaving become internalised and generalised across different situations. They do not now depend on the presence of the workers, but become consolidated and owned by the individual/ family as part of themselves. It is through this process that the client's sense of self-efficacy has been increased (Morrison 1995). Successful maintenance builds on each of the processes that have come before, as well as an open assessment of the conditions under which a person is likely to relapse (Prochaska and DiClemente 1986, p.10). Stability and support will be essential to sustaining change, especially with the many families who have such poor experience of problem solving (Morrison 1991).

Relapse

The cyclical model of change allows for the reality that few people succeed first time round. Change comes from repeated efforts, re-evaluation, renewing of commitment, and incremental success. Relapse is thus part of, rather than necessarily hostile to, change. Change is a battle between the powerful forces that want us to stay the same, and our wish to be different (Morrison 1991). It usually occurs gradually after an initial slip (often due to unexpected stress), rather than occurring spontaneously (DiClemente 1991, p.200). It can lead to a loss of all or most of the gains, resulting in giving up and a return to pre-contemplation. This can be counteracted by the worker, by giving feedback on how long it takes to accomplish sustained change. They should aim to keep the change effort going rather than becoming disengaged and stuck. Morrison (1995) noted that where it is noted quickly enough, and help is urgently sought and available from friends, family or professionals, all is by no means lost. This may lead to further work through the contemplation stage.

The assessment of change is a very uncertain process, and is often very fragile where it is achieved. It is important that we acknowledge that change is very slow and, as such, workers need to set realistic expectations of involuntary clients so as not to personalise disappointment, experience frustration, impatience and feelings of failure. Few workers are effectively trained to deal with negatively charged emotional material, reluctance, or non-compliant behaviour (Ivanoff, Blythe and Tripodi 1994).

There are a number of useful principles which workers can adopt when considering their role in encouraging change and these include:

- Change is possible
- Change comes through supportive relationships
- Change comes through new ways of thinking about problems and possibilities
- Changes can sometimes come from little things
- Change can grow from the ordinary and the everyday
- Change may come from a single opportunity or positive turning point which leads on to other good things
- Changes comes from tapping into strengths in a child's circumstances
- Change may sometimes come through chance – experiences or contacts – which if allowed may lead to positive outcomes
- Getting even some things right may be the best place to start
- Look for strengths and possibilities
- Relatives and other people in their informal social networks are likely to be around longest for a child
- The child can be one of the agents of change and development in their own lives
- Complex problems rarely have single answers – small steps may interact in positive and unforeseen ways
- Big plans have a habit of coming unstuck – it may be best not to have all the planning eggs in one basket

- ▶ 'One size fits all' solutions are unlikely to work
- ▶ 'The best may be the enemy of the good' – waiting to achieve the elusive best possible solution may mean missing the potential good of valuable intermediate steps.

Cautionary notes

Parental motivation and readiness for change are of considerable interest to child welfare workers. Readiness for change is a central component of the stages of change model. In the past, researchers have viewed readiness for change as 'a dichotomous phenomenon, a presence or absence of motivation' (DiClemente and Hughes 1990, p.218). Clients were either ready or they were not. Similarly, behaviour change has been described as 'a one-step process – one simply changes from one form of behaviour to another' (Gelles 1995, p.4). The change model is thought to have considerable heuristic value for practitioners (Sutton 1996) because it portrays readiness for change and behaviour change as phenomena that develop over time.

By suggesting that many behavioural problems are not quickly or easily remedied, the change model may encourage greater patience and persistence in change efforts. The model may promote less pejorative views of clients who are not ready for change and of those who relapse (Davidson 1998). Indeed, problem denial (pre-contemplation) can be seen as a common state and a potential starting point in the change process.

Stage-matched interventions are said to be more effective than interventions that are not matched to the stages (Prochaska 1995) but there is limited empirical support for this assertion (Littell and Girvin 2002). In sum, the weight of the empirical evidence does not confirm the existence of discrete stages, orderly progression through a sequence of stages, or the benefits of staged-matched interventions. Critics suggest that, like all stage theories, the change model imposes artificial categories on continuous processes (Bandura 1997; Davidson 1998; Sutton 1996). 'Debate has emerged as to whether the descriptive aspects of the model over-simplify or even misrepresent the more complex reality of human change' (Miller and Heather 1998, p.1).

Stage classification is not straightforward in child maltreatment cases. As the developers of the model observed, rarely is there 'a single, well-defined problem … reality is not so accommodating and human behaviour is not so simple… Although we can isolate certain symptoms and syndromes, these occur in the context of complex, interrelated levels of human functioning' (Prochaska and Norcross 1994, p.470). A parent can be pre-contemplating (not thinking about) one issue, contemplating change in another, and making change in a third area related to child maltreatment. People can be simultaneously involved in multiple stages in relation to a single behaviour and single-stage classifications are not accurate (Sutton 1996). Even if we could classify individuals according to change stages, the stage categories have multiple meanings and, hence, would include dissimilar cases. For example, the pre-contemplation category includes clients who deny they have a particular behaviour problem, along with those who acknowledge the problem but are not ready to work on it. These are different issues that call for different intervention strategies. Contemplation covers a wide range of thoughts and intentions, from wishful thinking that things were different to serious consideration of alternatives. Among clients in the action category are those who are making real behavioural changes and those who only say that they are working on their problems.

It is useful to have a framework for gauging the parental response to change efforts and Table 5.3 provides us with one useful option.

TABLE 5.3 POTENTIAL RESPONSES TO CHANGE EFFORTS

Genuine commitment	Tokenism
Parent recognises the need to change and makes real efforts to bring about these changes	Parent will agree with the professionals regarding the required changes but will put little effort into making change work While some changes may occur they will not have required any effort from the parent

Compliance/approval seeking	Dissent/avoidance
Parents will do what is expected of them because they have been told to do it. Change may occur but has not been internalised because the parents are doing without having gone through the process of thinking and responding emotionally to the need for change	Dissent can range from proactively sabotaging efforts to bring about change to passively disengaging from the process The most difficult parents are those who do not admit their lack of commitment to change but work subversively to undermine the process (i.e. sexual abuse perpetrators or perpetrators of Munchausen Syndrome by proxy)

(Horwath and Morrison 2000)

Why many interventions fail

There is too often a failure to consider where families are starting from (probably different from the professionals). Some examples of such problems that impede the appropriate choice and construction of plans include:

▸ Failure to make the purpose explicit: If we fail to make the purpose of the contact explicit, then the worker and the client may have different, even contradictory ideas of what the purpose is and will interpret each other's communications in the light of different ideas. As the subtle distortions continue, the two will be heading in entirely different directions.

▸ Premature change activities: Efforts to effect change will fail where the worker attempts change efforts without clearly understanding what the client wants and whether that change is feasible. Change efforts should be based on the client's understanding of the problem and what they want done about it. To urge change prematurely may create a barrier to communication and can lead to directive approaches that are often ineffective in the absence of trust.

Strengths-based working and over-optimism (Pearson 2013)

Strengths-based work with families has for some time been seen as an extremely useful tool to achieving change. However, as noted above, all families whose children are in their care will have some strengths and some periods where positive progress is seen. It can be easy for these to be assumed to override concerns or to represent a true picture rather than actual family life. The fact that Daniel Pelka attended school appropriately dressed and in clean clothes, that his siblings seemed well cared for and his mother's apparent concern about a fictional 'eating disorder' led professionals not to consider abuse as another reason for his distressing presentation and behaviour (Coventry LSCB 2013).

Parents may demonstrate a good and affectionate relationship with their children, but still not be able to prioritise them over, for example, their drug or alcohol dependence or a relationship with a person who poses a risk to the child. In the case of Baby T (Isle of Wight LSCB 2013) professionals observed what they took to be positive relationships from family with his four year old sister, S. The serious case review in relation to the serious injuries to Baby T and high levels of risk within the family, noted that, 'all records about the children's interactions with them are positive. However, it was evident that the mother often did not know who was caring for S, it was rarely the mother who took her to the early years provision where her attendance was poor' (Isle of Wight LSCB 2013). Fauth et al. (2010) make clear that it is important to understand 'the weight and severity of the evidence to ensure that appropriate action is taken, even when families exhibit positive factors' (p.50).

Motivation

Motivation is defined as 'the probability that a person will enter into, continue, and adhere to a specific change strategy' (Miller and Rollnick 1991, p.19). It is about a state of readiness or eagerness to change, which may fluctuate from one time or situation to another. Moore-Kirkland (1981) argued that motivation is not an attribute of the client but a product of the interaction of client, worker and environment. It is not a characteristic of the client's personality structure or psychological functioning. She argues that by viewing motivation as a transactional concept and a process rather than a trait, we are free to mobilise motivation in such a way as to build on and enhance the competencies of clients in their life experiences (p.28).

A transactional model of motivation enables us to assess several factors in relation to the change effort:

- ▶ Affective arousal: the level of emotional arousal related to the change

- ▶ Directionality: the goals or direction of change/movement

- ▶ The environment: as each person in the change effort perceives it.

None of these factors can individually explain or predict the level of motivation available for accomplishing a given task or for initiating change. Each of the components are interacting, interdependent forces affected and being affected by the others. As such, all components must be considered in assessing the motivation of a system, and each is necessary but not sufficient to explain motivation or to predict if change will occur. If we can identify the reluctant or disabling component, this can become the target for the initial intervention.

Morrison (1991) has argued that motivation comes from the interplay of internal and external factors and it is rarely the case that real change is accomplished only on the basis of personal motivation without the assistance of external reinforcement (p.93).

An alternative way of assessing the parent's motivation for problem solving is to locate them on the following scale. We need to be aware that many parents will not share the same views or the same level of motivation to change, and this should not be overlooked.

A scale for assessing the parent's motivation for problem-solving

- ▶ Shows concern and has realistic confidence:

  - » Parent is concerned about children's welfare; wants to meet their physical, social, and emotional needs to the extent he/she understands them

  - » Parent is determined to act in best interests of children

  - » Parent has realistic confidence that he/she can overcome problems and is willing to ask for help when needed

  - » Parent is prepared to make sacrifices for children.

- ► Shows concern, but lacks confidence:
  - » Parent is concerned about children's welfare and wants to meet their needs, but lacks confidence that problems can be overcome
  - » Parent may be unwilling for some reason to ask for help when needed; feels unsure of own abilities or is embarrassed
  - » Parent uses good judgment whenever he/she takes some action to solve problems.

- ► Seems concerned, but impulsive or careless:
  - » Parent seems concerned about children's welfare and claims he/she wants to meet their needs, but has problems with carelessness, mistakes and accidents; professed concern is often not translated into effective action
  - » Parent may be disorganised, not take enough time, or pays insufficient attention; may misread signals from children; may exercise poor judgment
  - » Parent does not seem to intentionally violate proper parental role; shows remorse.

- ► Indifferent or apathetic about problems:
  - » Parent is not concerned enough about children's needs to resist temptations (e.g. competing demands on time and money); this leads to one or more of the children's needs not being met
  - » Parent does not have the right priorities when it comes to child care; may take a cavalier or indifferent attitude; there may be a lack of interest in the children and in their welfare and development
  - » Parent does not actively reject the parental role.

- ► Rejection of parental role:
  - » Parent actively rejects parental role, taking a hostile attitude toward child care responsibilities

» Parent believes that child care is an imposition, and may ask to be relieved of that responsibility; may take the attitude that it isn't his or her 'job'

» Parent may seek to give up the responsibility for children.

(Magura, Moses and Jones 1987, p.25)

Resilience

Having developed assessment frameworks for risk and resistance it was clear that the notion of resilience needed to be included, as many children, despite the risks and the unwillingness of the parents to redress the concerns, were continuing to thrive. One of the main elements of the Scottish risk assessment approach (Calder, Sneddon and McKinnon 2012) had been the development of a matrix that considers both the positives as well as the negatives for the child to consider when and in what circumstances the development may become impaired. The revised contemporary risk assessment framework thus had three key components shown in Figure 5.5.

Figure 5.5 The 3R approach

The resilience/vulnerability matrix is essential in enabling meaningful analysis and is used to sort information gathered using the key headings of vulnerability, resilience, adversity and protective factors (see Figure 5.6).

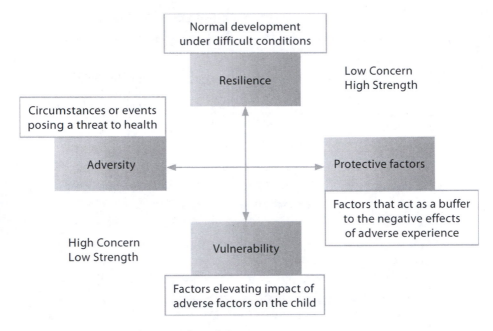

Figure 5.6 Resilience/vulnerability matrix
(Daniel, Wassell and Gilligan 2010)

The concept of resilience is fundamental to children's wellbeing. Many children who need additional help are experiencing difficult conditions. This may relate to their health, their progress at school or what is happening in their family or community. A resilience-based approach builds on the strengths in the child's whole world, always drawing on what the family, community and universal services can offer. Focusing on the positives and the strengths in a child's life is likely to help to improve outcomes by building a protective network around them. At the same time, it is always important to be alert to whether any adversity or vulnerability is putting children's wellbeing at risk and make sure this is taken into account. Home is important but so too is what is going on in the rest of a child's world. School and spare time activities, for example can provide opportunities for enhancing resilience. The existence of protective factors can help to explain why one child may cope better with adverse life events than another. The level of individual resilience can be seen as falling on a dimension of resilience and vulnerability. This dimension is usually used to refer to the intrinsic qualities of an individual. Some children are more intrinsically resilient than others because of a whole range of factors. For example, an easy temperament is associated with resilience in infancy.

A further dimension for the understanding of individual differences is that of protective and adverse environments. This dimension covers extrinsic factors and is therefore located in the parts of the 'My world triangle' (Figure 2.1) that are concerned with wider family, school and community. Examples of protective environment might include a supportive adult in a child's wider world, such as a teacher or youth leader, or a grandparent (Aberdeen Getting it Right Toolkit 2012).

Resilience

Resilience is defined as 'the capacity to transcend adversity – may be seen as a guiding principle when planning for young people whose lives have been disrupted by abuse and or neglect and who may require to be looked after away from home' (Gilligan 1997).

Rutter (1985) identifies three key factors associated with resilience: a sense of self-esteem and confidence, a belief in own self-efficacy and ability to deal with change and adaptation and a repertoire of social problem-solving approaches.

Resilience promotes protective factors that support positive outcomes. It is not solely safeguarding but protecting for growth. The protective factors it addresses are associated with long-term social and emotional wellbeing located at all levels of the young person's ecological social environment. The existence of these factors can help explain why one young person may cope better with adverse life events than another. It well captures the notion that there is no such thing as a child on their own but necessarily there need to be relationships with close carers and others. The effects of these relationships balance the intrinsic qualities of the person along with extrinsic factors.

The International Resilience Project uses a simple checklist of 15 items that indicate resilience (Grotberg 1997):

- ▶ The child has someone who loves him/her totally (unconditionally)
- ▶ The child has an older person outside the home he/she can tell about problems and feelings

- ▶ The child is praised for doing things on his/her own
- ▶ The child can count on her/his family being there when needed
- ▶ The child knows someone he/she wants to be like
- ▶ The child believes things will turn out all right
- ▶ The child does endearing things that make people like her/him
- ▶ The child believes in power greater than seen
- ▶ The child is willing to try new things
- ▶ The child likes to achieve in what he/she does
- ▶ The child feels that what he/she does makes a difference in how things come out
- ▶ The child likes himself/herself
- ▶ The child can focus on a task and stay with it
- ▶ The child has a sense of humour
- ▶ The child makes plans to do things

Resilience is a dynamic process that occurs in a context and is the result of the person in interaction with his or her environment (Rutter 1991). The concept of resilience provides a framework for understanding the varied ways in which some children fare well in the face of adversity. Although definitions of resilience vary, the consensus is that resilient children are those who achieve normal development despite their experience of past or present adversity. Resilience is not only dependent on the characteristics of the individual, but is greatly influenced by interactions and processes arising from the family or the wider environment. Resilience due to social influence may be particularly open to our influence.

Summary of factors associated
with resilience during school years

Individual factors associated with resilience	Family factors associated with resilience	Wider community factors associated with resilience
► Female	► Close bond with at least one person	► Neighbour and other non-kin support
► Sense of competence and self-efficacy	► Nurturance and trust	► Peer contact
► Internal locus of control	► Lack of separations	► Good school experiences
► Empathy with others	► Lack of parental mental health or addiction problems	► Positive adult role models.
► Problem-solving skills	► Required helpfulness	
► Communication skills	► Encouragement for autonomy (girls)	
► Sociable	► Encouragement for expression of feelings (boys)	
► Independent	► Close grandparents	
► Reflective, not impulsive	► Sibling attachment	
► Ability to concentrate on schoolwork	► Four or fewer children	
► Autonomy (girls)	► Sufficient financial and material resources.	
► Emotional expressiveness (boys)		
► Sense of humour		
► Hobbies		
► Willingness and capacity to plan		

(NCERCC/commissioning/resilience paper 1, undated)

Vulnerability

Vulnerability is the opposite of resilience and it is about those factors which threaten development. It is defined as '...those innate characteristics of the child, or those imposed by their family circle and wider community, which might threaten or challenge healthy development' (Daniel, Wassell and Gilligan 2010). Factors that make a child vulnerable include those intrinsic to the child, imposed by parents' views or expectations or arising from the wider family and environment. Vulnerability can be understood as a feature that renders a person more susceptible to negative consequences of adversity. Each individual has their own level of vulnerability and resilience to stressful life events, developed partly as a result of quality of attachments and other factors like individual temperament and community factors. Vulnerability helps our understanding of why some children suffer major adverse reactions to life events while others do not – while some people may fall to pieces at the break up of a relationship others do not. All young people are likely to be vulnerable at some time or other, but many of them will have recourse to protective factors which minimise the chances of poor outcomes (see Table 5.4).

TABLE 5.4 POTENTIAL SOURCES OF VULNERABILITY AND RESILIENCE FACTORS

Resilience	Vulnerability
Good attachment	Poor attachment
Good self-esteem/positive outlook	Young age (under 6)
Goals and aspirations	History of abuse
Sociability. Social networks outside the family/ belonging to organised, out of school activities	Innate characteristics in child/ family that threaten/challenge development
Peer acceptance and friendship	
High IQ (attainment as proxy)	A loner/isolation
Good school experience	Institutional care
Regular attendance at school	Early childhood trauma
Flexible temperament	Communication differences/ problems
Problem-solving skills	
Positive parenting	Inconsistent/neglectful care
Leisure activities	Physical disability/learning disability/behavioural problems
Talents and interests	

Cognitive ability to rationalise drug/alcohol problems in terms of illness	Perceptions of provocative behaviour by child
Being taught different ways of coping and being sufficiently confident to know what to do when parents are incapacitated	Powerless (highly dependent on, and susceptible to, others)
	Defenceless (unable to defend self against aggression)
An ability to separate, either psychologically or physically from the stressful situation	Non-assertive/passive

Adversity

Adversity is defined as 'any influence which increases the probability of onset, progression to a more serious state or maintenance of a problem condition'. (Daniel *et al.* 1999) Adversity is also defined as the experience of life events and circumstances which may combine to threaten or challenge healthy development.

When individuals experience adversities, they adapt, and these adaptations fit the types of adversities they've experienced. For example, being on the alert for the sound of footsteps and the angry utterances of a drunk parent with abusive tendencies will lead children to hide or escape the family home until the drunk person passes out. Such situations can result in hypervigilance, which can be protective when it leads individuals to avoid future frightening and dangerous situations. Children who behave this way are displaying adaptive behaviours whose intent is to ensure at least some wellbeing and even survival. They are coping with and adapting to noxious events.

Protective factors

Whilst a risk factor can be viewed as any influence which increases the probability of onset, or progression to a more serious state or maintenance of a problem condition, a protective factor can be seen as any influence that ameliorates or reduces risk or a problem condition. In contrast to risk factors – protective factors can decrease the probability of high-risk outcomes. Protective factors appear to be the building blocks to resilience. Rutter's (1985) four major protective processes that foster resilience are reducing negative outcomes by altering the risk or the child's exposure to the risk, reducing negative chain reaction following exposure to risk, establishing and maintaining self-esteem and self-efficacy and opening up opportunities. Protective processes work by developing positive self-esteem, an internal locus of control, goal setting abilities and planning behaviour.

Research has shown that children and adolescents who have experienced adversities tend to manage well in a variety of situations if they have engaged in protective processes. These can include a long-term caring relationship with at least one other person with whom they share personal and painful experiences. These persons also model pro-social behaviours that they encourage and reward in younger persons, who, in turn want to emulate these positive persons. The younger persons thus internalise favourable working models of themselves, others, and how the world works. These working models are likely to guide them toward pro-social ways of dealing with other stressors and adversities, or minimally, serve to counteract inner working models that channel thoughts, emotions, and behaviours toward destructive actions. Unfortunately, it is difficult if not impossible, to determine which protective factors are causally related to which risk factors. The pattern of little effect for one risk variable applies (unfortunately) also for protective factors, thus, we need to move beyond looking at single protective factors to examining overall processes that foster adaptive functioning.

Summary of factors relating to adversity and protective factors

Adversity	Protective factors
Life events/crisis	One consistent supportive adult
Illness/loss/ bereavement	A mentor or trusted adult with whom the child is able to discuss sensitive issues
Separation/family breakdown	Supportive older sibling
	Special help with behavioural problems
Domestic violence	Community networks
Asylum seeking status	Sympathetic, empathic and vigilant teachers
	Sufficient income support and good physical standards in the home
Serious parental difficulties (e.g. drug abuse/alcohol misuse)	Practical and domestic help
	Regular, long-term support for the family from services

Parental mental illness	Parent acknowledges the difficulties and is able to access and accept treatment
Bullied	An alternative, safe and supportive residence for mothers subject to violence and the threat of violence
	Regular medical and dental checks including school medicals
	Factual information about puberty, sex and contraception

Sample questions to gather the required information (Calder, Sneddon and McKinnon 2012)

RESILIENCE

Child	Parent	Environment
Does the child have a significant or primary attachment figure?	Do the parents/carers show evidence of unresolved childhood trauma?	Are there longstanding concerns across the wider family?
Has the child experienced repeated change of placement?	Are the family in continual crisis?	Are new interventions creating new problems for the child or family?
Has it been possible to contain/ work with the child's reactive behaviours?	Is this a family seeking asylum?	Currently and historically is there no willingness or potential to overcome adversity?
Is the child presenting with abusive behaviours?	Are the parents/carers isolated from their culture/community of origin?	
Does the child present with unpredictable behaviours?	Do the parents/carers have a long history of untreatable substance misuse or mental health problems?	
Is there evidence of the child's coping strategies?	Are multiple risk factors present such as mental health, conflict between parents/carers/other family members, alcohol, criminality (consideration needs to be given to the accumulative impact of these factors on the parent/ carer's ability to care for their child)?	
Are there more than four children in the home?		

Vulnerability

Child	Parent	Environment
Was this an unwanted child/difficult birth?	Is there evidence of parental problems such as domestic violence, addiction, mental health problems, poverty?	Does the family have access to community resources or support groups?
Has the child been previously abused or neglected?	Were the parents/carers abused as children?	Has the family experienced racism or other isolating factors?
Does the child demonstrate behaviour problems – poor sleep pattern, difficult feeder, difficulties around toilet training	Is there evidence of a poor partner relationship or is there a history of multiple partners?	Does the family have financial difficulties?
Is this an asylum seeking child/is the child being detained or in an immigration center?	Is this a single parent household?	Does the family have poor/unsuitable housing?
Was the child born at a time of crisis?	Is the parent/carer under 20 years of age or immature?	Is the family home overcrowded?
Is there evidence that the child resembles a hated partner or spouse?	Does the parent/carer have unrealistic expectations of the child?	Does the family lack extended family support?
Was the child born with developmental impairments, or disabilities that developed post birth?	Does the parent/carer have a criminal record?	Does the family have poor support networks?
Is the child very young and dependent on the parent/carer?	Is the family living in social chaos?	Is the family homeless?
Is there evidence of the child experiencing insecure attachments?	Are the parents asylum seeking/being held in detention/living here illegally?	Is the family residing in a detention centre/secure accommodation?
Does the child find it hard to make and keep friends?		

Adversity

Child	Parent	Environment
No significant or primary attachment figure	Evidence of unresolved childhood trauma	Long-standing concerns across wider family
Repeated changes of placement	Living in recurrent and/or constant crisis	Interventions create new problems for child or family
No capacity to contain or work with the child's reactive behaviour	Asylum status	Currently and historically no willingness or potential to overcome adversity
Child presenting with abusive behaviours	Isolated from culture/community of origin	
Unstable unpredictable presenting behaviour	Longstanding untreatable substance misuse or mental health problems	
Evidence of coping strategies	Multiple risk factors present	
More than four children in the home		

Protective factors

Child	Parent	Environment
Does the child keep good health?	Does the parent/carer demonstrate motivation to change?	Can the child/parent/carer access appropriate services?
Does the child have a positive self-esteem?	Does parent/carer accept responsibility for problems and a willingness to receive help?	Is there evidence of a supportive extended family?
Is this an older child?		Is there regular contact with extended family?
Does the child have an outgoing temperament?	Does the parent/carer have mental health problems which are responsive to treatment?	Does the parent/carer have access to good child care?
Does the child demonstrate self-control?		
Does the child have a different status than other siblings in the home?	Has the parent/carer been a victim of abuse?	Does the parent/carer have access to volunteer networks?
Is the child able to take action to keep self-safe?	Has the parent/carer overcome their own childhood abuse?	Does the family have good social support?
Does the child have clear and functional coping strategies?	Does the parent/carer demonstrate effective parenting?	Do the family live in a safe and secure neighbourhood?

cont.

Child	Parent	Environment
Does the child have a good relationship with siblings?	Is there a history of domestic abuse?	Is there evidence of family cohesion?
Does the child attend school or nursery regularly?	Is there evidence that the parent carer has capacity for change?	Do the family have access to adequate health care and education resources?
Does the child attend out of school activities?	Do you consider the parent/carer to be an adequate parent who is resilient and a good parental role model?	Is the family settled in their home?
	Are there relatively few sources of stress?	Is there a history of previous professional support?
	Does the parent/carer reject the perpetrator?	Do the family have sufficient income and good physical living standards?
	Is the parent/carer supported by partner?	
	Is there evidence of a cohesive parental relationship?	
	Does the parent/carer have the ability to separate positive from disruptive behaviour?	
	Was the parent/carer's own childhood positive?	

A resilience matrix for analysing information

Figure 5.10 offers a simple blank matrix that allows workers to plot their findings to allow a visual picture of what they have found as a preface to considering the weighting required.

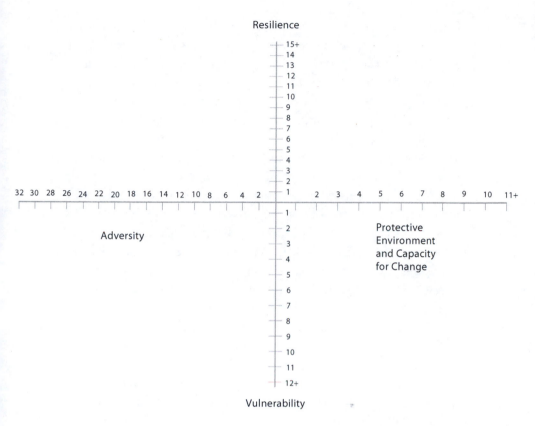

Figure 5.7 Blank risk matrix

The content of the two axes are dynamic and will change over time. The impact of various risk and protective factors at various points in life changes – someone resilient at one stage in life may not be at the next. Someone may be resilient in one area (developmental domain) but not in another. Children's resilience will be affected by what happens to the adults with whom they live. It will, therefore, be important to try to predict how changes in the adults may affect the children. A good example would be kinship care. A grandparent may agree to take on a child but the circumstances could be influenced by future events, such as the ease of management of contact visits from parents. Or a grandparent may have underestimated the pressure that a young child would bring to the household emotionally and financially. Predicting possible trajectories for a child will help to make sure contingencies are built in to preserve a child's protective environment. If these contingencies are not considered, a child's resilience could be weakened by subsequent adverse events.

There are some factors which may be both protective and also suggest vulnerability or adversity (e.g. removing an abuser from a domestic violence situation may be protective to both mother and child but can result in poverty which increases adversity). In making decisions about where to plot this information, where the meanings may be not so straightforward, practitioners need to exercise judgment in making sense of these different aspects of information and weigh the competing influences. Judgment will be needed to weigh which factors are most important. It will also be helpful to look at the interactions between factors as this may influence whether the impact is negative or positive.

Once these judgments have been made, it will be possible to see what needs to be done to help the child and family in order to strengthen protective factors and resilience, and reduce adversity and vulnerabilities. Achieving small improvements is a good way to accumulate success rather than having overambitious aims.

Having plotted the factors on the matrix and given some thought to the child's needs, the desired outcomes for this child should be plotted against the eight Scottish wellbeing indicators of: safe, healthy, achieving, nurtured, active, respected, responsible and included. Action may be needed against only some or against every indicator but the help has to be proportionate to the issues identified (Aberdeen Getting it Right Toolkit 2012).

Figure 5.7 indicated the likely consequences under consideration with a clear indication on what needs to happen next. Children who are vulnerable in situations of continuing adversity are likely to require a child protection response whilst those in the resilience–protective factor quadrant are likely to only require universal provision. The resilience matrix offers all agencies a useful tool to consider where a child may be, and to anticipate harm rather than simply reacting to it as many thresholds invite.

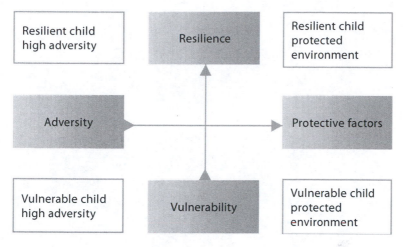

Figure 5.8 Outcome indicators

An integrated contemporary risk assessment framework

The progression of the risk framework over a decade has seen it expand from assessing risk, to assessing resistance and factoring in resilience considerations. It has also seen a fundamental shift from risk being a social work exclusive activity to it being a multi-agency activity. It is a reflection of the growing complexity of casework and the need to build capacity to respond, the need to try and stem the reactive responses and become more proactive (and hopefully preventive). Many cases held currently as child-in-need cases are in reality yesteryear's child protection. It is also in recognition that staff who fear risk assessment frequently have the capacity to harvest the richest crop of information to populate the required risk framework.

Figure 5.9 offers a visual representation of the integrated contemporary risk assessment framework. I am currently working to develop more substantive and specific assessment materials and guidance to support early help with troubled families, and in so doing introducing accessible, more succinct and user-friendly guidance to thresholds for service accessibility with a greater clarity on respective roles and responsibilities.

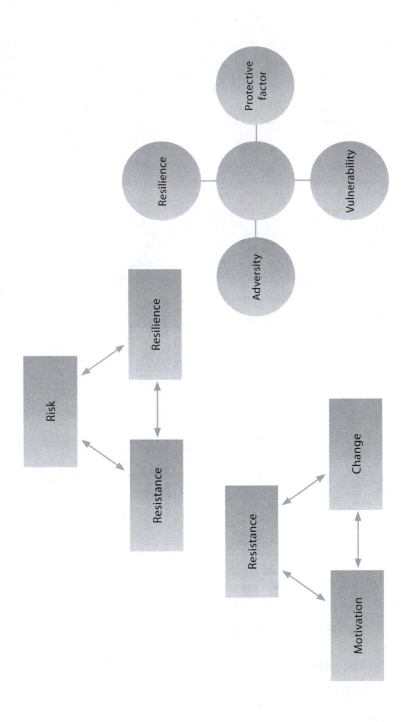

Figure 5.9 Evidence-based risk indicators

The book series will then shift the generic risk framework into more specific areas to capture the complexity and required depth of the cases currently being worked.

Shifting risk to an interagency audience

Calder, Sneddon and McKinnon (2012) were commissioned by the Scottish Government to take RASSAMM to a new audience, as the numerous problems set out in this book have resulted in a wide range of child protection cases not crossing the threshold into child protection. The difficulties of allocating child protection work to anyone not holding a social work qualification has compounded the problem, as cases are frequently downgraded to family support – children in need.

In reviewing a wide range of risk factors, we produced a number of indicator checklists that can be used by other agencies to recognise risks through their observations and knowledge of the child and their family. Although they may feel that risk is outside their remit, because of the demise of the signs and symptoms of different types of abuse in central guidance post-Munro, the checklists prove a useful prompt for naming concerns and communicating them effectively to social care staff:

▸ **Child considerations**

» Developmental delay

» Mental health difficulties

» Learning disabilities

» Behavioural difficulties

» Difficult temperament

» Premature birth/low birth weight/early prolonged separation at birth

» Babies born with drug/substance withdrawal

» Very young – highly dependent – under five years old

» Cries frequently, difficult to comfort

» Difficulties in feeding/toileting

» Severity of abuse/harm and impact on child

» Repeat victim

» Fearful of parent or caregiver

» Large number of children in family

» Periods of separation from parents/primary caregiver

» Direct or indirect exposure to domestic violence

» Adopted, fostered or stepchild

» Historical abuse of siblings by carers

» Engaging in self-harm

» Involved in substance misuse

» Out of parental control

» Antisocial behaviour/relationships

» Poor school attendance

» Demonstrating sexually inappropriate behaviour

» Child is perpetrator of abuse

» Subject to statutory/child protection interventions

» Illness requiring ongoing medical treatment

» Young carer

» Meaning of child for parents dominates their relationship

» Child's account is minimised or not believed

» Child not seen or given chance to talk to workers

» English is not first language of child/parent

▶ **Parents /caregivers**

» Poor understanding of child's needs and development

» Unrealistic expectations of child

» Unable or unwilling to meet child's needs

» Poor attachment

» Antisocial, sadistic or aggressive behaviour

» Hostile/resistant parent/carer/family

- » Lack of compliance or engagement
- » Refuses access to child
- » Parents colluding
- » No shared understanding of concerns
- » Minimisation of concerns in relation to injury or incident
- » High stress levels such as poverty, isolation, loss
- » Parents' experiences of being parented was poor/abusive
- » Low self-esteem/poor identity
- » History of multiple relationships
- » Communication difficulties
- » Limited life skills and problem solving abilities
- » Poor impulse control
- » Lack of trust
- » Parental psychopathology
- » Evidence of rejection or critical behaviour
- » Previous history of harm towards children
- » Violent or poor self-control
- » Pre-meditated harm/abuse
- » Evidence of grooming/control of the child
- » Unwilling/unable to protect the child
- » History of violence
- » Violence in past relationships
- » Rigid authoritarian attitude
- » Deceitful or secretive
- » Alleged perpetrator remains in household
- » Number and frequency of visitors to family home is unknown
- » Breaches of legal orders/agreements – legal and civil
- » Carer defers to partner for response

» Physical illness which impairs parenting ability

» Partner is not biological parent of child

» New partners whose background is unknown

▶ **Child/parent interaction**

» Poor relationship with parents

» Lack of empathy for the child

» Adult prioritises own needs over child's

» Lack of interest in child and insensitive to their needs

» Repeated rejection, threats or requests for child to be placed in alternative care

» Child perceived as difficult by parent

» Attributing negative attitudes and labels to child's behaviour

▶ **Social and environment**

» Extended family stressors

» Social isolation and loneliness

» Lack of/or absence of social supports

» Physical or psychological isolation

» Multiplicity of problems

» Highly mobile families

» Home environment chaotic, hazardous or unsafe

» Chaotic sleeping arrangements – child/adult

» Emotional stressors (conflict, finance, illness)

» Separation conflict

» Family misuse substances

» Discrimination

» Conflicts of family honour

» Unwillingness or inability to deviate from cultural norms

» Child cared for away from home

» Unconvincing, superficial compliance

» Poor engagement with universal services – health and education

» Failing to make proper use of support services

» Concerns relate to all children

» Dangerous, violent and unsupportive neighbourhood

► **Professional considerations**

» Lack of resources

» Limited agency understanding of concerns

» Limited service response

» Service interventions do not effect positive change

» Family fear of anxieties about professional intervention

» Inexperienced staff

» Inadequate opportunity for staff supervision and reflection

» Working in isolation

» Unquestioning acceptance of explanations and self-reporting

» Difficulties in challenging cultural, racial, religious practices or beliefs

» Fear of over or under reacting

» Listening to carers rather than children

» Lack of understanding of professional roles – individual/ interagency

» Insufficient contact with family and child

» Poor recording

» Failure to critically challenge, review family circumstances within and across agencies

» Performance driven practice over practice driven performance.

═════════ **Key messages from the chapter** ═════════

This chapter has offered a comprehensive contemporary risk assessment framework that embraces risk, resistance and resilience and related areas.

It offers an optimally desirable risk template with a pick and mix approach given timescales and work pressures.

However, the more gaps in the assessment completed the greater the chances of error – snapshots are dangerous and rarely representative.

Depth and time are key, as well as the cross checking of information with other professionals involved.

It is important that workers have some understanding of different uses for words, different professional focus and assessment tools when receiving information to ensure correct and shared interpretation.

The assessment requires a coordinated multi-disciplinary approach.

Keeping the child as the central focus is key, as is eliciting their wishes and feelings in the context of the home environment and understanding of relationships and norms.

CHAPTER 6

Good Practice in Section 47 Inquiries

Julie Archer

Introduction and context setting

The complex nature of social work cannot be underestimated, and for practitioners within both police and social work the effective protection of those at risk of significant harm has to be achieved in an ever-changing sociopolitical context. Even the briefest of histories takes us through the early work of entirely separate agencies; through the development of joint police and social work training and the introduction of the *Memorandum of Good Practice* (Home Office and DoH 1992), later updated by *Achieving Best Evidence* (Ministry of Justice 2011); the development of child abuse investigations teams within the police; the introduction of the refocusing debate and the introduction of the assessment of need and the disappearance of risk from the agenda.

Social work has been reorganised to reflect the separation of assessment and care management: the development of joint investigation teams; the introduction of the assessment framework; the Climbié inquiry and the move of the police away from joint working with social care; the further separation of referral teams from assessment through the development of the Multi Agency Screening Hub (MASH) referral centres; many updates of the core guidance *Working Together* (DH 2006); the single assessment; the impact of the Rotherham inquiry in response to child sexual exploitation; and of many other serious case reviews during that time. And of course the impact of the current financial climate, which requires both police and social care to be ever more efficient and effective – and all of this with potentially devastating consequences for anyone caught up in the media frenzy when things go wrong. All of these changes and trends influence what happens and how organisations respond to vulnerable children and somehow, in this ever-changing context, social workers need to be able to respond consistently and robustly to establish which children have suffered significant harm and whether it is likely to occur again. Munro (2010) suggests that we need to be more forensic in our approach. What does a more forensic investigation look and feel like and how can we make that fit with services that are geared up to offer an assessment of need? This chapter will attempt to explore some of the issues facing practitioners in this field and to apply the stepwise process as a model for effective practice. It is written with the legislation and guidance for England and Wales in mind, but many of the practice issues and suggestions will have much wider application.

Issues to consider

Section 47 of The Children Act 1989, is it an inquiry or investigation? Seeing the child and legal framework, the application of the Achieving Best Evidence Guidance, criminal processes, and differing thresholds and points to prove in law.

Legal framework

I am often asked whether a section 47 is an inquiry or an investigation. I generally respond with inquiry as Section 47 of the Children Act 1989 refers to the duty that a local authority has to make inquiries where there is a suspicion that a child may or has suffered significant harm. The real question is whether it matters and whether there is a difference. A simple dictionary definition (*Oxford English Dictionary*) suggests that inquiry means 'the act of asking for information' and investigation means 'formal or systematic examination or research'. So whilst the difference is subtle, it is actually quite significant. Since these terms fit with the notion that early in the referral process we are inquiring, that is asking questions about whether the child's welfare is safeguarded, and that when we reach a threshold which suggests that a child may not be safe we need to investigate the child's circumstances more formally and systematically, and thus the decision is reached that a case has crossed the threshold into a child protection investigation. There are formal points at which this decision-making is made (all referrals require a managerial decision and outcome within 48 hours) and within the strategy discussion consideration should be given as to whether inquiries should be made under Section 47. The use of the phrase 'child protection investigation' is generally fairly easily understood by all parties, although it is a phrase that can create much anxiety for parents and children. For me, the key issue is not which label (investigation or inquiry) we should apply, but that we undertake the task in a systematic and purposeful way, that we are clear about the reasons some referrals cross the threshold and that we make best use of the knowledge and frameworks for helping to identify risk factors and thresholds (Warner 2003; Thorpe and Bilson 1998) so that decision-making is clear, consistent and accountable.

In order to be effective within a child protection investigation social workers need a clear understanding of the legal framework within which we operate. When practitioners understand this, it builds confidence and enables them to use their authority appropriately and effectively and to challenge practice and decisions that may be contrary to best practice. Not fully understanding is tantamount to building on dry sand. Weak foundations inevitably fall down at some point. However, in reality, the legal framework is not simple and each step is a series of small decisions that result in the overall picture. All too often our natural human desire to simplify things (Kahneman 2012) results in practitioners and managers erroneously thinking that Section 17 means with consent and Section 47 means without consent. A simple question by which we can illustrate this is to ask whether or not the child can be seen without the knowledge or consent of the caregiver. Most practitioners will answer with a confident yes, ask them to tell you what the legal basis for that decision is and uncertainty and a loss of confidence are immediately apparent. The reality is that whilst the question is simple, the answer in legal terms is not. The practitioner and manager must consider as a minimum, whether the threshold for suspicion of significant harm has been met, who has parental responsibility, whether the parents' action in withholding consent is reasonable, whether the actions of the local authority are reasonable, proportionate and justifiable, the age and ability of any child to be involved in decision-making, and whether delay or seeking consent will put the child at greater risk of harm. Finally, just when we have perhaps reached a decision to see a child without consent, we are faced with the contradictions contained within *Achieving Best Evidence* (Ministry of Justice 2011) that on the one hand 'the child may in exceptional circumstances be seen without the consent or knowledge of the caregiver' and that without consent 'the interview cannot take place. A strategy discussion between the police and social services should consider whether it is appropriate to make an application for an Emergency Protection Order (EPO)'. All this while the clock ticks via the Police and Criminal Evidence Act (PACE) or local authority expectations about seeing the child within a given timescale. So, practitioners and their managers need to not only know the answer, but also to be able to understand and apply the complexities of the legal framework in practice, under pressure, and record it to a standard that will satisfy any legal redress.

Furthermore, we have in operation two key organisations who operate from very different legal perspectives and thresholds. Social Care operate within the civil framework where the burden of proof is 'on the balance of probability' and the Police operate within the criminal framework where the burden of proof is 'beyond all reasonable doubt'. The confusion of these two thresholds is nowhere more sadly illustrated than in the inquiry into the death of Peter Connolly:

> The panel concludes that nothing less than injuries that were non-accidental beyond all reasonable doubt would have caused him to be moved to a place of safety. When such injuries did occur they were catastrophic, and he died of them.

The challenge for practitioners is to better understand each other's legal context and to make judgments about a child's wellbeing and safety from an arena in which ambiguity and uncertainty prevail in a climate where managers, the courts, the public and the media increasingly want proof beyond all reasonable doubt. The best practitioners and managers recognise this and are able to resist the distortion that this creates and work with ambiguity and uncertainty to rule differing possibilities in/

out, resulting in finely balanced judgments. The best practitioners understand that all offences have points to prove in law, and that being unable to evidence them does not mean that something harmful did not occur, but that we must use the evidence we have to safeguard the child as best we can.

════════════════════ Issues to consider ════════════════════

Does the context operate in such a manner that it pushes us towards creating more hostility and resistance than engagement? What does it really take to engage families in the Section 47 process, can it really be achieved? And what are the risks in trying to achieve it? Who else do we need to engage (other agencies) and are we really effective at it?

Engagement, hostility and resistance

Stop and think for a moment about a time when someone made (or tried to make) you do something you didn't want to do; connect for one moment with the sheer frustration, rage even, about that loss of control over your own life, and we begin to understand that 'hostility and resistance' are not labels to be applied, but in fact are a really natural human response to a stressful situation beyond one's control. Whilst research (Fauth *et al.* 2010) struggles to define hostility and resistance, as practitioners in our day-to-day conversations and thinking (if not our recordings), we use these labels to describe some of our service users. Underpinning such views and behaviour is the challenge of trying to empower and engage parents and their children in a complex process, whilst remaining authoritative in our practice in an uncertain and ambiguous context.

Children and their families may be fearful of the good intentions of social workers, as well as influenced by their media portrayal, but somehow, together we have worked effectively to keep the child safe and at the heart of our practice. For a parent, to be introduced to social workers who are concerned that their child may be 'at risk of significant harm', it is a potentially catastrophic moment. It takes real skill from practitioners to introduce themselves within a Section 47 inquiry:

to properly explain the process in terms that can be understood by adults and children who are at their most vulnerable; to explain their rights and the rights of the child and obtain informed consent from both parents and children without sharing any information that may compromise the inquiry or criminal investigation; whilst monitoring the worker's own and the child's safety, and recognising that some adults and children will struggle to develop trusting relationships and may consequently lie or withhold the truth; and all of this before the bell for the end of the school day or in time to do a medical examination. The best practitioners understand that these are not labels, but they are behaviours in a context, which make sense at the time, and that to be effective we must persist with empathy and authority and without minimising the risks to the child and to ourselves as professionals. In order to achieve this at the very minimum we need to understand the complexities of the process and the psychological exchange, and to take all possible action to crate an arena in which it is safe enough to explore risk, uncertainty, harm and ambiguity. We might look like we are knocking on the door armed only with our powers of persuasion and a diary, but the best practitioners are juggling so much more.

Issues to consider

The need to understand the difference between an inquiry and an investigation and to be confident about your use of power and authority. The ability to focus on finding out what happened and whether significant harm has/is likely to occur whilst simultaneously assessing the broader need of the child and family. How do we manage the anxiety that runs like a vein through the child protection process without becoming authoritarian or permissive? How do we effectively change hats when moving from Section 17 to Section 47 – managing those initial early conversations with children, families and professionals to ensure that they understand and can participate in the process.

Role clarity and purpose

Morrison (2005) describes six factors leading to good outcomes, starting with role clarity, leading to role security and emotional competence and empathy. This model is helpful in understanding how critical it is that social workers are clear about their role. It is not sufficient to know that you are there as a social worker, often there will be complex negotiations about the balance of power and the roles of others, such as the police and medical staff other local authority practitioners. It is not unusual that the worker has been visiting the family wearing a different hat (family support, disability social worker, fostering supervisor), all of which carry subtle differences in the way they are perceived by children, families, carers and professionals, and the worker now has to review and re-establish their role within a different legal framework. That shift in framework has an impact on the power dynamics, and unless the worker is absolutely clear about the difference, about what can and cannot be shared, and about the basis of their authority, they cannot act with any degree of clarity. A moment of uncertainty or confusion can leave the door open for service users to take control in a manner that is detrimental to the safety of the child – after all, this is a terrifying situation for a parent who will do whatever they think it takes at that time to reduce the perceived threat. Without the role security and confidence that come from role clarity, the worker's ability to act authoritatively will be compromised. 'Role security is established when the worker's confusions, anxieties and dilemmas can be brought to supervision and resolved thus providing the secure base from which the practitioner goes out to undertake the practice task' (Morrison 2005, p.57).

All of this takes place in a potentially compromised context in which speed/timescales can inhibit the opportunities for dealing with those uncertainties. In reality, most social workers learn how to do Section 47 investigations through observed practice or as a second worker and it is possible for them to appear competent and confident through copying without understanding the practice of others. We must ensure that we build in to the process the opportunity to explore uncertainty and ambiguity, as well as that which may seem obvious to more experienced practitioners/managers.

Issues to consider

WT guidance, single/joint or parallel, making strategy discussions effective, links to managerial oversight, effective co-working.

Investigative strategy

Working Together (HM Government 2015) provides the statutory guidance requiring social care, the police and health professionals to discuss all cases where significant harm is suspected. As guidance, it gives a reasonable framework to follow in terms of what should be considered. The challenge in practice is to make it a discussion that is actually helpful to the investigation. All too often, opportunities are missed early on to clarify understanding, and errors that could have been avoided are there from the outset. For example, there is a lack of clarity about the initial referral, so agreement is reached that social care will 'go and have a look' and come back and let the police know what happened. Whilst potentially, in many cases that might be the right strategy, the opportunity has been missed to jointly assess initial risks (to children and staff): to share an understanding about the legal basis for intervention, including whether or not consent will be required for any aspect of the investigation; to share an understanding about whether the threshold has been reached and why; to hypothesise about possibilities generating potential new lines of inquiry; to agree what will and won't be shared with various family members; to agree ways to ask about concerns without asking leading or suggestive questions; to consider possible criminal offences and raise awareness of possible points to prove; to identify what is not known and agree how to fill the gaps; to identify what unique factors need to be taken into consideration for this child and family (culture, language, communication method, routines, impact of medication, etc.); and, of course, whether the investigation should be single or joint.

Considering whether an investigation should be single or joint has the potential to oversimplify the process. In reality, there are only a very few situations in which there is no role for the police (perhaps in a few cases of emotional abuse where other concerns have not been identified, and even those could be considered under wilful ill-treatment). In all other situations of suspected significant harm, there is almost always a possible crime to be investigated. In fact, since the Rotherham inquiry into child sexual exploitation (CSE), the police have lost any discretion they may once have had not to investigate a possible crime, yet those which result in a joint investigation are still a relatively small number of cases; and this may be more about the availability of staff than the needs of the investigation. However, there is another way to look at this, that of two parallel investigations. Social care are investigating whether significant harm has occurred, the police investigating whether a crime has occurred. Each will hold information that needs to be shared and some tasks may need to be done jointly. Some tasks are better done by one skill set (e.g. formal video statement from children is often better led by the police who practice this interview style regularly and understand the range of possible offences and points to prove), so the two investigations happen in parallel, avoiding duplication and repetition, with each understanding and respecting the other's legal framework and context. This is a much more subtle way of co-working effectively, rather than simply identifying as joint, those cases which require a police officer and social worker to jointly interview a child or carer.

There are also inconsistencies within both organisations about who conducts strategy discussions. In some authorities only a team manager/sergeant undertakes them, in others social workers and police officers do. This in itself can create challenges. If managers and sergeants hold the discussions, the staff actually doing a joint visit/investigation may miss out on critical planning discussions, and without managerial input, decisions about resources and thresholds may not be consistently made. The creation of co-located police, social work and health teams responsible for multi-agency assessment and screening (MAST) or multi-agency safeguarding teams or hubs (MASH) has real potential to allow for the development of effective use of the strategy discussion, however, it is essential that they remain meaningful and do not become a tick box exercise with a template to complete that becomes a greater priority than the effective communication and understanding required within a child protection investigation.

It can be really helpful within the strategy discussion to encourage everyone to suggest different explanations for how 'x' may have happened or what might be happening within the family. This can help generate lines of inquiry that can be explored during the investigation. For example, points to clarify with paediatricians, photos/observations of the home environment (cots, seats/chairs, play mats, furnishings, etc.);

issues to be explored within parent/carer interviews. However, at this early point during an investigation, we should be seeking explanations about what is happening from parents, rather than offering possibilities to them.

One of the challenges for social workers is that of how to raise concerns without contaminating evidence, and again, the strategy discussion is the place to identify appropriate phrasing, as it will have the benefit of the police understanding about the rules of evidence for criminal law. Equally, whatever is agreed has to be sufficiently detailed so that the social worker is not required to be overly vague or dishonest. For example, if you are talking to the parents of a child with a serious injury and the parental explanation is absent or vague it can be helpful to say:

'So what we have here is a serious injury with a discrepant explanation (Dale *et al.* 2002), we need to consider all the possible ways that this could have occurred, lets start with what you (Mum/Dad) think...'

Having established their explanation (and written it down) we can then explain that our role is to consider ALL possible explanations, and ask them to say what the other possibilities are that we have to consider (many parents will know that we have to consider the possibility that they may have caused it) – this allows us to have this conversation without getting into a polarised position about truth/denial. We can move from there to consider any other possible explanations (e.g. medical, family views, etc.) so that the parent understands that we have written down all the possibilities and that our investigation will explore them all.

NB: When using this approach, plan for it within the strategy discussion as there may be a possibility that the police may want to interview parents prior to you having a conversation of this nature.

Issues to consider

How do we avoid common errors in assessment and follow a process that supports robust 'forensic' style assessment? How do we ensure that the investigative process respects difference? How does stepwise fit with the government guidance in Working Together 2015 and The Single Assessment? How can we ensure that the investigation is culturally informed and that children who are disabled have a voice in the investigation?

Investigative process and the links to stepwise

It would be easy to assume that if we followed the neat flowcharts within *Working Together* (HM Government 2015) the process would be clear. However, the guidance really only covers the key investigative stages and the content of a strategy discussion, which is as intended, guidance, rather than a rigid and prescriptive step-by-step protocol. Unfortunately, the only thing to fill the gap is the assessment guidance and that in itself is insufficient for a child protection investigation. What we need therefore, is a framework that supports the use of professional judgment, encourages a systematic and forensic approach to investigation, promotes robust assessment and meets the needs of children and families with a wide range of needs and from a diverse range of ethnic minorities.

There is a vast amount of literature which guides and promotes social workers and police officers in working with minority ethnic children, families and communities. The challenge is in translating this into practice that respects difference and uses power appropriately whilst keeping the child's safety at the heart of the investigation. Useful guidance can be found on the Bolton Safeguarding Children Board website,[1] which suggests 12 key practice issues to consider when working with difference, and reminds us that 'All communities value and love their children. All communities want to teach their children how to participate and prosper in the world'.

The cultural review (McCracken 1998 in CWDC 2009) is also a useful tool in encouraging practitioners to challenge assumptions and think about where their knowledge comes from. Some of these questions can usefully find their way into the planning stage or strategy discussion.

For children with learning or communication difficulties, special attention will need to be paid in the planning stages to the needs of the child, their understanding and the most effective means of obtaining a first account from them. Any interview, whether or not it is to be video recorded, will require detailed preparation and it may be appropriate to use a trained intermediary (Ministry of Justice 2011) or interpreter (e.g. British Sign Language (BSL), or the use of specific tools such as 'In My

---

1   http://boltonsafeguardingchildren.org.uk/documents/2013/10/bscb-annual-report-2011-2012.pdf

Shoes'.[2] *Achieving Best Evidence in Criminal Proceedings* (Ministry of Justice 2011) provides some guidance about the preparation and assessment of child witnesses. The challenge in practice is in ensuring that those with the knowledge about the child's communication and understanding are fully involved in the planning and interviewing of the child. In many organisations specialist workers for children with disabilities may operate in a different context to their child protection colleagues, with the consequence that they do not always have the familiarity with the investigative process nor the relationships with their colleagues in the police. The solution is not to remove the investigation from specialist disability teams as this will leave investigators floundering with a lack of knowledge about disability but to ensure that the three strands of practice wisdom (disability, child protection and criminal investigations) are knitted together so that the child can have a voice within the investigative process.

If we consider that a Section 47 is an assessment (of the nature of harm and the likelihood of recurrence) we must also attend to what is known from research about common errors in assessment and human reasoning. Munro (1999) analyses those common errors and identifies themes around failing to revise assessments, failing to use all available evidence and failing to check facts and information. An alternative framework for investigations, that allows us to operate within the *Working Together* (HM Government 2015) guidance and to build in strategies to avoid some of the common pitfalls is the stepwise model (Raynes 2003). A suggested adaptation is given in Table 6.1. This framework includes a more thorough and conscious planning and hypothesising, which naturally results in better quality information gathering and the testing of hypotheses, all of which support good practice and help workers avoid common errors in assessment.

---

2   www.inmyshoes.org.uk/In_My_Shoes/Introduction.html

TABLE 6.1 THE STEPWISE APPROACH TO ASSESSMENT
ADAPTED FOR SECTION 47 INVESTIGATIONS

> **Plan**
Purpose of assessment, timescale, how will family members be engaged
and empowered in the process? What is the role of the police/social worker,
single or joint investigation, how will information sharing be managed (what
can and can't be shared)? strategy discussion, tasks and responsibilities,
communication, access to consultation, consent and legal status. What are
the risks to the child and staff? How will staff safety be managed? How will
the timing of child, and carer interviews be managed? Is a medical likely to be
needed?

> **Hypothesise**
About all the possibilities. Be clear about the possibility of deliberate harm and
the likelihood that family members may be likely to want to obscure the truth
and present their best selves. How will assumptions be avoided? Ensure that
when hypothesising we really think about the possibilities (e.g. what are the
possible ways this double fracture to the radius and ulna could have occurred?).
Use the forum of the strategy discussion to do some hypothesising as this may
generate new lines of inquiry and new tasks with the investigation. Consider
the different possible meanings of what a child is alleged to have said, and the
meaning of any previous allegations or retractions (it is incredibly powerful
to acknowledge, for example, within a strategy meeting, that a child who
has previously retracted an allegation of sexual abuse has not lied – they just
became overwhelmed or were coerced and this led to the need to 'un-say it')

> **Gather information**
Always do a genogram and include the father even if he is not known; he
still needs to be identified and included, and any decision to restrict his
involvement must be conscious and deliberate, rather than unconscious or
based on assumptions.
Gather information about all siblings and family members not just the
index child. Make questions to other agencies as open and curious as possible
in order to obtain the information they have not realised is relevant. Ask each
agency to provide a chronology and combine them to look for patterns.
Other agencies – what do they need to be asked, how will they be
engaged?
Take care to bring depth and breadth to questioning – for example, if the
referral does not mention substance misuse, domestic violence or parental
mental ill health we should still make inquiries about these given the high rate
of occurrence in cases of significant harm (Brandon *et al.* 2008)
Complete checks of the child protection register, MARAC, MAPPA,
voluntary domestic abuse services (many women will access these services
long before they come to the attention of police and social care) and substance
misuse agencies, etc.
How will the child's views be sought? Where and when will we talk to
them? Take the time to plan the interview (however briefly) regardless of
where and when it takes place. Who, where and when will parents/carers be
interviewed; again plan the interview using the same adapted *Achieving Best
Evidence* (Ministry of Justice 2011) structure as for children

> ► **Test information**
> Checking back, what evidence is there to confirm hypotheses? What new hypotheses are emerging? Review the quality of the information, look for:
> » Information from more than one source (beware the same information from multiple sources, that is not the same as multiple sources)
> » Patterns and history
> » Different types of information (observation, child's own words, agency records)

> ► **Analyse information**
> Use of supervision, consultation and reflection. Challenge bias and assumption and the over reliance on instinct or a disconnect with the child's lived experience.
> Is there sufficient information for immediate protective decision-making? What information is missing or requires further assessment? Have protective/vulnerability factors been considered alongside harm, likelihood of occurrence and recurrence, parental motivation and capacity to change? What framework has been used to assess and analyse risk?

> ► **Decide on care plan**
> What is the outcome of the Section 47 investigation? Have the child's views been clearly identified and has sufficient weight been given to them? Has consideration been given to factors that may be inhibiting the child's ability to convey their views? Are the child's needs clearly identified?

Issues to consider

How do we apply this guidance to the social work role? Understanding that we are conducting 'early investigative interviews' in both single and joint investigations and that we need to adapt the structured interview for the social work context when children disclose during the course of planned work, that we are visiting children who may not know initially why we are there. The loss of Achieving Best Evidence training for social workers and consequential de-skilling. How do we get that back and where else can we practise the skills of asking open questions (stat visits, assessment work, there are many opportunities). It needs to be seen as part of a skill set that is used in other situations, not just formal police-led statements.

Achieving best evidence

Many local authorities no longer provide Achieving Best Evidence training for their staff, and it may be a fair point to ask why they should do a course on a par with the police when in reality there is no intention for social workers to lead a video statement with a child, even though that is possible within the guidance of Achieving Best Evidence. From a police perspective, they are the ones with the regular practice at taking statements and they would not wish to hand the lead interviewer role to a social worker with all the attendant risks of contaminated evidence that may result, and contaminating evidence/asking the wrong question is one of social workers' biggest fears. However, the removal of this training from many agency programmes (whether it's intended or unintended) results in a gap in knowledge for social workers without which they can neither challenge poor practice nor support effective practice What is actually needed is sufficient training for social workers on this subject relevant to their context.

In practice, social workers are frequently working with children long term who disclose what is/has happened once they have a trusting relationship, or the worker is required to make an unannounced and unexpected visit to a child, for example in school, and conduct an interview (without leading or contaminating) to establish what has happened, whether it might be significant harm, whether immediate protection is needed, or whether a crime may have occurred. This does require the worker to have and understanding of the Achieving Best Evidence framework, to be able to apply a framework for a structured early investigative interview and to have some understanding about possible offences, points to prove and the gathering of evidence. That knowledge and skill set should not be left to chance; appropriate and contextualised training with the opportunity to practice the skills will be far more effective.

═══════════════════ **Issues to consider** ═══════════════════

In reality, why would any child tell us what's really going on in their family? For the courageous few who do society, community and the system convey such powerful messages of denial that suppression and retraction become an inevitable part of the process. Social workers need to understand this and avoid being pressured into 'truth and lies' dialogue. In addition, we need to understand attachment and trauma and begin to make sense of not only the words that children say, but their behaviour and to make judgments about what all of this means within the context that they are living. The child's voice is so much more than what they say and yet we are still challenged to achieve this in a one off visit of short duration.

Fergusson (2014). Denial, suppression and retraction. Muldaly and Goddard (2006) – 'truth is longer than a lie'.

The child's voice

One of the difficulties of operating with the child protection system is that it is heavily weighted toward children telling us what is happening in their lives. This fails to take into account that in any abusive or neglectful environment the child is psychologically dependant on a potentially abusive caregiver for their safety. Skilled practitioners will understand that it is both what the child says and does not say, along with their behaviour and the context that will lead us to a judgment about what is most likely to have occurred. Practice can be compromised when practitioners are unconsciously guided to seek the truth about what has happened from both children and their carers. Almost inevitably, each will give their perspective, possibly re-framed to make them appear what we and they want them to be (good, effective, better parents) and confusion about the truth can dominate the investigation. It's more helpful to think about the truth as 'the truth is out there – somewhere'. A social worker's role is to take all the information (observations, conversations, statements, medical information, history, context), maintain a stance of respectful uncertainty and reach a judgment about what we think is most likely to have occurred.

In order to do this we need to spend enough time with children to engage them, explain our role, build trust (including clarifying confidentiality), establish a rapport, invite the child to talk, question and clarify, summarise and close the interview by talking about what will happen next. For many of the children we talk to, their ability to trust adults has already been severely impaired and it is unrealistic to expect a one-off visit to achieve all of these things, and yet, if we don't get the first interview right we risk potentially putting children at further risk. Social workers need to be supported and encouraged to reconnect with their skills in communicating with children and allowed the time that this will take. It is of concern that Fergusson (2014) identifies a pattern that even the most effective child interviewers felt pushed by the constraints of time into asking direct questions or rushing/missing rapport and introductions, and on average, social workers spent 5–16 minutes alone with children. That is simply not enough to allow children the opportunity to talk effectively, nor is it enough time to allow social workers to grasp the complexities of what a child may be telling us, which is well summed up below:

> That's always the problem with these people, they don't want to believe the truth, they just want to believe the easiest side, the side that is…the simplest, basically…They don't want to hear the truth because the truth is so much harder to understand and so much longer than a lie about the truth. (12-year-old girl in Muldaly and Goddard 2006)

Within this context, the application of an adapted structured interview from *Achieving Best Evidence* (Ministry of Justice 2011) could support effective practice, along with encouraging social workers to be more playful and engaging with children (Fergusson 2014). An interview structure would look similar to that used in formal statements, but differ slightly in practice due to the context being one in which a child has not necessarily decided that they wish to talk to someone about what has been happening to them. See Table 6.2 for an adapted interview structure for child protection investigations.

TABLE **6.2** ADAPTED INTERVIEW STRUCTURE FOR
CHILD PROTECTION INVESTIGATIONS

Introductions and rapport
What is the purpose of your visit/interview?
What do you know/What don't you know/What may you want to know?
How will you introduce yourself and explain your role? How will you explain any change to your usual role with the child/family?
How will you explain the purpose of your visit (without leading)?
What will you say about your connection with the police?
What assumptions have you made about the child/family/parent?
What barriers are there to engaging the child? How will you overcome them?
What will you do to put the child at ease and build rapport?

Ground rules (Davies and Townsend 2008)

If you don't know the answer to a question do not guess. It's ok to say 'I don't know'

If you don't understand something I say, please tell me and I will try to say it using different words

If I misunderstand something you say, please tell me. I want to understand everything you say

Please remember that I was not there (present) when it happened but I do need to understand. So tell me everything you can remember, even things you don't think are important

It's important to only talk about things that really happened

Do you need any other ground rules? If so, what are they?

Free narrative

How will you raise the subject for discussion (without leading)?

How will you invite the child to give an account?

How will you support the child to freely recall events?

What will you do/say if the child says nothing of concern?

Questioning

What topics do you already know you need to cover?

Can you identify some open questions that you can ask that may help you explore these?

What unknowns are there? How can you ask about them without leading?

Closure

Towards the end of the interview may be a good time to explore the child's wishes and feelings about what they would like to happen. How will you go about this?

What will you say about what happens next?

What questions do you think the young person may ask? How will you answer?

═══════ Issues to consider ═══════

Analysis and evidence-based practice – not a search for proof. We operate within the arena of ambiguity and uncertainty, distinguishing between probability and possibility, exploring risk and triggers in order to come to a judgment about what may have happened and what may happen in the future. The implications of substantiated and unsubstantiated concerns in terms of child safety.

Reaching conclusions

Reaching a conclusion is much easier if the practitioner was clear at the start about their role and the context in which the inquiry took place. They will be starting the analysis from a point where multiple hypotheses have been actively considered and confirmed, where information gathering has been robust, inclusion of fathers, and the child's views will have been heard and given weight. There should be different types of evidence and ambiguity and uncertainty identified and clarified as much as possible. What remains is for the practitioner to assemble all of this information and come to a judgment about whether of not harm occurred, whether it was significant, what the most likely cause of the harm is, how likely it is to recur whether the parents are motivated to change their behaviour if required, and whether they have the capacity to change their behaviour. This is not intended as an oversimplification of the risk assessment framework, but to provide a working model for practitioners, particularly those undertaking short, intense Section 47 inquiries; to make safe, analytical, justifiable, evidence-based judgments in a complex context.

Having such a framework leads practitioners away from the inadvertent and misunderstood over reliance on whether an incident was Non-accidental injury (NAI) (a phrase that should be banned) as illustrated in the Daniel Pelka inquiry:

> For professionals from Children's Social Care or the Police to defer to medical staff for the provision of the primary evidence to confirm or otherwise whether an injury to a child was the result of abuse or not, could be unhelpful, particularly when no definitive view one way or the other can be given. To do so could lead to any following investigation being inappropriately downgraded and implies that other aspects of the child's life are less significant for the purposes of assessing the existence of child abuse.
>
> Serious Case Review Re: Daniel Pelka Coventry Safeguarding Children Board (2013)

Having reached a professional judgment the social worker must then ensure that their analysis and outcome are accurately understood by both family and professionals alike. It is at this critical moment that children can be left more vulnerable, particularly those where the inquiry is unsubstantiated and this outcome is misunderstood/ misinterpreted (by families or professionals) to mean 'it did not happen', 'there is no risk', 'he/she made it up', 'I can get away with more now'. For those children for whom the outcome is substantiated the likelihood is that they will be more overtly safeguarded by either a family support plan or, if recurrence is likely, a child protection plan.

Supervision and managerial oversight

Fergusson (2011) states: 'The worker's state of mind and the quality of attention they can give to children is directly related to the quality of support, care and attention they themselves receive from supervision, managers and peers', and this supports the well established view that effective supervision is at the heart of a safe and effective child protection system (Munro 2010; Morrison and Wonnacott 2010). It is not just supervision that is important, but good supervision.

> The fact that supervision takes place is no guarantee that service users will be beneficiaries of the process. It is only good supervision that adds to the capacity of the practitioner to do a complex task, often in difficult circumstances. Morrison (2005)

Morrison, Wonnacott and Frankel (2009) further expanded the original model to the supervision of assessment and risk management (see Figure 6.1). The model complements the use of the stepwise model by practitioners, as it covers the development of clarity of purpose at the start, active hypothesising early on and the exploration of the nature of relationships and power dynamics in the child/family/professional network.

Clarify focus and model of risk assessment
Reflect on workers initial assumptions about risk
Identify information required to assess risk
Exploring worker–family network dynamics
Overall analysis of interaction between risk and
protective factors, and judgment of level of risk
Managing risk-defensible decision and risk management plans

Figure 6.1 Supervising assessment and management of risk
(Morrison, Wonnacott and Frankel 2009)

Additionally, the supervision of staff and cases within the Section 47 process must also be considered within the organisational context. The vast majority of case discussions will be informal (i.e. outside of planned (monthly) supervision sessions), which requires the supervisor to have the capacity to create a safe psychological climate in which ambiguity and uncertainty can be explored, assumptions can be noticed and alternatives can be considered. Those agencies which are most effective at this will be demonstrating many of the features of the collaborative cycle (Morrison 2005) within a positive organisational culture. The challenge for managers and supervisors is that the pace of work at the front door is continually challenging capacity, and in many organisations the process has been further broken down by systems of screening/assessment/ investigation so that by the time a case is allocated for a child protection investigation it is possible that three or four workers have already been involved in gathering and recording early information, which then becomes open to interpretation/misinterpretation. Such systems need to ensure not only that the quality of information is good, but that it is recorded accurately and that those reading it have a clear understanding of how it was obtained. Supervision also plays a role in challenging the 'short circuit' (Morrison 2005) that can occur in busy contexts with an emotionally laden workload.

What good practice in Section 47 might look like and how we might achieve it, not just training but also the way we work with families and other agencies, systemic issues.

Conclusion

Since Erooga and Masson (1990), there has been little written about how to undertake a Section 47 inquiry and what good practice in Section 47 inquiries is. The quality of a Section 47 could be considered by the following standards, (see Table 6.3) yet these standards cannot have timescales and measures easily added since each inquiry is unique to that child, his/her family and context, and as we have discovered to our cost, the addition of measurement does not in itself ensure quality, it merely makes it measureable.

TABLE 6.3 WHAT WOULD A GOOD SECTION 47 INQUIRY LOOK LIKE?

- ▶ Involvement with, and engagement of other agencies
- ▶ The child/carer's experience of the investigation is as positive as it can be
- ▶ The child/carers understand the investigative process
- ▶ Medicals are timely and appropriate
- ▶ Decision-making is timely, consistent and appropriate
- ▶ Achieving Best Evidence interviews are timely
- ▶ Suspect interviews are timely
- ▶ Risk is assessed as thoroughly as possible within the timescales and decisions about the safety of the child are evidence-based.

It is possible to provide some simple tips for practitioners (see the following top tips) that will help support good practice. However, the investigation of whether a child has suffered significant harm, or is likely to in the future is a complex process, which requires judgment, knowledge, emotional intelligence and confidence in order to achieve a level of competence. This can only be carried out in an organisational context that allows for the exploration of ambiguity and uncertainty within a framework of risk management, which allows practitioners both the freedom and support to use their extensive skills and knowledge, and which provides contextually relevant training for social workers on the front line.

══ Top tips for good practice in Section 47 inquiries ══

Investigate whether significant harm has occurred, or may occur in the future

Avoid just focusing on the event in the referral. At the early stage keep a very open mind and use lots of open questions to add depth and breadth to your inquiry.

Make each conversation count

The temptation to rush out and see the child is huge. That needs to be balanced against the need to take into that conversation a good understanding of what may have been happening in the family. Encourage the other people you are talking to, to be curious about what they know, think, feel, assume and don't know in relation to the family.

Hypothesise and encourage other professionals to hypothesise

This will help you add depth and breadth to your enquiry and will help you avoid falling in to the 'fixed thinking' trap. For example, how do you think this may have occurred? Can you think of an alternative explanation?

Plan your interview of the parent/carer and of the child

It is essential to clarify your role and the purpose of your visit with the child and family, particularly when you have been a long-term worker with the family, and to explain your relationship with the police. It is better to plan this conversation with caregivers properly (strategy discussion), so that you are clear what you can/cannot share at this point. If in doubt, consult with the police – all too often we each make assumptions about what the other understands and will do, and at this point it can lead to an ill-timed sharing of key investigative information. The adapted structured interview will be appropriate for both child interviews and parent/carer interviews.

Go at the child's pace

Slowly, slowly slowly… Again the temptation is to rush, to get things finished and be driven by other people's timescales, etc. and this can interfere with your capacity to build rapport and engage the child. Use your skills to build rapport whilst at the same time gathering general information about the chid and his/her experiences.

Co-work

The interviews of the child and of the parent should always be undertaken by two staff. This is not explicit within the guidance but is absolutely best practice.

═══════════ **Key messages from the chapter** ═══════════

There are many similarities and many differences between standard risk assessment and those required in the conduct of section 47 enquiries. The principal differences relate to the approach required for evidence to be admissible in the criminal courts and the snapshot timeframe afforded staff that is difficult to capture as being representative.

There is a need to plan the approach carefully and not simply to develop a plan at the end of the assessment process.

Children who have been exposed to patterns and processes of harm often have been over long periods so the professional attention to the relationship development is key if they are to disclose things they may have encoded as normal as they grew up.

References

Aberdeen City Council (2012) *Getting it right for every child in Aberdeen: Operational Guidance 2012*. Available at www.aberdeengettingitright.org.uk/docs/OperationalGuidance2012.pdf.

Adcock, M. (2001) 'The core assessment: How to synthesise information and make judgements.' In J. Horwath J (ed.) *The Child's World: Assessing children in need* London: Jessica Kingsley Publishers.

Archer, J. (2002) *Good Practice in Section 47 Enquiries*. Halifax: Archer Training & Consultancy.

Argyris, C., and Schön, D. (1978) *Organizational learning: A theory of action perspective*. Reading, Mass: Addison Wesley.

Ayre, P. and Calder, M.C. (2010) 'The deprofessionalization of child protection: Regaining our bearings.' In P. Ayre and M. Preston-Shoot (eds.) *Children's Services at the Crossroads: A Critical Evaluation of Contemporary Policy for Practice*. Lyme Regis: Russell House Publishing.

Bandura, A. (1997) *Self-efficacy: The Exercise of Control*. New York: WH Freeman.

Barry, M. (2007) *Effective Approaches to Risk Assessment in Social Work: An International Literature Review. Research Findings No. 31*. Edinburgh: Scottish Executive.

Batty, D. (2004) 'The blame game.' *The Guardian*, 3 September, 2004.

Beach, L.R. and Connolly, T. (2005) *The psychology of decision making*. Thousand Oaks, CA: Sage.

Beck, U. (1992) *Risk Society: Towards a New Modernity*. London: Sage.

Becker, S. and Bryman, A. (eds.) (2004) *Understanding Research for Social Policy and Practice: Themes, Methods and Approaches*. Bristol: Policy Press.

Beckett, C. (2003) 'The language of siege: Military metaphors in the spoken language of social work. *British Journal of Social Work* 33, 625–639.

Betts, B. (2015) In *CLG Committee: Rotherham highlights a failure of Ofsted inspection* (2015) Available at www.parliament.uk/business/committees/committees-a-z/commons-select/communities-and-local-government-committee/news/report-rotherham-child-sexual-exploitation

Bolton Safeguarding Children (2013) *BSCB annual report 2011–2012*. Available at http://boltonsafeguardingchildren.org.uk/documents/2013/10/bscb-annual-report-2011-2012.pdf

Boushel, M. and Lebacq, M. (1992) 'Towards empowerment in child protection work.' *Children and Society 6*, 1, 38–50.

Brandon, M., Belderson, P., Warren, C., Howe, D., Gardner, R., Dodsworth, J. and Black, J. (2008) *Analysing Child Deaths and Serious Injury Through Abuse and Neglect: What can we learn? A biennial analysis of serious case reviews 2003–2005*. London: DCSF.

Brearley, P. (1982) *Risk and social work*. London: Routledge & Kegan Paul.

Brophy, J., Brown, L., Cohen, S. and Radcliffe, P. (2001) *Child Psychiatry and Child Protection Litigation*. London: Royal College of Psychiatry.

Bunting, L. (2005) *Females Who Sexually Offend Against Children: Responses of the Child Protection and Criminal Justice Systems*. London: NSPCC.

Caddick D and Watson B (2001) rehabilitation and the distribution of risk. In Parsloe P (ed.) risk assessment in social care and social work. London: Jessica Kingsley Publishers.

Calder, M.C. (1995) 'Child protection: Balancing paternalism and partnership.' *British Journal of Social Work 25*, 6, 749–766.

Calder, M.C. (1999) 'A conceptual framework for managing young people who sexually abuse: Towards a consortium approach.' In M.C. Calder (ed.) *Working with Young People Who Sexually Abuse: New Pieces of the Jigsaw Puzzle* (109–150). Lyme Regis: Russell House Publishing.

Calder, M.C. (2000) *A Complete Guide to Sexual Abuse Assessments.* Lyme Regis: Russell House Publishing.

Calder, M.C. (2002a) 'A framework for conducting risk assessment.' *Child Care in Practice 8*, 1, 1–18.

Calder, M.C. (2002b) 'Structural changes in the management of young people who sexually abuse in the UK.' In M.C. Calder (ed.) *Young People Who Sexually Abuse: Building the Evidence Base for Your Practice* (265–308). Lyme Regis: Russell House Publishing.

Calder, M.C. (2003a) 'The assessment framework: A critique and reformulation.' In M.C. Calder and S. Hackett (eds.) *Assessment in Childcare: Using and Developing Frameworks for Practice* (3–60). Dorset: Russell House Publishing.

Calder, M.C. (2003b) 'Risk and child protection.' *CareKnowledge,* 9 September, 2003. London: Pavilion.

Calder, M.C. (2003) *RASSAMM.* Leigh: Calder Training & Consultancy Limited.

Calder, M.C. (2007) *The Silent Minority: Domestic Abuse Perpetrated within Ethnic Communities: A review of the literature with recommendations for risk assessment.* Leigh: Calder Training and Consultancy.

Calder, M.C. (2008) 'A framework for working with resistance, motivation and change.' In M.C. Calder (ed.) *The Carrot or the Stick? Towards Effective Practice with Involuntary Clients in Safeguarding Children Work* (120–140). Lyme Regis: Russell House Publishing.

Calder, M.C. (2010) 'A Framework for Assessing Resistance, Motivation and Change.' *Presentation to Flinsthire Conference Working with Resistant Families: Challenges and Possibilities.* 17 December 2010.

Calder, M.C. (2011) 'Competence and Credibility: Developing Assessment Tools to Support Professional Judgement in Child Protection Work.' *Keynote presentation to International Symposium Decisions, Assessment, Risk and Evidence in Social Work.* Belfast. 26 April 2011.

Calder, M.C. (2012) 'Contemporary approaches to risk assessment.' *Keynote presentation to Contemporary risk assessment and signs of safety approach.* University of Birmingham. 8 May 2012

Calder, M.C. (2015) 'Competence and Confidence in Court Proceedings.' *Presentation to Safer Futures Development Day.* Salford. May 2015.

Carson, D. and Bain, A.J. (2008) *Professional Risk and Working with People: Decision-making in Health, Social Care and Criminal Justice.* London: Jessica Kingsley Publishers.

Cash, S.J. (2001) 'Risk assessment in child welfare: The art and science.' *Children and Youth Services Review 23*, 11, 811–830.

Children's Workforce Development Council (2007) *Advice on Developing and Implementing an Integrated Local Children's Services Workforce Strategy.* London: CWDC.

Cicchinelli, L. (1995) 'Risk assessment: expectations and realities.' *The APSAC Advisor 8*, 4, 15–21.

Clark, D. (2009). Talking Truth to Power. *Solace.* 28 May. Available at www.solace.org.uk/blog.asp?blog_id={BAFE30D7-AACA-40D2-B460-415DE4AD4C8C}

Cleaver, H., Wattam, C. and Cawson, P. (1998) *Assessing Risk in Child Protection.* London: NSPCC.

Compton, B.R. and Galaway, B. (1989) *Social Work Processes* (6th edition). Pacific Grove, CA: Brooks/Cole Publishing Company.

Cooper, A. (2006) 'The Centre Cannot Hold: Child Care Social Work, Emotional Dynamics and Modern Organisations.' Annual childcare lecture given at the University of East Anglia. 22 May 2006.

Cooper, J. (2010) 'Munro review may adopt police risk assessment methods.' *Community Care 14*, 12. Available at www.communitycare.co.uk/2010/12/14/munro-review-may-adopt-police-risk-assessment-methods/, accessed 20 July 2015.

Cottrell, S. (2005) *Critical Thinking Skills: Developing Effective Analysis and Argument*. Basingstoke: Palgrave Macmillan.

Coventry Safeguarding Children Board (2013) *Serious Case Review Re: Daniel Pelka*. Coventry: Coventry LSCB.

Cowger, C.D. (1994) 'Assessing client strengths: clinical assessment for client empowerment.' *Social Work 39*, 3, 262–268.

Curtis, S. (1997) 'Action speaks louder than words in the third sector: Measures of effective practice that really count.' In *Australasian Evaluation Society International Conference 1997: Proceedings*. Curtin, ACT: Australasian Evaluation Society.

Dale, P., Davies, M., Morrison, T. and Waters, J. (1986) *Dangerous Families: Assessment and Treatment of Child Abuse*. London: Tavistock.

Dale, P., Green, R. and Fellows, R. (2002) *What Really Happened? Child Protection Case Management of Infants with Serious Injuries with Discrepant Explanations*. London: NSPCC.

Dalgleish, L. (2003) 'Risk, needs and consequences.' In M.C. Calder and S. Hackett (eds.) *Assessment in Childcare: Using and Developing Frameworks for Practice*. Dorset: Russell House Publishing.

Daniel, B., Wassell, S. and Gilligan, R. (2010) *Child Development for Childcare and Protection Workers* (2nd edition). London: Jessica Kingsley Publishers.

Davidson, R. (1998) 'The transtheoretical model: a critical overview.' In W.R. Miller and N. Heather (eds.) *Treating Addictive Behaviours* (25–38). New York: Plenum Press.

Davies, L. (2008) 'Reclaiming the language of child protection.' In M.C. Calder (ed.) *Contemporary Risk Assessment in Safeguarding Children*. Dorset. Russell House Publishing.

Davies, L. and Townsend, D. (2008) *Investigative Interviewing of Children: Achieving best evidence*. Lyme Regis: Russell House Publishing.

Dean, I. (2013) *Briefing on Working Together to Safeguard Children 2013*. London: London Safeguarding Children Board.

Depanfilis, D. and Wilson, C. (1996) 'Applying the strengths perspective with maltreating families.' *The APSAC Advisor 9*, 3, 15–20.

Department for Education and Skills (2006) *Every Child Matters: Change for Children Outcomes Framework*. London: DfES. Available at http://webarchive.nationalarchives. gov.uk/20130401151715/http://www.education.gov.uk/publications/standard/ publicationDetail/Page1/DFES-2063-2005, accessed 17 July 2015.

DOH (1988) *Protecting children: A guide for social workers undertaking a comprehensive assessment*. London: HMSO.

Department of Health (1995a) *The Challenge of Partnership*, London: HMSO.

Department of Health (1995b) *Child Protection: Messages from Research*. London: HMSO.

Department of Health (1999) *Working Together to Safeguard Children*. London: TSO.

Department of Health (1999) *Working Together: A Guide to Interagency Working to Safeguard and Promote the Welfare of Children*. London: TSO.

Department of Health (2000) *Framework for the Assessment of Children in Need and Their Families*. London: HMSO.

Department of Health (2013) *Working Together to Safeguard Children*. London: TSO.

Dhami, M.K. and Thomson, M.E. (2012) 'On the Relevance of Cognitive Continuum Theory and Quasirationality for Understanding Management Judgment and Decision Making.' *European Management Journal 30*, 4, 316–326.

DiClemente, C.C. (1991) 'Motivational interviewing and the stages of change.' In W. Miller and S. Rollnick (eds.) *Motivational Interviewing*. London: Guilford Press.

DiClemente, C.C. and Hughes, S.O. (1990) 'Stages of change profiles on outpatient alcoholism treatment.' *Journal of Substance Abuse 2*, 217–235.

Dingwall, R. *et al.* (1983) *The protection of children*. Hoboken, New Jersey: Wiley-Blackwell.

Doherty, M. E., and Kurz, E. M. (1996) 'Social judgement theory.' *Thinking and Reasoning 2*, 109–140.

Eraut, M. (1994) *Developing Professional Knowledge and Competence*. London: The Falmer Press.

Erooga, M. and Masson, H. (1990) *Investigations, Journeys into the Unknown. Step by Step Approach to Investigations*. London: NSPCC & Rochdale Child Protection Training Sub-Committee.

Fauth, R., Jelicic, H., Hart, D., Burton, S. and Shemmings, D. (2010) *Effective Practice to Protect Children Living in 'highly resistant' families*. London: Centre for Excellence and Outcomes in Children and Young People's Services.

Fergusson, H. (2011) *Child Protection Practice*. London: Palgrave McMillan.

Fergusson, H. (2014) 'What social workers do in performing child protection work: Evidence from research into face-to-face practice.' *Child and Family Social Work*. DOI: 10.1111/cfs.12142.

Fischhoff, B. (1975). 'Hindsight is not equal to foresight: The effect of outcome knowledge on judgment under uncertainty.' *Journal of Experimental Psychology: Human Perception and Performance, 1*, 3, 288–299.

Fitzpatrick, M. (2011) 'Munro child protection report lacks a truly scientific basis.' *Community Care*, 22 June. Available at www.communitycare.co.uk/blogs/social-care-the-big-picture/2011/06/munro-child-protection-report-lacks-a-truly-scientific-basis/, accessed 22 July 2015.

Fletcher, C. (1978) 9th Australian Conference on Child abuse & neglect.

Fletcher, C. (1993) *An idea whose time has gone?* Personnel Management, September.

Furlong, M. (1989), 'Can a family therapist do statutory work?' *Australian and New Zealand Journal of Family Therapy 10*, 4, 211–218.

Gambrill, E. (1990) *Critical Thinking in Clinical Practice: Improving the Accuracy of Judgements and Decisions about Clients*. Chichester: Wiley.

Gambrill, E. (1997) *Social work practice: A critical thinker's guide*. New York: Oxford University Press.

Gambrill, E. (1999) 'Evidence-based practice: An alternative to authority-based practice source.' *Families in Society 80*, 4, 341–350.

Gawlinski G et al (unpublished) Thurlow House Assessment Programme.

Gawlinski, G. and Otto, S. (1985) 'The anatomy of organisational melancholia.' In N. Heather, I. Robertson and P. Davies (eds.) *The Misuse of Alcohol*. London: Croom Helm.

Gelles, R.J. (1995) 'Using the Transtheoretical Model of Change to Improve Risk Assessment in Cases of Child Abuse and Neglect.' *Paper presented at the 4th International Family Violence Research Conference*. University of New Hampshire. 22 July 1995.

Gibb, M. (2009) *Building a Safe, Confident future. The Final Report of the Social Work Task Force*. London: DCSF.

Gibbons, J., Conroy, S. and Bell, C. (1995) *Operating the Child Protection System*. London: HMSO.

Gibbs, J., Dwyer, J. and Vivekananda, K. (2009) *Leading Practice: A Resource Guide for Child Protection Frontline and Middle Managers*. Melbourne: State of Victoria Department of Human Services.

Gilgun, J.F. (1999) 'CASPARS: Clinical assessment instruments that measure strengths and risks in children and families.' In M.C. Calder (ed.) *Working with Young People Who Sexually Abuse: New Pieces of the Jigsaw* (49–58). Dorset: Russell House Publishing.

Goddard, C.R., Saunders, B.J., Stanley, J.R. and Tucci, J. (1999) 'Structured risk assessment procedures: Instruments of abuse?' *Child Abuse Review 8*, 251–263.

Goleman, D. (1996) *Emotional Intelligence: Why It Can Matter More Than IQ*. London: Bloomsbury.

Grotberg, E. (1997) 'The international resilience project.' In M. John (ed.) *A Charge Against Society: The Child's Right to Protection*. London: Jessica Kingsley Publishers.

Grove, W. and Meehl, P. (1996) 'Comparative efficiency of informal (subjective, impressionistic) and formal (mathematical, algorithmic) prediction procedures: The clinical-statistical controversy.' *Psychology, Public Policy and Law 12*, 293–323.

Hallett, C. (1995) *Inter-agency Co-ordination in Child Protection*. London: HMSO.

Hammond, K.R. (1996) *Human Judgment and Social Policy: Irreducible Uncertainty, Inevitable Error, Unavoidable Injustice*. Oxford: Oxford University Press.

Hammond, K.R. (2000) *Judgements under stress*. New York: Oxford University Press.

Hammond, K. R., Hamm, R.M., Grassia, J. and Pearson, T. (1997) 'Direct Comparison of the Efficacy of Intuitive and Analytical Cognition in Expert Judgment.' In W.M. Goldstein and R.M. Hogarth (eds.) *Research on Judgement and Decision Making: Currents, Connections and Controversies* (144–180). Cambridge: Cambridge University Press.

Hanson, R.K. (1998) 'Using Research to Improve Sex Offender Risk Assessment.' Keynote presentation to the NOTA National Conference. University of Glasgow. 17 September 1998.

Hanson, R.K. (1999) 'Working with sex offenders: a personal view.' *Journal of Sexual Aggression* 4, 2, 81–93.

Hanson, R.K. and Bussiere, M.T. (1998) 'Predicting recidivism: A meta-analysis of sexual offender recidivism studies.' *Journal of Consulting and Clinical Psychology 66*, 2, 348–362.

Harrison, P. (2009) *Managing child welfare and protection services*. Dorset: RHP.

Harrison, R., Mann, G., Murphy, M., Taylor, A. and Thompson, N. (2004) *Partnership Made Painless: A Joined Up Guide to Working Together*. Lyme Regis: Russell House Publishing.

Heasman, P. (2008) 'Dimensions of risk: Professionals tipping the balance?' In M.C. Calder (ed.) *Contemporary Risk Assessment in Safeguarding Children*. Lyme Regis: Russell House Publishing.

Heilbrun, K. (1997). 'Prediction versus management models relevant to risk assessment: The importance of legal decision-making context.' *Law and Human Behavior, 21*, 347–359.

Hein, S. (2007) *Definition of emotional intelligence*. New York: Psychology Press.

Hill, M. (ed.) (1999) *Effective Ways of Working with Children and their Families*, London: Jessica Kingsley Publishers.

Holder, W. and Morton, T. (1999) *Designing a Comprehensive Approach to Child Safety*. Duluth, GA: National Resource Center on Child Maltreatment.

Hollows, A. (2001) 'Beyond Actuarial Risk Assessment: The Continuing Role of Professional Judgement.' Presentation to a one-day national conference on Risk Assessment: Developing and Enhancing Evidence-based Practice. TUC Congress Centre, London. 6 February 2003.

Home Office and Department of health (1992) *Memorandum of Good Practice*. London: HMSO.

HM Government (2015) *Working Together to Safeguard Children: A Guide to Inter-agency Working to Safeguard and Promote the Welfare of Children*. London: HMSO. Available at www.gov.uk/government/uploads/system/uploads/attachment_data/file/419595/Working_Together_to_Safeguard_Children.pdf, accessed 25 July 2015.

Hopkins, N. and Morris, J. (2015) 'Cyril Smith child abuse inquiry "scrapped after his arrest".' *BBC Newsnight*, 17 March, 2015. Available at www.bbc.co.uk/news/uk-31908431, accessed on 16 July 2015.

Horwath, J. and Morrison, T. (2000) 'Assessment of parental motivation to change.' In J. Horwath (ed.) *The Child's World: Assessing Children in Need*. London: DOH, NSPCC and The University of Sheffield.

Howe, D. (1992) 'Child abuse and the bureaucratization of social work.' *The Sociological Review 40*, 3, 491–508.

Howitt, D. (1992) *Child abuse errors: when good intentions go wrong*. London: Harvester Wheatsheaf

Isle of Wight LSCB (2013) Serious case review in respect of baby T. Available at www.iwight.com/azservices/documents/2706-BabyTSCRFinal051113.pdf.

Ivanoff, A., Blythe, B. and Tripodi, T. (1994) *Involuntary Clients in Social Work Practice*. New York: Aldine de Gruyter.

Janis, I. and Mann, L. (1977) *Decision Making: A psychological analysis of conflict, choice and commitment*. New York: The Free Press.

Jenkins, A. (1990) *Invitations to Responsibility: The Therapeutic Engagement of Men who are Violent and Abusive*. Adelaide: Dulwich Centre Publications.

Jones, R. (2015) 'Wounded Ofsted is inadequate to inspect child sexual exploitation policies.' *The Guardian*, 26 March, 2015.

Kahneman, D. (2012) *Thinking Fast and Slow*. London: Penguin.

Kahneman, D., Knetsch, J.L. and Thaler, R.H. (1990). 'Experimental Tests of the Endowment Effect and the Coase Theorem.' *Journal of Political Economy 98*, 6, 1325–1348.

Kassin, S.M. (2004) 'On the psychology of confessions.' *American Psychologist, 60*,3, 215–228

Kemshall, H. (2001) *Risk Assessment and Management of Known Sexual and Violent Offenders: A Review of Current Issues. Police Research Series Paper 140.* London: The Home Office.

Kemshall, H. (2002) *Risk, Social Policy and Welfare.* Buckingham: Open University Press.

Kemshall, H. (2003) *Understanding Risk in Criminal Justice.* Maidenhead: Open University Press.

Kemshall, H. (2008) 'Actuarial and clinical risk assessment: Contrasts, comparisons and collective usages.' In M.C. Calder (ed.) *Contemporary Risk Assessment in Safeguarding Children.* Lyme Regis: Russell House Publishing.

Kennington, R. (2008) 'Risk assessment in adult sex offenders.' In M.C. Calder MC (ed.) *Contemporary risk assessment in safeguarding children.* Lyme Regis, Dorset: Russell House Publishing, 232–29.

Kirby, P., Lanyon, C., Cronin, K. and Sinclair, R. (2003) *Building a Culture of Participation. Research Report.* London: DfES.

Kindler, R. (1990) *Risk assessment; a guide for decision makers.* Menlo Park, CA: Crisp Publications.

Klein, W.C. and Bloom, M. (1995) 'Practice Wisdom', *Social Work 40*, 6, 799–807.

Krill, D.F. (1990) *Practice Wisdom: A Guide for Helping Professionals.* Newbury Park: Sage.

Laming, H. (2003) *The Victoria Climbié Enquiry.* London: HMSO.

Laming, H. (2009) *The protection of children in England: a progress report.* London: DCSF.

Learner and Statham (2004) 'The role of the first line manager: New challenges.' *Management Issues in Social Care, Quarterly Bulletin, 10,* 1, 36–44.

Leung, P., Monit Cheung, K.F. and Stevenson, K.M. (1994) 'A strengths approach to ethnically sensitive practice for child protective service workers.' *Child Welfare 733*, 707–721.

Littell, J.H. and Girvin, H. (2002) 'Stages of change: A critique.' *Behaviour Modification 26,* 2, 223–273.

Littlechild, B. (2008) 'Child protection social work: Risks of fears and fears of risks – impossible tasks from impossible goals. *Social Policy and Administration 42*, 6, 662–675.

Loxley, A. (1997) *Collaboration in Health and Welfare: Working with Difference.* London: Jessica Kingsley Publishers.

Lupton, K. and Bayley, M. (2002) *Children's perspective on road safety. Workshop on children & traffic, 2-3 May.* Copenhagen.

Macdonald, K. and Macdonald, G. (2001) 'Perceptions of risk.' In P. Parsloe (ed.) *Risk Assessment in Social Work and Social Care.* London: Jessica Kingsley Publishers.

Magura, S., Moses, B.S. and Jones, M.A. (1987) *The Family Risk Scales.* Washington, DC: Child Welfare League of America.

Mailick, M. and Ashley, A.A. (1989) 'Politics of inter-professional collaboration: Challenge of advocacy.' *Social Casework 62*, 3, 131–137.

Maluccio, A (1979) 'The influence of the agency environment on clinical practice.' *Journal of Sociology and Social Welfare 6*, 734–755.

Margetts, T. (1998) 'Establishing multi-agency working with sex offenders: Setting up to succeed.' *NOTA News 25*, 27–38.

McCracken, G. (1998) In CWDC (2009) *NQSW Guide for Supervisors* (171). London: CWDC.

McNeish, D. and Newman, T. (2002) *What Works for Children? Effective Services for Children and Families.* Milton Keynes: Open University Press.

Middleton, L. (1997) *The Art of Assessment.* Birmingham: Venture Press.

Millar, M. and Corby, B. (2006) 'The Framework for the Assessment of Children in Need and their Families - A Basis for a "Therapeutic" Encounter?', *British Journal of Social Work, 36,* 887–899.

Miller, W.R. and Rollnick, S. (1991) *Motivational Interviewing: Preparing People to Change Addictive Behaviour.* New York: Guilford Press.

Miller, W.R. and Heather, N. (1998) 'The transtheoretical model of change.' In W.R. Miller and N. Heather (eds.) *Treating Addictive Behaviours.* New York: Plenum Press.

Milner, J. and O'Bryne, P. (2002) *Assessment in Social Work (2nd edition).* London: Palgrave Macmillan.

Ministry of Justice (2011) *Achieving Best Evidence in Criminal Proceedings: Guidance on Interviewing Victims and Witnesses, and Guidance on Using Special Measures.* London: Ministry of Justice.

Mitchell, T.R., Holtom, B.C., Lee, T.W., Sablynski, C.J. and Erez, M. (2001) 'Why people stay, using job emebeddedness to predict voluntary turnover.' *Academy of Management Journal 44,* 6, 1102–1122.

Monahan, J. (1993) 'Limiting therapist exposure.' *American Psychology, 48,* 242–250.

Moore Kirkland, L. (1981) 'The Use of Orientation Groups to Engage Hard-to-Reach Clients: Model, Method and Evaluation.' *Social Work with Groups, 12,* 2.

Moore, B. (1996) *Risk Assessment: A Practitioner's Guide to Predicting Harmful Behaviour.* London: Whiting & Birch Ltd.

Morrison, T. (1991) 'Change, control and the legal framework.' In M. Adcock, R. White and A. Hollows (eds.) *Significant Harm: Its Management and Outcome* (85–100). Croydon: Significant publications.

Morrison, T. (1995) 'Learning, Training and Change in Child Protection Organisations.' Keynote presentation to the National Child Protection Trainers Conference. 15 March 1995.

Morrison, T. (1997) 'Emotionally competent child protection organisations: Fallacy, fiction or necessity?' In J. Bates, R. Pugh, and N. Thompson (eds.) *Protecting Children: Challenges and change* (193–211). Aldershot: Arena.

Morrison T. (1998) 'Partnership, collaboration and change under the Children Act.' In M. Adcock and R. White (eds.) *Significant Harm: Its Management and Outcome* (2nd edition) (121–147). Croydon: Significant Publications.

Morrison, T. (2004) 'Effective Collaboration in a Time of Change.' Keynote presentation to Manchester BASPCAN conference. 30 January 2004.

Morrison, T. (2005) *Staff Supervision in Social Care* (3rd ed.) Brighton: Pavilion Publishing.

Morrison, T. (2009a) 'The Roll and Toll of Emotions in Safeguarding Work.' Podcast available at www.safeguardingchildrenea.co.uk/safeguarding-events/tony-morrison-seminar-reaffirms-why-we-need-emotional-intelligence/

Morrison, T. (2009b) 'The Strategic Leadership of Complex Practice: Opportunities and Challenges.' Founders lecture to BASPCAN conference. Swansea. 14 September 2009.

Morrison, T. and Wonnacott, J. (2010) *Supervision: Now or Never Reclaiming Reflective Supervision in Social Work.* Available at www.in-trac.co.uk/supervision-now-or-never/, accessed 26 July 2015.

Morrison, T., Wonnacott, J. and Frankel, J. (2009) *EPD Guide For Supervisors.* London: CWDC.

Morton, T. and Salovitz, B. (2003) *Essential safety constructs in child maltreatment cases.* Duluth: Child Welfare Institute.

Muldaly, N. and Goddard, C. (2006) *The Truth is Longer Than a Lie. Children's Experiences of Abuse and Professional Interventions.* London: Jessica Kingsley Publishers.

Munby, J. in Re. M (Care Proceedings: Judicial Review) [2003] 2FLR 171 p.183.

Munro, E. (1998) *Understanding Social Work: An Empirical Approach.* London: The Athlone Press.

Munro, E. (1999) 'Common errors of reasoning in child protection work.' *Child Abuse and Neglect. 23,* 8, 745–758.

Munro, E. (2005a) 'A systems approach to investigating child abuse deaths.' *British Journal of Social Work 35.*

Munro, E. (2005b) 'Improving practice: child welfare as a systems problem.' *Children and Youth Services 16,* 27, 375–391.

Munro, E. (2007) *Child Protection SAGE Course Companions.* London: SAGE Publications.

Munro, E. (2008) *Effective Child Protection.* London: Sage Publications.

Munro, E. (2009) 'Managing societal and institutional risks in child protection.' *International Journal of Risk Analysis 29,* 7, 1015–1023.

Munro, E. (2010) *The Munro Review on Child Protection: Part 1: A Systems Analysis.* London: Department for Education.

Munro, E. (2011a) *The Munro Review of Child Protection. Part 1: A systems Analysis.* London: Department for Education.

Munro, E. (2011b) *The Munro Review of Child Protection: Interim report – A child's journey.* London: Department for Education.

Munro, E. (2011c) *The Munro Review of Child Protection: Final report – A child centred system.* London: Department for Education.

Munro, E. and Calder, M.C. (2005) 'Where has child protection gone?' *Political Quarterly 76,* 3, 439–445.

Ofsted (2015) *Ofsted Social Care Annual Report 2013/14.* London: Ofsted. Available at www.gov.uk/government/publications/ofsted-social-care-annual-report-201314, accessed on 16 July 2015.

O'Sullivan, T. (2005) 'Some theoretical propositions on the nature of practice wisdom.' *Journal of Social Work 5,* 2, 221–242.

Parton, N. (ed.) (1996) *Social Theory, Social Change and Social Work.* London: Routledge.

Parton, N. (ed.) (1997) *Child Protection and Family Support: Tensions, Contradictions and Possibilities.* London: Routledge.

Parton, N. (1998) 'Risk, advanced liberalism and child welfare: The need to rediscover uncertainty and ambiguity.' *British Journal of Social Work 28,* 5–27.

Parton, N. (2000) 'Some thoughts on the relationship between theory and practice in and for social work.' *British Journal of Social Work 30,* 4, 449–463.

Parton, N. (2004) 'From Maria Colwell to Victoria Climbié: Reflections on public inquiries into child abuse a generation apart.' *Child Abuse Review 13,* 2, 80–94.

Parton, N. (2006) *Safeguarding Childhood.* London: Palgrave Macmillan.

Parton, N., Thorpe, D. and Wattam, C. (1997) *Child Protection: Risk and the Moral Order.* Basingstoke: Macmillan Press.

Perry, B. (2006) 'Applying principles of neurodevelopment to clinical work with maltreated and traumatised children.' In Boyd Webb (ed.) *Working with traumatised youth in child welfare.* New York: Guilford Press.

Perry, J. and Sheldon, B. (1995) *Richard Phillips Inquiry Report,* London: City of Westminster, and Kensington and Chelsea and Westminster District Health Authority.

Peterson, M.A. (ed.) (2001) 'Editor's Note. Evidence: Its meaning in health care and in law.' *Journal of Health Policy, Politics and Law 26,* 2.

Plant, M. and Plant, M. (1992). *Risk-takers: Alcohol, drugs, sex and youth.* London: Routledge.

Power, M. (2004) *The Risk Management of Everything: Rethinking the Politics of Uncertainty.* London: Demos.

Prentky, R., Harris, A., Frizzell and Righthand (2000) 'An actuarial procedure for assessing risk with juvenile sex offenders.' *Sexual Abuse: A Journal of Research and Treatment 12,* 2, 71–93.

Prochaska, J.O. (1995) 'Common problems: Common solutions.' *Clinical Psychology: Science and Practice 2,* 101–105.

Prochaska J.O. and DiClemente C.C. (1986) 'Towards a comprehensive model of change.' In W.N. Miller and N. Heather (eds.) *Treating Addictive Behaviours: Processes of Change* (3–27). New York: Plenum Press.

Prochaska, J.O. and Norcross, J.C. (1994) *Systems of Psychotherapy: A Transtheoretical Analysis* (3rd edition). Pacific Grove, CA: Brooks/Cole.

Rai, G.S. (1994) 'Complexity and co-ordination in child welfare agencies.' *Administration in Social Work 18,* 1, 87–105.

Rajan-Rankin, S. and Beresford, P. (2011) *Critical Observations on the Munro Review of Child Protection.* Paisley: SWAN.

Ramchandani, P., Joughin, C. and Zwi, M. (2001) 'Evidence-based child and adolescent mental health services: Oxymoron or brave new dawn?' *Child Psychology & Psychiatry Review, 6,* 2, 59–64.

Raynes, B. (2003) 'A stepwise process of assessment.' In M.C. Calder and S. Hackett (eds.) *Assessment in Child Care – Using and Developing Frameworks for Practice.*Lyme Regis: Russell House Publishing.

Reason, J. (1997) *Managing the Risks of Organizational Accidents.* Burlington, VT: Ashgate.

Reason, J. (2000) 'Human error: Models and management.' *British Medical Journal 320*, 768–770.

Reder, P. and Duncan, S. (1999) *Lost Innocents: A Follow Up Study of Fatal Child Abuse.* London: Routledge.

Reder, P. and Duncan, S. (2003) 'Understanding communication in child protection networks.' *Child Abuse Review 12*, 82–100.

Reder, P., Duncan, S. and Gray, M. (1993) *Beyond Blame: Child Abuse Tragedies Revisited.* London: Routledge.

Rist, G. (1997) *The history of development, from western origins to global faith.* London: Jed books.

Rodwell, M.K. and Blankebaker, A. (1992) 'Strategies for developing cross-cultural sensitivity: Wounding as metaphor.' *Journal of Social Work Education 28*, 2, 153–165.

Rose, N. (1998) 'Governing risky individuals: the role of psychiatry in new regimes of control.' *Psychiatry, Psychology and the Law 5*, 2, 177–195.

Ruch, G. (2007) 'Reflective practice in contemporary child-care social work: The role of containment.' *British Journal of Social Work 37*, 659–680.

Rutter, M. (1985) 'Resilience in the face of adversity: Protective factors and resistance to psychiatric disorder.' *The British Journal of Psychiatry 147*, 598–611.

Rutter, M. (1989) 'Intergenerational continuities and discontinuities in serious parenting difficulties.' In D. Cicchetti and V. Carlson (eds.) *Child Maltreatment: Theory and Research on the Causes and Consequences of Child Abuse and Neglect.* New York: Cambridge University Press.

Rutter, M. (1991) *Maternal Deprivation Reassessed.* London: Penguin.

Ryan, M. (2000) *Engaging Men.* London: TSO.

Saleebey, D. (ed.) (1992) *The Strengths Perspective in Social Work Practice.* New York: Longman.

Saleebey, D. (1996) 'The strengths perspective in social work perspective: extensions and cautions.' *Social Work 41*, 3, 296–305.

Samra-Tibbets, C. and Raynes, B. (1999) 'Assessment and planning.' In M.C. Calder and J. Horwath (eds.) *Working for Children on the Child Protection Register: An Inter-agency Practice guide* (81–117). Aldershot: Arena.

SCIE (2009) *Personalisation Briefing: Implications for Commissioners.* London: SCIE.

Scott, D. and O'Neill, D. (1996) *Beyond Child Rescue: Developing Family Centred Practice at St Lukes.* Sydney: Allen & Unwin.

Sheldon, B. (2001), 'The validity of evidence-based practice in social work: A reply to Stephen Webb', *British Journal of Social Work, 31*, 801–809.

Sheppard, M. (1995) 'Social work, social science and practice wisdom.' *British Journal of Social Work 25*, 3, 265–293.

Shlonsky, A. and Wagner, D. (2005). 'The next step.' *Children & Youth Services Review 27*, 4, 409–427.

Smale, G., Tuscon, G., Biehal, N. and Marsh, P. (1993) *Empowerment, Assessment, Care Management and the Skilled Worker.* London: HMSO.

Smith, A. and Rosenthal, D. (1995) 'Adolescent's perceptions of their risk environment.' *Journal of Adolescence 18*, 229–245.

Smith, R. (2008) 'From child protection to child safety: Locating risk assessment in the changing landscape.' In M.C. Calder (ed.) *Contemporary Risk Assessment in Safeguarding Children.* Lyme Regis: Russell House Publishing.

Stalker, K. (2003) 'Managing risk and uncertainty in social work – A literature review.' *Journal of Social Work 3*, 2, 211–233.

Stanley, J. and Goddard, C. (1997) 'Failures in child protection: A case study.' *Child Abuse Review 6*, 1, 46–54.

Stanley, J. and Goddard, C. (2002) *In the Firing Line: Violence and Power in Child Protection Work*. Chichester: Wiley.

Statham, D. (ed.) (2004) *Managing Frontline Practice in Social Care*. London: Jessica Kingsley Publishers.

Stewart, A. and Thompson, C. (2004) *Comparative Evaluation of Child Protection Assessment Tools*. Queensland: Griffith University.

Stoke-on-Trent Safeguarding Children Board (2015) *Resistant Families: Working with Resistant and Non-compliant Families*. Available at www.safeguardingchildren.stoke.gov.uk/ccm/navigation/professionals/resistant-families/, accessed 24 July 2015.

Sutherland, P. (1992) *Cognitive development today*. London: Paul Chapman Publishing Ltd.

Sutton, S. (1996) 'Can "stages of change" provide guidance in the treatment of addictions? A critical examination of Prochaska and DiClemente's model.' In G. Edwards and C. Dare (eds.) *Psychotherapy, Psychological Treatments and the Addictions* (189–205). Cambridge: Cambridge University Press.

Taylor, B.J. (2010) *Professional Decision Making in Social Work* (110). Exeter: Learning Matters.

Taylor, R. (2015) 'We need to talk about the dangers of overestimating risk.' *Community Care*, 21 April, 2015.

Thomas, T. (2002) *Children, Family and the State: Decision Making and Child Participation*. Bristol: Policy Press.

Thorpe and Bilson (1998) In E. Munro (2008) *Effective Child Protection* (2nd edition). London: Sage Publications.

Tomison, A.M. (1999) 'Ensuring the Protection of Children: The Role of Child Protection Services in the Identification, Assessment and Treatment of Maltreated Children.' Keynote address to the NSW Department of Community Services, Entry Parameters for Child Protection Conference, Sydney. March 20–21 1999.

Topss UK Partnership (2004) *The National Occupational Standards for Social Work*. London: Topss. Available from www3.shu.ac.uk/HWB/placements/SocialWork/documents/SWNatOccupStandards.pdf, accessed 17 July 2015.

Towl, G. and Crighton, D. (1996) *The Handbook of Psychology for Forensic Practitioners*. London: Routledge.

Turnell, A. and Edwards, S. (1999) *Signs of Safety: A solution and safety oriented approach to child protection*. New York: WW Norton.

Unicef (1989) *UN Convention on the Rights of the Child*. London: Unicef UK. Available from www.unicef.org.uk/Documents/Publication-pdfs/UNCRC_PRESS200910web.pdf, accessed 17 July 2015.

Utting, R. (1997) *People Like Us*. London: TSO.

Vaughan, G. and Hogg, M. (1995) *Introduction to Social Psychology*. Melbourne: Prentice-Hall.

Walker, S. and Beckett, C. (2003) *Social Work Assessment and Intervention*. Lyme Regis: Russell House Publishing.

Walker, S. and Beckett, C. (2010) *Social Work Assessment and Intervention* (2nd edition). Lyme Regis: Russell House Publishing.

Ward, D. and Mullender, A. (1991) 'Empowerment and oppression: An indissoluble pairing for contemporary social work.' *Critical Social Policy 11*, 21–30.

Ward, J. and Bayley, M. (2009) 'Young people's perceptions of "risk".' In B. Thom, R. Sales and J. Pearce (eds.) *Growing Up With Risk*. Bristol: The Policy Press.

Wardlaw, G. (1982) *Political Terrorism: Theory, Tactics and Counter-Measures*. Cambridge: Cambridge University Press.

Warner, J. (2003) 'An initial assessment of the extent to which risk factors, frequently identified in research, are taken into account when assessing risk in child protection cases.' *Journal of Social Work 3*, 3, 339–363.

Warner, S. (2003) 'Critical reflections on communicating with children: Making the tactics of training and intervention in child protection explicit.' *Education and Child Psychology 20*, 1, 109–123.

Webb, S.A. (2001) 'Some considerations on the validity of evidence based practice in social work.' *British Journal of Social Work 31*, 1.

Weick, A., Rapp, C., Sullivan, W.P. and Kisthardt, W. (1989) 'A strengths perspective for social work practice', *Social Work, 34*, 4, 350–354.

Welch, V., Lerpiniere, J. and Young, E. (2014) *Scottish First-line Managers' Views of Newly Qualified Social Workers' Preparedness for Practice*. Glasgow: CELCIS.

White, K. and Grove, M. (2000) 'Towards an understanding of partnership.' *NCVCCO Outlook* Issue 7, Spring.

Winkworth, G. and McArthur, M. (2006) 'Being "child centred" in child protection: What does it mean?' *Children Australia 31*, 4, 13–21.

Wonnacott, J. (2012) *Mastering Social Work Supervision*. London: Jessica Kingsley Publishers.

Yatchmenoff, D. (2008) 'A closer look at client engagement: Understanding and assessing engagement from the perspectives of workers and clients in non-voluntary child protective service cases.' In M.C. Calder (ed.) *The carrot or the stick*. Lyme Regis, Dorset: RHP.

Youll, P. and Walker, C. (1995) 'Great expectations? Personal, professional and institutional agendas in advanced training.' In M. Yellolly and M. Henkel (eds.) *Learning and Teaching in Social Work: Towards Reflective Practice*. London: Jessica Kingsley Publishers.

Subject index

Author index